Structure and Structural Change in the Chilean Economy

Also by Geoffrey J. D. Hewings

STRUCTURE AND STRUCTURAL CHANGE IN THE BRAZILIAN ECONOMY
(*Co-edited with Joaquim J. M. Guilhoto*)

Structure and Structural Change in the Chilean Economy

Edited by
Patricio A. Aroca
and
Geoffrey J. D. Hewings

palgrave
macmillan

First published 2006 by
PALGRAVE MACMILLAN
Houndmills, Basingstoke, Hampshire RG21 6XS and
175 Fifth Avenue, New York, N. Y. 10010
Companies and representatives throughout the world

PALGRAVE MACMILLAN is the global academic imprint of the Palgrave Macmillan division of St. Martin's Press, LLC and of Palgrave Macmillan Ltd. Macmillan® is a registered trademark in the United States, United Kingdom and other countries. Palgrave is a registered trademark in the European Union and other countries.

ISBN–13: 978–0–230–00496–2 hardback
ISBN–10: 0–230–00496–2 hardback

This book is printed on paper suitable for recycling and made from fully managed and sustained forest sources.

A catalogue record for this book is available from the British Library.

Library of Congress Cataloging-in-Publication Data

Structure and structural change in the Chilean economy / edited by Patricio A. Aroca and Geoffrey J.D. Hewings.
p. cm.
Includes bibliographical references and index.
ISBN 0–230–00496–2 (cloth)
1. Chile–Economic policy. 2. Structural adjustment (Economic policy)–Chile. I. Aroca, Patricio. II. Hewings, Geoffrey.

HC192.S74 2007
338.983–dc22 2006046065

10 9 8 7 6 5 4 3 2 1
15 14 13 12 11 10 09 08 07 06

Printed and bound in Great Britain by
Antony Rowe Ltd, Chippenham and Eastbourne

Contents

List of Tables

List of Figures

List of Contributors

Renato Aguilar is associate professor (docent in Swedish) at the Department of Economics of the University of Gothenburg, Sweden. He was born in Chile. His main areas of interest are mathematical economics, econometrics, and development economics. He has also done some work in labor economics, production function analysis, and poverty and income distribution. Renato.Aguilar@economics.gu.se

Roberto Alvarez is a doctoral student at the Anderson School at UCLA in the area of global economics and management. He earned his B.S. in economics (1996) from University of Chile and M.A. in economics (2006) from UCLA. His research has focused on the evaluation of export promotion programs, industry productivity growth and technological innovation. ralvarez@anderson.ucla.edu,

Patricio Aroca is Professor and Head of IDEAR at Universidad Católica del Norte, Antofagasta, Chile, and Affiliated Research Professor at REAL, University of Illinois. He earned his B.S. in business (1983) from the Austral University (Chile), M.A. in economics (1987) from University of Chile, M.Sc. in Policy Economics (1994), and a Ph.D. in economics (1995) from the University of Illinois at Urbana-Champaign. He specializes in econometrics, natural resources and regional economics, and more specifically works with input-Output analysis, spatial econometrics, regional growth and labor interregional migration. From 1997 to 2000 was dean of the Faculty of Economics and Business of the Catholic University of the North and consultant for institutions like World Bank, IADB, UNCTAD, CELADE-ECLAC. paroca@ucn.cl

Nelson Correa is a Ph.D student at Santa Anna School of Advanced Studies, Pisa, Italy. He received his B.S. in economics from the Universidad de Concepción (Chile). He has worked for the Economic Commission for Latin America, United Nations. His publications are mainly focused on empirical industrial organization, trade and development in Latin America. n.correa@sssup.it

Jorge Dresdner is Associate Professor at Universidad de Concepcion, Chile. He received his Ph.D. at Uppsala University, Sweden. His main areas of research are Labor Economics, and Natural Resource Economics. jdresdne@udec.cl

J. Rodrigo Fuentes obtained his Ph.D. and Master of Arts in Economics, University of California Los Angeles (UCLA), Master of Science in Finance and BA in Economics, Universidad de Chile. His current position is Senior Economist at the Central Bank of Chile and Lecturer at the Catholic University of Chile. He was Dean of the Graduate School of Economics and Business Administration at the Universidad de Chile. He has been visiting professor in UCLA, AB Freeman School of Business at Tulane University, Graduate School at the National University of Tucumán. He has published several papers in national and international journals and he has been consultant for international and domestic agencies. rfuentes@bcentral.cl

Geoffrey J.D. Hewings is Director of REAL, Professor of Geography and Regional Science, of Economics and of Urban and Regional Planning at the University of Illinois at Urbana-Champaign. He has served as a visiting professor at the University of Queensland (Australia), Bar Ilan University (Israel), Tianjin and Renmin Universities (China), University of Indonesia and Kagawa University (Japan). His major research interests lie in the field of urban and regional economic analysis with a focus on the design, implementation and application of regional economic models. hewings@ucn.cl

Marcelo Lufin, is a doctoral student in urban and regional planning at the University of Illinois at Urbana-Champaign specializing in the analysis of regional systems with a particular emphasis on the application of social network analysis. lufin@uiuc.edu

Mariano Bosch Mossi is a Ph.D. Student at the London School of Economics and Political Science, UK. Recently, he has published on regional growth in Chile, Brazil and Mexico. m.bosch@lse.ac.uk

Wilson Peres is Head of the Technological and Industrial Development Unit, Economic Commission for Latin America, United Nations. wperes@eclac.cl

Nola Reinhardt is a Professor of Economics at Smith College and former chair of the department. She received her Ph.D. in 1981 from the University of California at Berkeley. Her area of interest is economic development, with a concentration on Latin America and East Asia. Her

recent work has focused on assessing the impact of the 1980s/90s economic reforms in Latin America on the structure and performance of the region's economies. She co-edited, along with Wilson Peres, a special issue of the journal *World Development* (28:9) on the topic, and is currently investigating the region's savings behavior under the reforms. She has also worked on the comparative study of trade and development policies in Latin America and East Asia, especially Chile, Malaysia and Thailand. Her past work has focused on Latin American agricultural development, especially in Colombia and Central America.
nreinhar@email.smith.edu

Johanna D. Robles is a Ph.D. student of the urban and regional planning program at University of Illinois at Urbana-Champaign, USA, and Associate Researcher at IDEAR, Universidad Católica del Norte, Antofagasta, Chile. He work has focused on the spatial impacts of foreign direct investment. jdrobles@ucn.cl

Eduardo Saavedra is Associate Professor and Chair of the Department of Economics and Business at Universidad Alberto Hurtado, Chile. He is currently visiting professor at Georgetown University. He received his Ph.D. in Economics at Cornell University in 1999 and he has been researching on industrial organization and the economics of regulation since then. He used to be advisor of the Ministry of Economics and Energy in Chile and has also worked as international consultant on institutions reforms in several other developing countries.
saavedra@uahurtado.cl

Raimundo Soto is Associate Professor of the Department of Economics at Pontificia Universidad Católica de Chile, Chile. He has been visiting professor at The World Bank, Federal Reserve Bank of Minneapolis, Universidad Mayor de San Simón, Bolivia and numerous central banks in Latin America. He has worked extensively on issues in macroeconomics, regional economics, and econometrics and published his work in leading journals. He holds a Ph.D. from Georgetown University. He is also the editor of *Cuadernos de Economía*. rsoto@faceapuc.cl

Fernando Vial is an Associate Professor and Head of Department of Economics at Universidad Católica del Norte, Chile. He received his Ph.D. from the University of Illinois at Urbana-Champaign where he worked on the development of integrated network analysis of spatial systems. fvial@ucn.cl

Miguel Atienza Úbeda is Ph.D. in Economics, Universidad Autónoma de Madrid and MPhil from the Institute of Development Studies (IDS),

University of Sussex. He is Assistant Professor at the Department of Economics, Universidad Católica del Norte, Antofagasta, Chile. His specialization is in urban and regional economics and his main research is oriented to spatial agglomerations, and human development.
miatien@ucn.cl

Sergio Zúñiga is an Associate Professor at the Escuela de Ingeniería Comercial (Business Administration School), Universidad Catolica del Norte, Coquimbo, Chile. He earned his B.S. in business (1987) at the Universidad Austral (Chile), M.A. in Finance (1993) at the Universidad de Chile, and a Doctorate in Financial Economics (1999) at the Universidad de Barcelona, Barcelona, Spain. For several years, he has worked on the behavior and structure of interest rates in Chile. He has published several papers on this subject on the principal refereed journals of Chile: *Economía Chilena* (Central Bank of Chile), *Cuadernos de Economia* (Catholic University of Chile), *Estudios de Administración* (University of Chile), and *Revista de Análisis Económico* (Instituto Latinoamericano de Doctrina y Estudios Sociales, ILADES-Georgetown University) among others. sz@ucn.cl

Preface

This volume has benefited from significant support from myriad organizations whose financial commitments have enabled the editors to meet on a frequent enough basis to steer this volume to production. A great deal of work has been undertaken on the macro economy of Chile but relatively little attention has been directed to problems at the sub-national level. This volume provides a sampling of some of the important insights that can be gained from regional or spatial perspectives.

The editors would like to thank Werner Baer, the Jorge Paulo Lemann Endowed Professor of Economics at the University of Illinois for his continuing support of research initiatives centered on Latin America. He has been a strong advocate in fostering continuing ties between the University and its distinguished Latin American alumni through the promotion of exchanges, conferences and books such as this one. We also want to thank to Adam Swallow from WIDER for his wise advice and assistance in the publication process. Guo Dong read through the manuscript carefully and helped immensely in preparing the final version. Mary Payne provided superb copy-editing, revealing in the process the importance of a set of "independent eyes" in the final reviewing of the manuscript.

Finally, the editors would like to thank our spouses, Yilly and Adrianna, for their support and understanding of our absences – even when we were still at home. Ms. Katie Button at Palgrave Macmillan has been a delight to work with and we thank her for her patience and support.

1 Introduction and Overview

Patricio A. Aroca and Geoffrey J.D. Hewings

The Chilean economy over the last three decades has been a source of continuous interest and fascination for economists, political scientists and development analysts. Moving from a regime with significant protectionist policies to one with a very open economy, embracing free trade reforms, negotiating multilateral and bilateral agreements, the macroeconomic indicators suggest that the economy has prospered. In this book, a collection of chapters has been assembled to explore the macroeconomic picture in more detail and to complement this with both more detailed sectoral evaluation and an analysis of the impacts at the regional level. The latter contributions reflect an increasing need to drill down from the macroeconomic perspective to explore the degree to which economic development has or has not contributed to reducing disparities in level of welfare across the country.

What was most surprising was the initiation of free trade reforms occurred from 1973 during a period when Chile was ruled by military government (with significant inputs from University of Chicago trained economists). The period between 1973 and 1982 witnessed both trade and financial liberalization that together with stabilization policies resulted in low inflation rates. These efforts were complemented with labor reforms, changes to the social security, education, and health systems and the initiation of administrative decentralization. This period began with a fall in GDP greater than 14 percent in 1974 (the oil crisis) and after a recovery, the economy suffered another collapse in 1982 but recovered such that between 1987 and 1997 it grew at an average annual rate of 8%. From 1990, democratically elected governments have managed to continue the pace of reform while achieving noteworthy growth rates.

Important questions arise – how has this been accomplished? What were the major engines for this growth? How effectively did the benefits of growth filter down to the constituent regions of the country? These questions provide the basis for many of the contributions to this book.

The chapters are grouped into three sections, Macroeconomic Analysis, Sectoral Analysis and Regional Analysis.

Macroeconomic Analysis

Reinhardt *et al.* provide an overview of the major economic reforms enacted over the period 1970-2000. As they note, the macroeconomic performance masked some less comfortable features of Chile's economy; while poverty has been reduced, they note that it averaged 20% of the population in 1999-2001, with extreme poverty accounting for one fourth of this figure. Further, as chapter 2 will explore, income distribution remains one of the most unequal in Latin America. Using a structural change index, their analysis reveals that high structural change corresponded to periods of low investment, and vice versa although more disaggregated data showed a somewhat different trend; the greatest degree of structural change occurred in the 1970s, in both the crisis and growth periods. However, it is still the case that structural change was lower during the high-investment and rapid-growth period of the mid 1980s to the mid 1990s.

Reinhardt *et al.* pose the question as to whether the outcomes from the reforms confirm expectations. The result is a mixed outcome; for the most part they appear to have been successful. The issue of aggregation plays an important role; for example, the decline in the share of manufacturing since 1985 (after accommodating changes in the national accounts base) masked the fact that specific sectors have been able to maintain or recover, especially those involved in the processing of natural resources. The problem would appear to lie in labor productivity; while it has increased for manufacturing as a whole at a rate faster than the rest of the economy, it has been low for some industry groups, especially those likely to be challenged by significant international competition. The authors provide important insights from their comparison of Chile's experience with East Asian countries where manufacturing growth (and manufacturing productivity growth) appear to have provided the major engines for economic development. They leave one question for continued monitoring and analysis: while Chile's economic reforms generated a decade of rapid economic growth, has the underlying economic structure developed in such a way that it will provide a strong foundation for the continued development of the economy?

Saavedra and Soto's macroeconomic perspective focuses on the role of the state as an institution and explores a variety of facets that delve into the structure of governance and the changes that have accompanied reform over the past three decades. Their thesis is that economic reform without strong supporting institutional reform may generate significant problems that may serve to dampen the anticipated economic benefits. In particular, they focus on the role of judicial reform with respect to the needed redesign of institutions that regulate, control and facilitate the operation of fair market performance and competition as well as to ensure the implementation of governance mechanisms to make the changes viable. In their assessment, the institutional structure of Chile's economy, the state apparatus most particularly, is incompatible with the efficient functioning of the market that the reforms were meant to open. The absence of profound changes in State administration, in the administration of justice and in the regulatory agencies and competition institutions will potentially impede the Chilean economy from reaching the high sustained growth rates needed to lead the country to full economic development.

Sectoral Analysis

The structural change index utilized in chapter 2 by Reinhardt *et al.*, suggested that there were important variations in the behavior and contribution to change when one disaggregated below macro aggregates such as manufacturing or services. In this part of the book, contributors examine a variety of sectoral issues.

Alvarez and Fuentes explore the impacts of trade reforms on the manufacturing sector, again looking at a more disaggregated view of this part of the economy. They point out the major changes that occurred between 1974 and 1979 in the effective rates of protection (ERP) enjoyed by the manufacturing industry, especially compared to other sectors in the economy. At the beginning of this period (1974), there was high ERP dispersion across the manufacturing sectors but there were almost no differences at the end of the period. These large changes in relative prices affected the allocation of resources within the economy. Alvarez and Fuentes challenge those who claim that the reforms initiated a deindustrialization process in Chile; while the share of manufacturing in GDP did decline between 1975 and 1985, the 1986-1999 average corresponds to the period prior to reforms; the major differences between the later and earlier period lie in the composition of the sectors within manufacturing. Essentially, as Reinhardt *et al.* noted, sectors more closely associated with natural resources and labor intensive activities have increase their importance, in terms of total value added, in the manufacturing industry while those sectors that are more capital intensive account for one fourth of the total value added, which is lower than their share in 1974. They found significant shifts in the structure and level of productivity in the manufacturing industry after the trade liberalization; of considerable importance was the finding that increases in productivity are closely associated with changes in technical efficiency for the manufacturing industry as a whole and for most manufacturing sectors. They do not find strong evidence of technological changes in the manufacturing industry.

While Alvarez and Fuentes did explore the role of manufacturing in exports, Reinhardt focuses attention on Chile's export structure in chapter 5. The author notes that in contrast to the Asian economies where the basis for new export success was created through a wide array of government interventions in favor of new export activities, the Chilean government, adhered fairly strictly to the neoliberal doctrine of non-intervention in the 1970s, becoming directly supportive of export activities only after the economic crisis of the early 1980s. As others have noted, Chile's exports have come to be dominated by sectors related to natural resources; these are commodities that are vulnerable to severe price fluctuations. With rising real wages and appreciating currency, Reinhardt feels that these factors will threaten the profitability and continued international competitiveness of Chile's principal exports. The issue raised is whether Chile should continue to invest to expand or at least protect its existing comparative advantage or invest to seek new comparative advantages.

Inflation has proven to be one of the persistent problems in many Latin American countries; Zúñiga explores the role of inflation targeting in Chile to see whether the received wisdom that inflation targeting generates a real product stabilization with a cost in an apparent increase in financial instability applies in the Chilean case. Of note, the Chilean central bank became independent in 1990; however, data preclude a "before" and "after" evaluation of the success or otherwise of targeting since independence. Using a sophisticated econometric specification, the three regimes we analyzed. These were an initial stage towards independence of the Chilean Central Bank (1990:5 -1995:5); the second represents the period in which the Central Bank used the interbank real daily rate as a tool of monetary policy (1995:05 - 2001:08) and the third regime represented the period in which the Central Bank employed a nominal daily interest rate (2001:08 - 2002:12). One of the most important findings from this analysis was that although volatility has increased towards the last regime, the responses are smoother, suggesting an increase in the anticipative capacity of the market. This appears to be associated with more degrees in the transparency of Chilean monetary policy, a finding that parallels research in the US that found market anticipation of the actions of the US Federal Reserve Board beginning in the 1980s.

Given the role the agricultural exports play in the Chilean economy, it is appropriate that a chapter be devoted to this sector. As Aguilar and Dresdner note, after World War II agriculture was singled out as a main cause of the problems affecting Chile's economy at that time. Chile had been suffering of persistent high inflation during a quite long period and problems in agriculture were thought to be a main cause, generating a broad consensus about the need to introduce deep structural transformations in the agriculture. Of paramount importance was land reform that together with other important innovations in processing succeeded in significantly transforming the agricultural into one of the leading technological, export and growth sectors of the Chilean economy in the 1990s. The authors point out the important role that prior investments in human capital in agriculture played, investments that date back to the 1930s. In essence, they provided the necessary conditions that enhanced the adoption of new techniques, spurring the significant productivity advances that have been well documented. In contrast, the econometric analysis was not able to draw a strong, formal relationship between domestic (macroeconomic) policies and agricultural development; on the other hand, the real exchange rates played a major role, especially in changing the terms of trade for agricultural exports. Of course, the successes in agriculture also aided those forward-linked industrial sectors responsible for processing much of the agricultural outputs.

Regional Analysis

Macroeconomic analysis tends to ignore what goes on inside an economy; however, most economies are characterized by significant core-periphery dichotomies, often exacerbated by a strong primate city. For many Latin American countries, the disparities in levels of regional welfare have been large and persistent, notwithstanding long-standing government intervention. Aroca *et al.* take up some of the newly developed tools of spatial econometrics to analyze the importance of geography in regional growth. This perspective is used to characterize growth features in the Chilean economy. Spatial econometric analysis is used to examine the spatial dependence of regional per capita GDP in Chile for the last four decades, avoiding earlier problems that treated regions in isolation from each other. The indicators of spatial dependence show a dramatic increase of the GDP's spatial interdependence in the last 15 years. This coincides with the collapse of the reduction of disparities between the Chilean regions. It has also been shown that during this period, the formation of clusters, especially in the north, has been remarkably intense. The idea of unconditional convergence during this period can be strongly rejected; only when the fixed effects are included does the convergence parameter takes its usual sign and value. The existence of highly significant fixed effects for all regions denotes the lack of a common steady state.

We have also shown that the FDI has been a major contributor to the consolidation of the Northern cluster throughout the 1990s provoking a polarization between dynamic and lagging regions. Public investment has not been able to promote lagging regions. Further, location factors are attracting FDI to natural resources exploitation; since natural resources are spatially concentrated, FDI will continue increasing the spatial dependence, while the Chilean FDI abroad has been focused in manufacturing and services thus of little direct help others regions in Chile that are poor in natural resources, reducing the likelihood that they will catch up with the northern regions. These findings provide an additional perspective to Reinhardt's study of exports; not only is Chile sectorally concentrated in exports, but spatially as well. Thus, there is a tension between national policies promoting the development of a multicountry market (MERCOSUR) and those attempting to reduce internal disparities between regions. It is a problem shared by many other countries in Latin America.

Úbeda delves into the New Economic Geography (NEG) to explore the degree to which the core-periphery model that has become such a prominent feature of this literature provides valuable insights into the Chilean experience. The analysis of industry location factors in Chile between 1985 and 1997 reveal the existence of different patterns of location among regions especially in the case of the Metropolitan Region and northern and southern regions of the country and possibly contribute to maintain a core-periphery structure that has retarded the regional dispersion of industrial activities.

However, the NEG model that was estimated revealed that internal trade costs were not a significant factor for industry location. It would be possible to say that some regions with relatively poor paved roads endowment have attracted more employment than the rest. This unexpected result could be related with the relevance of raw materials intensity as a dispersion force. Some firms need to be located close to the sources of raw materials even if internal trade costs are high.

The main centripetal forces in the economic geography of Chile between 1985 and 1997 were the external scale economies arising from the relative specialization of the Metropolitan Region in activities from the same industrial branch and, above all, the relative productivity of labor that, in the Metropolitan Region, had a positive effect on industrial labor growth, one that was significantly higher than in the rest of the country. The main centrifugal force was the intensity in the use of raw materials, used as a proxy of regional comparative advantage in natural resource endowment. These results imply the existence of a location pattern that, at the very least, contributes to preserve the primacy of the Metropolitan Region and to delay the process of regional dispersion of activities. The location pattern may be characterized as comprising two parts. The first part is a core region, with a diversified industrial fabric and mainly oriented to the domestic market; the second part comprises various peripheral regions, predominantly export-oriented and highly specialized in the production of raw materials intensive manufactures where productive linkages tend to be weak and give rise to few external scale economies.

Vial *et al.* turn their attention to the labor market; if the findings of the previous chapter suggest persistence of core-periphery dimensions in development, does this translate into regional separate labor markets? In a competitive economy with homogenous space, and with no significant costs on factor and information mobility, similar workers in the same type of occupation should obtain similar wages no matter where they live. Regional wage differentials for identical workers would be cleared by movements of labor and capital that sought to take advantage of those differences. The analysis used a two-level model; in the first level, attention was directed to sector characteristics; in the second level, individual worker characteristics were included. While significant regional variations were found, part of the explanation may lie in differences in cost of living between regions; there seemed to be only small variations across space when attention was directed to sectoral-regional differences. Hence, the source of variation may be found in the human capital components of wage setting.

Finally, Robles and Hewings return to the issue raised in chapter 8 about the role of foreign direct investment (FDI). There have been many studies made concerning the impact of FDI, either as a determinant or as a dependent variable, but very few studies have considered the determinants of FDI at a regional level. The case of Chile is interesting because the patterns for FDI tend to be clearer over time; the regions tend to specialize in their activities and in the ways in which they attract FDI. Hence, it would seem important to investigate the determinants for FDI across regions and to explore whether there are certain regions that are able to attract more FDI than others. The use of panel data specifications was appropriate and revealed for the main dependent variables (authorized and realized FDI) that the fixed effects specifications were significant. As FDI has evolved from the primary to the tertiary sector, the determinants have also evolved, making necessary the search for other factors that could explain the attraction of FDI. For the case of the services sector, the analysis revealed that it was not market-seeking FDI, since the typical factors considered for this kind of FDI were not significant. Hence, it appeared that this type of investment was market-capture FDI. Consideration of spatial effects or more specific factors such as trade arrangements, or the inclusion of Chile into to larger trade markets, would need to be tested in future work.

Remaining Challenges

Unfortunately, no book of this size can embrace the full range of issues associated with structural change. The sample of contributions explores facets of macroeconomic, sectoral and regional dimensions of change. Underlying these issues are other important concerns. For example, an economy whose exports are dominated by resource-based activities needs to evaluate the environmental dimensions of this dependency; sustainability needs to be addressed from both an economic and an environmental perspective. The challenges range from depopulation of fish species on the one hand to the impacts of large-scale copper mining on the other hand.

The issue of poverty has been raised but not formally addressed; closely allied with poverty are issues of both unemployment and underemployment and especially its concentration in urban areas. The issues raised in chapters 9 and 11 provide the basis for future explorations of this dimension of economic development, a dimension that is increasingly been shown to have important features of spatial concentration.

One of the dilemmas raised by Reinhardt was Chile's response to deepening its dependence on those export sectors in which it currently enjoys an international competitive advantage versus the option of diversifying into new, potentially competitive sectors. The experience with the success of agriculture, as Aguilar and Dresdner remind us, may be traced in part to significant investments in human capital (education) dating from the 1930s. It remains to be seen whether anyone has enough confidence in ability of analysts to forecast the future so that strategic investments can be made now in human capital to position the Chilean economy to be competitive one or two decades from now.

Finally, the physical geography of Chile presents significant logistical problems; greater integration with the MERCOSUR countries, with a proposed Free Trade Area of the Americas, with Asia or the European Union will be heavily dependent on decisions about logistics. Transportation infrastructure, like investments in human capital, consumes scarce resources now to yield benefits later. The synergism between trade partnerships and transportation presents one of the greatest challenges for almost all Latin American countries.

Part I

Macroeconomic Analysis

2 Structural Change in the Chilean Economy: The Sectoral Impact of Economic Reforms, 1970-2000

Nola Reinhardt, Wilson Peres and Nelson Correa

Introduction

The economic reforms introduced in the 1970s in Chile, and later in most of the Latin American countries, were expected to generate significant change in economic structure. Proponents of the reforms argued that the interventionist import-substitution policies of the past had created a structure that was distorted in a number of significant ways: resources had been artificially drawn into import-competing activities that were alien to the country's comparative advantage; resources were being inefficiently managed by the state; and firms were seeking rents rather than increased productivity due to lack of competitive pressures. A return to market-based signals would result in an allocation of productive resources that more closely followed the comparative advantage of the country, resulting in greater efficiency and growth.

In a previous work (Reinhardt and Peres, 2000), we examined the overall changes in economic structure in the Latin American region following the reforms. There we found that the reforms did indeed lead to some of the expected changes in economic structure, but not always, and not always with the anticipated outcomes. In this chapter, we focus in depth on the Chilean case, using the same methodology developed previously. We use a structural change index (SCI) to examine changes in economic structure between productive sectors as well as within the manufacturing sector. Our database for manufacturing is the PADI software developed by ECLAC. In this program, data for Chile are taken from the ENIA (Yearly National Industrial Survey), which presents information for 29 manufacturing sectors at the four-digit level of the International Standard Industrial Classification (ISIC).[1]

It is particularly instructive to consider structural change in the Chilean economy because it has led the region in economic reform. According to Stallings and Peres (2000), it is the only country in Latin America that has reached the third or "consolidation" stage of the region's New Economic Model. The results, according to some analyses, have been impressive. Chile's 5.0% average annual per capita GDP growth rate in the 1990s was higher than that of any other country in the region and well above the regional average of 1.5%. Other positive indicators are its low inflation rate, its high savings and investment ratios, and its fiscal surplus from 1991 to 1998. At the same time, however, there is a darker underside to Chile's economic performance, emphasized in other analyses. Although the record high poverty rates of the 1980s have been significantly reduced, poverty in the 1990s has remained persistently high, still averaging 20% of the population in 1999-2001, with extreme poverty accounting for one fourth of this figure. Equally disturbing is the fact that income distribution remains one of the most unequal in the region. And Chile's urban unemployment rate was above the regional average from 1990 to 1994 and again in 1999-2000; by 2002 it was almost 10%.[2] Furthermore, Chile's economic performance is less satisfactory if we consider the entire 30 years since reforms were first introduced, as we discuss below.

An analysis of the economy's structural change helps us to understand these different facets of Chile's economic performance. It also suggests some lessons for other countries following a similar reform path.

Reform Implementation and Economic Structure

In Chile, as elsewhere in the region, the import substitution policies of the 1950s and 1960s had supported the growth of the manufacturing sector. By 1970, this sector accounted for 26% of Chile's total output. Mining, which accounted for some 80% of exports, was only 7% of total output, and agriculture accounted for another 9%. The reforms introduced after

---

[1] PADI is based on ENIA data for 1979-99; for previous years, it uses information from *Industrias Manufactureras*, Instituto Nacional de Estadística (INE), several years. The ENIA does not include firms with employment between 1 and 8 people, that is to say microfirms. For 1970-1980, PADI uses a single deflator for all manufacturing sectors. From then on, it has a deflator for each ISIC sector. The PADI database has been widely used for analysis on structural change in Latin America (see, for example, Bielschowsky and Stumpo, 1995, and Katz and Stumpo 2001). However, we know of only one work based on PADI that studies the Chilean case in detail (Stumpo, 2000).

[2] Poverty data from ECLAC 2002. All other data from ECLAC 2000 and 2001, and INE website.

1973 dismantled the structure of protection and subsidies that had underpinned this economic structure. Given Chile's rich natural resource base, the liberalizing reforms of the Pinochet regime were expected to induce a shift of resources away from heavy, import-substitution manufacturing towards the primary sector. The latter would expand in response to the greater relative attractiveness of exporting following the elimination of protectionism. Overall efficiency would be enhanced by this redirection of resources along the lines of international comparative advantage.

The gains were expected to be dynamic as well as static. Greater economic competition would force firms to seek continued productivity improvements. Greater efficiency would lead to greater investment, which in turn would lead to economic growth. Investment would also be stimulated by the privatization of the large state sector, including both industrial and financial enterprises. Although exports were to be the leading sector, general economic growth would lead to growth in non-tradables as well. All told, the structural changes induced by the reforms would lead to an improved standard of living for the population.

The Chilean reforms were dramatic in their scope and intensity. A good measure of reform implementation is the set of indexes developed for Latin America by Morley *et al.* (1999) focusing on five reform areas: trade, finance, capital account, tax, and privatization, with a general reform index that includes all five. The indexes range from 0 (lowest level of reform implementation) to 1 (highest level). Chile's overall index jumped from 0.316 in 1973 to 0.576 by 1975, taking it from below to above the regional average. Continuing reforms through the rest of the decade brought the index to a high of 0.788 by 1981 – a level that would not be reached by the regional average until more than ten years later.

Figure 2.1 highlights two main features of Chilean economic performance after the reforms: investment and GDP growth. Investment is presumably the main vehicle for the restructuring of the economy in response to the new economic signals under the reforms. It was anticipated that resulting efficiency gains would spur more rapid economic growth. While the performance on these two indicators has been quite strong from the mid-1980s to the late 1990s, the experience before that time was variable and, on the whole, disappointing. Investment averaged only 16% of GDP in the 1974-84 period, falling from 21.2% in 1974 to a low of 12.8% by 1976, recovering to a high of 22.7% in 1981, and then collapsing to a low of 9.8% in 1983. By 1987 it had recovered to 22.2%, and from 1987-1998 it averaged a strong 24.9%. Overall economic growth similarly has been quite variable. An initial sharp recession after the reforms was followed by a period of recovery and growth lasting until 1981, at which time the economy collapsed. The economic crisis was followed by a period of recovery and then by a period of strong growth from 1986-1998. The Asian crisis resulted in a sharp contraction of economic growth after 1998, from which the economy is only gradually emerging. Given these fluctuations, the average annual GDP growth rate during 1973-2001 was only 4.1%, although this is still more than a full percentage point above the average for Latin America.

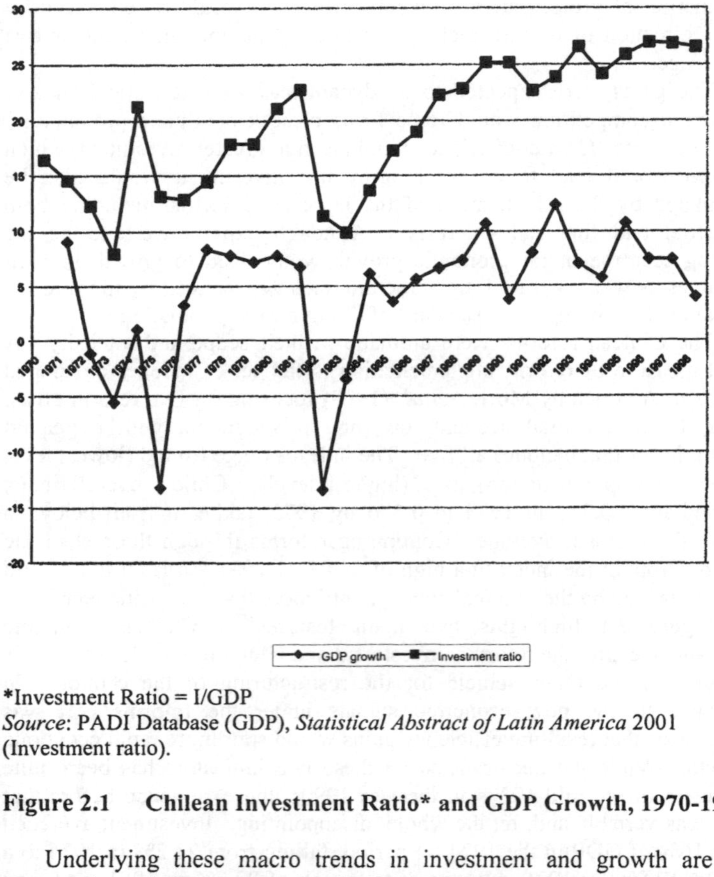

*Investment Ratio = I/GDP
Source: PADI Database (GDP), *Statistical Abstract of Latin America* 2001 (Investment ratio).

Figure 2.1 Chilean Investment Ratio* and GDP Growth, 1970-1998

Underlying these macro trends in investment and growth are the structural trends in sectoral development under the reforms. Using share data for different economic sectors, we can measure the overall extent of structural change in the economy by calculating a "structural change index" or SCI. The SCI measures the shift in the share of output in the various categories over a given time period:

$$SCI = \sum_i | s_{ie} - s_{ib} | / 2$$

where s_{ie} is the share of category *i* at end of period, and s_{ib} is the share of category *i* at the beginning of the period.[3] The value of the index ranges from 0 (no change in shares) to 1 (complete change).

Table 2.1 shows the development of Chile's economic structure between 1970 and 2000 in terms of broad sectors of economic activity, while table 2.2 provides a slightly more disaggregated picture of changes within the three broad primary, secondary, and tertiary sectors. For purposes of this analysis, the "primary" sector is defined as agriculture and mining (natural resource activities), "industry" includes manufacturing and construction, and services are divided into two broad categories of basic services (primarily utilities) and others. From the data in table 2.1, we can see that the expected structural change indeed occurred, with industry declining while the primary and tertiary sectors expanded. The more disaggregate data in table 2 also show a general decline in the industrial subsectors, while the primary subsectors increased, as did all but one of the service subsectors.

Table 2.1 Sector Shares, Four Sectors, 1970-2000

Sector	1970-1985a: 1977 prices				1985b-2000: 1986 prices			
	1970	1975	1980	1985a	1985b	1990	1995	2000
Primary	15.6	18.3	15.6	19.2	19.8	19.5	17.8	19.7
Industry	33.3	27.2	27.2	26.1	23.2	24.4	23.9	21.1
Basic svc	6.8	7.6	7.8	8.2	9.4	9.6	11.2	13.3
Other svc	44.3	47.0	49.4	46.5	47.7	46.5	47.0	46.0
Period		70-75	75-80	80- 85a		85b-90	90-95	95-00
SCI		.06	.03	.04		.01	.02	.03

Primary sector: agriculture and mining; *Industry*: manufacturing and construction; *Basic services*: utilities and transportation/storage/communication; *Other services*: finance, trade, and personal services.
Source: ECLAC *Statistical Yearbook*, various years.

Nevertheless, the trends have not been uniform in their direction or intensity. The results reported in table 2.1 show that overall structural change was greatest during the two crisis periods, 1970-75 and 1980-85, and considerably lower during the rapid growth periods of the mid 80s to mid 90s. Comparing to the trends in figure 2.1, we see that high structural change thus corresponded to periods of low investment, and vice versa. However, the more disaggregate data presented in table 2 show a somewhat different trend. The pattern of greater change in the two crisis periods no longer holds. What we see instead is that the greatest degree of structural change occurred in the 1970s, in both the crisis and growth

[3] Since any change in one share is matched by an equal change in other shares, the total must be divided by 2 to remove double counting.

periods. It is still the case, however, that structural change has been lowest during the high-investment and rapid-growth period of the mid-80s to the mid-90s.

Table 2.2 Sector Shares, Nine Sectors, 1970-2000

	1977 prices				1986 prices				%	%	
Sector	1970	1975	1980	1985 a	1985 b	1990	1995	2000	Chg 1970-85	Chg 1985-00	Over-all chg
Agri	8.8	10.3	8.4	10.1	8.8	9.9	9.2	8.5	+12.9	-3.4	+
Mini	6.8	8.0	7.3	9.1	11.0	9.6	8.6	11.2	+33.8	+1.8	+
Mfg	25.6	21.6	21.8	20.9	18.4	18.7	18.1	16.1	-18.4	-12.5	-
Cons	7.7	5.6	5.3	5.3	4.8	5.7	5.8	5.0	-31.2	+4.2	-
Util	1.8	2.3	2.2	2.6	2.8	2.1	2.7	2.9	+44.4	+3.6	+
Tran	5.0	5.3	5.7	5.6	6.6	7.6	8.5	10.4	+12.0	+57.6	+
Fina	11.4	13.8	15.6	14.6	18.7	18.6	18.9	18.7	+28.1	n.c.	+
Trad	17.1	13.9	18.7	16.0	14.8	16.3	18.6	18.7	-6.4	+26.4	+
Pers.	15.7	19.4	15.1	15.9	14.1	11.7	9.6	8.6	+1.3	-39.0	-
Period	70-75	75-80	80-85a		85b-90	90-95	95-00				
SCI		.10	.07	.05		.05	.04	.05			

Source: ECLAC *Statistical Yearbook*, various years.

Disaggregating further, we see in both tables that the greatest change in the 1970s took place in the first half of the decade, with much of the continued high change in the second half being a reversal of the previous trends. All sectors except for construction, transportation, and financial services reversed their direction of change in the second half of the decade. The shift into agriculture and mining was reversed, manufacturing stabilized, and personal services dropped sharply. A similar pattern is evident in the 1980s: in the second half of the decade, only agriculture continued to change in the same direction as in the previous crisis period.

This pattern of fluctuating shares rather than steady trend is evident for most sectors over the entire 30-year period. Unfortunately, because of a change in the base period for price corrections after 1985, we cannot compare shares before 1985 to those thereafter. However, we can look at direction of change in each subperiod. Overall, the two consistent trends have been the decline of manufacturing and the growth of transportation/storage/communication. Manufacturing lost 18.4% of its share in the 1970-85 period, and another 12.5% in the 1985-2000 period, with only two periods of extremely modest gains during the post-crisis recoveries. While the decline of this sector following the elimination of most ISI incentives was expected, it may be problematic that manufacturing has continued to lose share more than two decades after the reforms.

With respect to the two primary sectors, agriculture and mining, while they have indeed posted an overall gain, there has not been a continuous trend. Rather, their performance has been quite erratic, with their share alternately expanding and contracting between five-year periods. This reflects the greater instability of primary production and marketing, which raises concerns for these sectors as growth engines.

These broad changes in Chile's economic structure bear some similarities to other Latin American countries. Table 2.3 presents data on structural change for eight countries for which data was available. These data are not strictly analogous, since the base years for price corrections differ, but the direction of change can still be compared. The most salient result is that the share of industry declined during the crisis period of the 1980s in all the countries for which data was available. In half the countries, industrial share turned around after 1985, but in the other half, including Chile, it did not. On the other hand, Chile follows the pattern of most of the other countries of increasing share of agriculture during the 1980s crisis, and declining share overall in the post-crisis period.

It is also instructive to compare Chile's structural change to that of the East Asian economies, countries that have also followed an outward-oriented export-led growth strategy. Indeed, many observers have grouped Chile with these economies for that reason. Table 2.4 presents the available data for sector shares in five Asian countries, from 1980 up to the year of the Asian financial crisis. From these data, we can see that the share of agriculture declined steadily in all five countries, while the share of industry increased steadily in every country except the Philippines. This pattern of change is strikingly dissimilar to that of Chile.

Table 2.3 Change in Sector Shares, Nine Latin American Countries

	1980-85[a]					1985-2000[b]				
Country	Agri	Min	nd	Basic Svcs	Other Svcs	Agri	Min	nd	Basic Svcs	Other Svcs
Argentina	+	NC	-	-	+	-	+	-	NC	+
Bolivia	+	-	-	+	+	-	-	+	+	+
Colombia	-	+	-	-	+	-	+	-	-	+
Ecuador	+	+	-	-	-	+	-	+	+	-
Mexico	NC	NC	-	-	+	-	-	+	+	-
Peru	na	na	a	na	na	+	-	+	NC	-
Uruguay	+	-	-	-	+	-	+	-	+	+
Venezuela	na	na	a	na	na	-	+	-	-	+
Chile	+	+	-	+	-	-	+	-	+	-

[a] Mexico: 1980-88; not available for Peru and Venezuela.
[b] Mexico: 1988-2000.
Source: ECLAC Statistical Yearbook, various years.

Table 2.4 Structural Change in Five Asian Countries, 1980-1997

Country/sector	1980	1990	1997	Direction of change
Indonesia				
Agriculture	30*	19	16	-
Industry	34*	39	44	+
Services	36*	41	40	+
Malaysia				
Agriculture	22	19	9	-
Industry	38	39	44	+
Services	40	42	47	+
Philippines				
Agriculture	23	22	19	-
Industry	37	35	32	-
Services	40	43	49	+
South Korea				
Agriculture	16	9	6	-
Industry	41	43	43	+
Services	43	48	51	+
Thailand				
Agriculture	23	12	11	-
Industry	29	39	40	+
Services	48	48	49	+

*1977 data.
Source: UNESCAP, 1997, 1998; World Bank, 1998.

Table 2.5 presents the evolution of the structure of employment in Chile. To keep it consistent with the categories of table 2.1, we had to concentrate on the 1987-98 period. The most significant result is that tradable sectors continued their long-term decline, while both groups of services increased their participation, a result compatible with the secular trend pointed out by Stallings and Peres (2000).

Table 2.5 Employment Shares, Four Sectors, 1987-1998

	1987	1990	1996	1998
Primary	9.2	8.0	8.4	7.6
Industry	26.5	28.6	26.2	24.3
Basic Services	8.1	8.2	8.4	9.2
Other Services	56.2	55.2	56.9	58.9

Source: ECLAC *Statistical Yearbook*, various years.

Manufacturing Sector: Structure, Employment and Productivity

Manufacturing Structural Change Indexes in Comparative Perspective

We have seen that, contrary to the pattern in most of the Asian countries and many of the Latin American ones, manufacturing has declined in Chile in the three decades since the reforms. This decline has not been uniform across all manufacturing industries, however. Indeed, the structure of the manufacturing sector has undergone significant change.

Table 2.6 Structural Change Index, Manufacturing Value Added, 1970-99

Country	1970-80	1980-90	1990-99
Argentina	0.07	0.12	0.09
Brazil	0.13	0.08	0.09
Chile	0.21	0.09	0.11
Colombia	0.10	0.09	0.13
Mexico	0.07	0.07	0.06
Peru	0.16	0.12	0.16
Venezuela	0.15	0.15	0.16
Total [a]	0.11	0.09	0.09

[a] SCI for 7 countries, calculated as sum of each country SCI weighted by country's share of beginning year total value added.
Source: Calculated from the PADI data base.

Table 2.6 presents manufacturing structural change indexes for the seven medium and large Latin American countries. In the 1970s, Chile's manufacturing sector experienced significantly more change than in the other countries. This is consistent with the data in tables 2.1 and 2.2, that showed that the greatest overall structural change in Chile took place in the 1970s. It is also interesting to observe that manufacturing change in Chile in that decade of reform was considerably greater than that experienced by the other countries in their 1990s reform decade.[4]

The same pattern emerges with manufacturing employment, as table 2.7 demonstrates. In Chile, the greatest change in employment structure took place in the 1970s, and again, this change was much greater than that experienced by the other countries in the1990s. It is interesting to note that there was virtually no difference between countries in the extent of

[4] It is also interesting to note that Venezuela, which had the lowest reform effort, had the highest structural change index in the 1990s - tied with Peru, a country whose reform effort was substantial.

structural change in manufacturing employment in that decade, although their reform effort varied widely.

Table 2.7 Structural Change Index, Manufacturing Employment, 1970-99

	1970-80	1980-90	1990-99 [b]
Argentina	0.09	0.09	0.09
Brazil	0.14	0.06	0.08
Chile	0.16	0.08	0.09
Colombia	0.09	0.07	0.08
Mexico	0.08	0.09	0.09
Peru	0.14	0.19	0.09
Venezuela	0.12	0.06	0.09
Total [a]	0.11	0.08	0.09

[a] SCI for 7 countries, calculated as sum of each country SCI weighted by country's share of beginning year total employment.
[b] 1990-96 for Peru; 1990-97 for Venezuela; 1990-98 for Chile and Colombia.
Source: Calculated from the PADI database.

Table 2.8 Manufacturing Employment, 1990-1999

	1990	1999	% change
Argentina	802,777	608,113	- 24%
Brazil	5,784,303	3,311,782	- 43%
Chile	369,817	380,043	+ 3%
Colombia	488,800	424,197	- 13%
Mexico	3,275,199	3,540,119	+ 8%
Peru	480,177	539,842	+12%
Venezuela	464,400	431,818	- 7%
Total	11,665,472	9,235,915	- 21%

Source: PADI database.

Although the magnitude of structural change in manufacturing value-added was similar across countries in the 1990s, the magnitude and direction of manufacturing employment growth in that decade differed considerably between countries, as table 2.8 shows. Chile is one of only three countries exhibiting positive manufacturing employment growth in the 1990s. However, the overall increase was small, slightly over 10,000 workers or a 3% increase for the decade. This is striking considering that Chile's overall economic growth was high during most of this decade.

Trends in Value-Added and Employment Shares by Manufacturing Industry Group

Given that there has been considerable structural change within Chile's manufacturing sector in the 30 years since the reforms were introduced, which industries have been growth sectors, and which have been stagnant or declining? Of particular interest is the question of whether there has been any pattern to the trends based on the resource intensity, and presumably therefore the comparative advantage, of each industry. To carry out this analysis, we have divided manufacturing industry into the following groups:

AG (*agricultural processing*): of grains, oils, fruits and vegetables, fish, meat and dairy, wine, non-alcoholic beverages, tobacco; ISIC 311,313,314.

NR (*natural resource processing*): products of wood, rubber, glass, ferrous metals; ISIC 331, 341, 351, 354, 355, 362, 369, 371. It does not include ISIC 353 (petroleum refineries).

LA1 (*basic labor-intensive products*): textiles, clothing, shoes, and leather; ISIC 321, 322, 323, 324.

LA2 (*other labor-intensive products*): furniture, printing and publishing, some chemicals, ceramics, and plastics; ISIC 332, 342, 352, 356, 361, 390.

MM (*capital and technology intensive products*): metal-working, machinery, and scientific equipment; ISIC 381, 382, 383, 384, 385.

CO (*copper and other non-ferrous metals*): including silver, gold, tin, lead, and molybdenum; ISIC 372.

Table 2.9 Manufacturing Value Added in Millions of US$, by Type of Industry*

Group	1970	1975	1980	1985	1990	1995	1997	1999
AG	864.9	878.3	1,540.8	1,374.9	1,954.4	3,230.7	3,363.9	3,302.8
NR	742.0	679.0	1,076.3	1,087.2	1,506.7	2,257.8	2,331.9	2,275.4
LA1	652.7	359.1	552.7	382.2	606.6	674.0	594.1	458.8
LA2	444.7	385.1	752.0	580.5	999.1	1,663.0	1,817.9	1,826.0
MM	833.4	638.9	626.9	367.5	763.1	1,180.5	1,448.6	1,258.0
CO	1,406.1	658.8	973.7	1,178.0	1,313.4	1,069.5	1,445.7	945.6
Total	4,943.7	3,599.2	5,522.3	4,970.2	7,143.2	10,075.4	11,002.0	10,066.

*In 1985 dollars. The PADI database uses just one deflator for the whole manufacturing sector. This particularly affects the comparison of 1970 data with those for 1980.

Table 2.9 presents data on trends in value-added for each of these groups. From these data, we can see that overall manufacturing value-added has approximately doubled in the 30-year period, although it declined in the recessions of 1974-75, the early 1980s, and the late 1990s. The most dynamic group has been food processing, which almost quadrupled, followed by the natural resource intensive industries, which tripled. These two groups experienced overall growth in each of the three decades.

Labor-intensive industries alternately shrank and expanded in the 1970s and 1980s. The basic labor-intensive industries declined overall in the 1990s, while other labor-intensive industries experienced strong and steady growth after 1985. The metalworking and machinery industries experienced a sharp and steady decline until 1985, after which they steadily increased until the late 1990s. Even with the drop after 1997, value-added in this group in 1999 was almost four times its low in 1985, although only around 50% above its 1970 level. The copper industry has experienced considerable fluctuations, with no clear overall trend in value-added.

Table 2.10 Manufacturing Value-Added Shares by Industry Group

Group	1970	1980	1990	1999
AG	17.5	27.9	27.4	32.8
NR	15.0	19.5	21.1	22.6
LA1	13.2	10.0	8.5	4.6
LA2	9.0	13.6	14.0	18.1
MM	16.9	11.4	10.7	12.5
CO	28.4	17.6	18.4	

Source: Calculated from Table 9.

The changes in the structure of the manufacturing sector resulting from these differential growth rates can be seen clearly in the share data presented in table 2.10. Considering first the decade of the reforms, we see a shift in productive structure within manufacturing that is consistent with the general expectations. The two main ISI sectors, basic consumer-goods industries (LA1) and capital goods industries (MM), lost share in the 1970s. On the other hand, the primary processing industries (AG and NR) sharply increased their share. The "other labor-intensive" industries (LA2) also increased their share, which may seem surprising until we realize that the largest industry within this group is chemicals, which could also be considered natural-resource intensive.[5] This industry increased its share within the LA2 group from 43% to 50% in the 1970s. Conversely,

[5] While we follow the current ECLAC practice —based on a detailed analysis of the firms included in this category— of classifying this industry as labor-intensive (see Benavente *et al.* 1997), other studies have classified many of the chemical products as natural-resource intensive (UNIDO, 1981; CEPAL, 1992).

copper and other non-ferrous metals (CO) decreased in share over the 1970s. Most of this fall took place in the first half of the decade, when copper prices experienced sharp fluctuations in the world market and production in Chile was disrupted because of political upheaval.

Considering the entire three decades, we see the same pattern of change. The strongest growth industries have been those based on agriculture and other natural resources, whose combined share of manufacturing value-added increased from 32.5% in 1970, to 55.4% in 1999. The LA2 group, of which chemicals accounted for 59% of the total by 1999, doubled their share of manufacturing value-added from 9% to 18.1%. The groups losing share were the basic labor-intensive industries, the capital and technology-intensive industries, and the non-ferrous metals.

Another key facet of structural change in manufacturing is the distribution of manufacturing employment by industry group, shown in table 2.11. For four groups, employment share trends have mirrored those of value-added shares; both shares up for AG and LA2, both down for MM and LA1. For NR, both increased in the 1980s, but since then employment share has fallen while value-added share continued to increase. The opposite is true for CO, where value-added share has fallen while employment share has increased.

Table 2.11 Employment Shares by Manufacturing Industry Group

Sectors	1970	1980	1990	1998
AG	19.5	26.7	29.9	33.2
NR	17.6	19.2	17.6	17.6
LA1	24.3	20.4	19.4	12.9
LA2	12.0	13.8	15.1	17.0
MM	24.5	16.5	15.6	15.7
CO	2.2	3.3	2.4	3.7

Source: Calculated from PADI database.

Leading and Lagging Manufacturing Sectors: Productivity and Growth Implications

The differences we have identified between the LA1 and LA2 sectors deserve further consideration because they run against the common perception that all labor-intensive sectors have performed poorly in Chile since the reforms, both in absolute terms and in relation to the NR and AG industries. Figure 2.2 shows the sharp contrast in the external competition faced by the LA1 and LA2 groups. In the two growth periods of the three decades under consideration (1978-1982 and 1990-1998), the coefficient of imports to total supply —defined as imports divided by imports plus gross production value— of the LA1 group grew very fast, particularly during the 1990s, reaching a level close to 36%. In contrast, the LA2 group experienced a rapid growth in its coefficient immediately following the reforms, i.e., during the most important period of structural change. The coefficient peaked in 1977 and fell sharply during the 1978-82 growth period. It then stabilized for a decade, before starting to grow moderately in the 1990s to reach some 22% by the end of the decade.

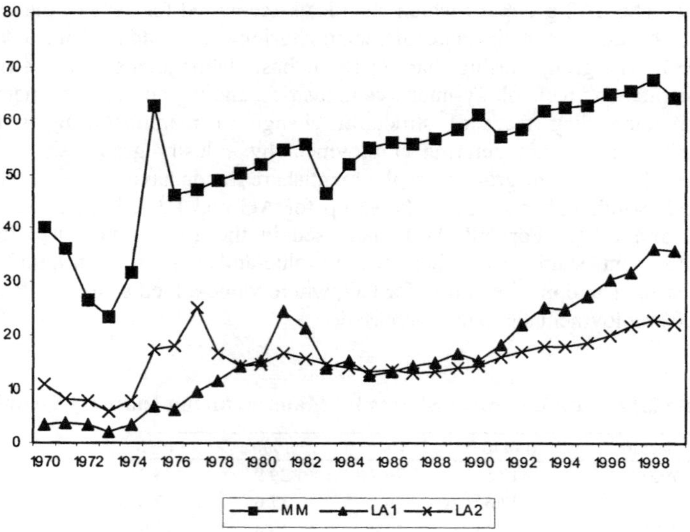

Source: PADI Database

Figure 2.2 Imports as a Percentage of Total Supply, Three Industry Groups

All this suggests that LA2 industries were able to adapt quickly to the new economic framework created by the reforms and could rapidly recover their share of the domestic market. This group includes some industries that build on Chile's natural-resource base and thus its natural comparative advantage (furniture, chemicals, ceramics). Conversely, the basic labor-intensive industries experienced a continuous deterioration in market share. Strong foreign competition in products like garments and footwear created an insurmountable pressure: by the late 1990s, value added in the LA1 group was below the 1970 level.

The strong implication is that Chile does not have an advantage in unskilled-labor-intensive products, except those that also are intensive in natural resources. This is consistent with a recent finding that Latin

America as a whole is not competitive in unskilled labor-intensive manufactures, given that the large Asian countries have a much greater population with no education or only primary schooling (IDB, 2001).

The decline in the MM sector can also be understood in terms of increased import pressure, as figure 2.2 demonstrates. The import to total supply coefficient for MM increased sharply immediately after the reforms, stabilized at around that level for the next decade, and then began to increase slowly but steadily from the mid-1980s to 1998. The performance of the MM sector followed these trends: MM value-added share dropped precipitously in the 1970s, stabilized in the 1980s, and finally began to grow in the 1990s, when the group was able to regain some of its competitive capacity. Nevertheless, these industries were not able to recapture their earlier domestic market share.

As we have seen, the copper industry has lost its dominance of the manufacturing sector, with non-ferrous metals declining from being the largest manufacturing group in 1970, to being the second smallest in 1999. At the same time, copper has been an extremely volatile industry, as figure 2.3 shows clearly.

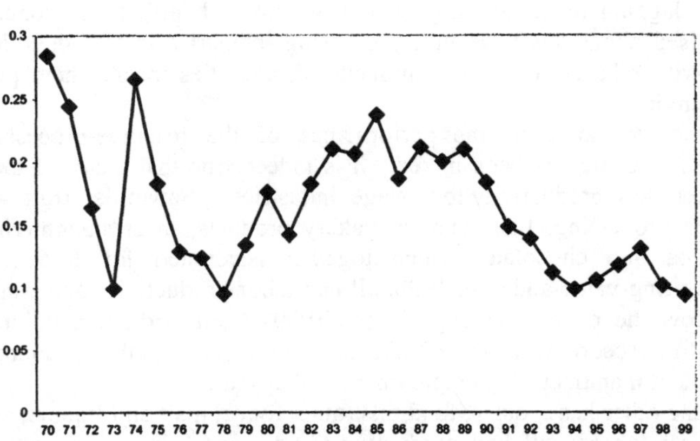

Source: PADI database.

Figure 2.3 Share of Copper in Manufacturing Value-Added (current prices)

The performance of this sector cannot be related to changes in import competition. Indeed, it might have been expected to be the strongest growth industry under the reforms. The steady decline of the copper industry in the 1990s is particular problematic, as it is the sector that has received much of the country's net investment in the post-1985 growth period. According to Moguillansky (1999, p. 80), mining investment accounted for 15.7% of total fixed capital formation from 1986 to 1997. The fluctuations in value-added in this sector since 1985 have reflected sharp swings in global copper prices. Although copper production actually increased steadily in the second half of the 1990s (INE, 2001), copper value-added fell dramatically in 1998 and 1999 as copper prices reached twenty-year lows. Moguillansky suggests that the wave of investment in Chile's extractive industries is coming to an end, which raises the troubling question of which sector can propel the economy forward in coming years.

We saw earlier that agriculture, another strong growth sector in the 1970s and 80s, has also declined steadily as a share of total GDP in the 1990s (table 2.2). On the other hand, the manufacturing industries that process natural resources have clearly been one of Chile's growth sectors. While this may represent a step up from unprocessed raw materials, the growing dominance of these industries within the manufacturing structure seems to suggest a weakening of the Chilean economic structure, since these dynamic sectors are generally believed to have lower productivity than the lagging manufacturing sectors we have identified. A concern often raised about these resource-processing industries is that their low productivity relative to other manufacturing activities makes them poor growth engines.

In reality, however, the performance of the resource-processing industries in Chile has been mixed. It is indeed true that many of them have been low-productivity/low wage industries. Sawmills, fruit and vegetable processing, fish canning, bakery products, meat slaughtering, and cocoa and chocolate, which together accounted for 13.5% of manufacturing value-added in 1998, all had labor productivity and wages well below the country average in the 1990s (Reinhardt, this volume, chapter 6). According to the ENIA, these industries together accounted for 27.5% of manufacturing employment in that year.

On the other hand, dairy, food oils, other foods, malt and liquors, soft drinks, and tobacco all had productivity and wages above the country average, and these industries among them accounted for a greater 16.4% of manufacturing value-added in 1998. Wine, with another 1.8% of manufacturing value-added, was a hybrid: higher than average productivity but lower than average wages. At the same time, however, employment in these higher productivity industries was considerably lower at only 9.4% of the manufacturing total in 1998.

Despite these differences in productivity within the natural-resource sector, a striking finding is that overall value-added per worker in these sectors was higher than in the MM, LA1, or LA2 sectors, as table 2.12 reveals. Indeed, only the non-ferrous metals group has consistently had higher labor productivity than these other natural resource based manufactures. These findings should be interpreted with some caution, however, given the fact that these data do not include small enterprises. Furthermore, the relatively higher productivity of Chile's dynamic industries does not necessarily mean that these industries will be good growth engines for the Chilean economy. Valid concerns remain about the ability of these industries to create linkages to other industries.[6] Another concern for the food-processing and other natural-resource based industries is their generally low income-elasticity of demand.

Table 2.12 Value-Added per Worker, by Manufacturing Group (1985 dollars)

Group	1970	1980	1990	1998
AG	13,125	20,005	17,709	25,869
NR	12,485	19,450	23,240	35,134
LA1	7,951	9,399	8,504	10,603
LA2	10,914	18,862	17,962	28,914
MM	10,074	13,161	13,251	22,889
CO	190,423	103,373	148,524	76,420
Avg without CO	10,692	16,323	16,206	25,568
Avg, all groups	14,615	19,170	19,381	27,428

Source: PADI database

Whatever the future implications of the changing structure of the manufacturing sector, to date overall manufacturing labor productivity has been rising. This outcome cannot be explained simply in terms of the shift within manufacturing from lower to higher productivity sectors, since the declining share of the extremely high-productivity non-ferrous metals group would have depressed the total. Rather, the increase in overall manufacturing labor productivity is due to rising productivity within each group except CO, as table 2.12 shows.

One issue that has been debated regarding the dynamics of manufacturing productivity in particular, and that of the Chilean economy in general, has been whether the country's growth pattern has exhibited greater heterogeneity among its economic sectors. Within manufacturing, data plotted in figure 2.4 show that heterogeneity, using as a proxy the Pearson variation coefficient for manufacturing productivity,[7] has indeed

---

[6] For example, Cimoli and di Maio (2002) have shown the deterioration of linkages among manufacturing sectors and between manufacturing and other activities and suggested that, because of this, we should consider the Chilean case as one of de-industrialization.

[7] The Pearson variation coefficient is calculated as the ratio between the standard deviation and the mean of the productivities at the sector level.

increased over time. Most of the increase occurred in the high growth periods of the late 1970s, the crisis years of the early 1980s and the 1990s, while the low growth decade of the 1980s shows quite a stable value for the coefficient. Chile's Pearson coefficient is significantly higher than the Latin-American average, which increased from 0.49 in 1978 to 0.65 in 1999.

This increased variation in productivity between manufacturing sectors may have been a positive factor for a small open country aiming at specialization of its economic structure. Increasing heterogeneity *among* sectors did not necessarily imply that heterogeneity *within* sectors grew. The expectation was that greater competition would increase homogeneity within industries by driving less productive firms out of the market. Evidence presented by Pavcnik (2000) shows that exit of less efficient plants did indeed contribute to increased industry productivity in both import-competing and exporting industries in Chile between 1979 and 1986, a period when overall manufacturing heterogeneity increased sharply. The dynamics since the mid-1980s is still an open question.

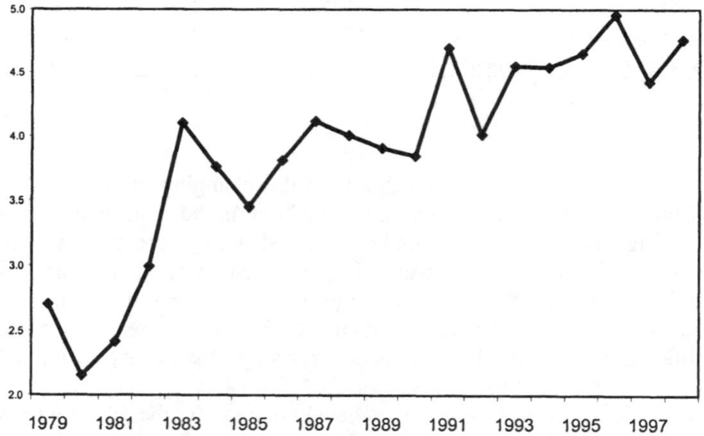

Source: PADI database

Figure 2.4 Pearson Coefficient of Manufacturing Productivity

How have employment growth and productivity trends been related? Figure 2.5 shows the changes in these two variables over time. What stands out from this picture is the fact that the strongest growth in manufacturing labor productivity has occurred during periods of slow-growing or declining manufacturing employment. Immediately after the reforms, both manufacturing employment and labor productivity fell. From 1975 to 1981, employment continued to decline while manufacturing productivity rose sharply, indicating that a decrease in X-inefficiency played a large part in productivity increases as firms adjusted to greater international competition. This source of productivity growth, while useful during the adjustment process, is of course limited. It can also be problematic if the labor released from these sectors is not absorbed in other productive sectors. Once manufacturing employment finally began to expand after 1983, productivity growth stagnated for most of the decade.

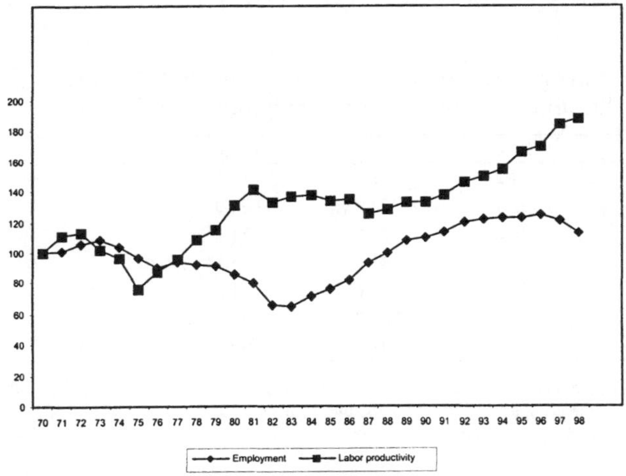

Source: PADI database.

Figure 2.5 Indexes of Manufacturing Labor Productivity and Employment (1970=100)

From 1987 to 1993, sustained increases in overall manufacturing productivity occurred along with sustained increases in overall manufacturing employment, a very positive outcome and one that is consistent with the high level of investment during this period. Each group, with the notable exception of non-ferrous metals, has enjoyed a period in which value-added, employment, and productivity have all risen: 1988-96 for MM, 1991-97 for NR, 1990-96 for AG, 1988-92 for LA1, and 1985-95 for LA2. After 1993, disappointingly, although overall productivity growth has increased sharply, overall manufacturing employment has stagnated. As we noted earlier, manufacturing employment growth for the decade of the 1990s as a whole has been weak, and the share of manufacturing employment has declined steadily in favor of the services sector.

Despite this productivity growth, the overall manufacturing productivity gap with the United States has widened, as can be seen in table 2.13. This means that international competitiveness has diminished as Chile has fallen further behind the technology frontier. This has not occurred uniformly across industries, however. Two groups of industries, the natural resource based and the "other labor-intensive," did narrow the productivity gap during 1970 to 1998 overall, although with a widening gap in the 1980s. The other sectors have all experienced a considerable widening of the productivity gap (or, in the case of non-ferrous metals, a considerable decrease in the productivity advantage).

Table 2.13 Labor Productivity as Percentage of United States Productivity, by Manufacturing Industry Group*

Sectors	1970	1980	1990	1998
MM	31.2	28.4	19.1	20.3
AG	39.4	30.7	22.0	30.0
NR	30.8	39.3	31.2	41.6
LA1	53.2	41.6	25.1	25.0
LA2	28.0	38.8	31.0	45.8
CO	514.0	223.7	297.3	130.9
Total	45.0	41.8	29.8	30.8

*The PADI database uses just one deflator for the whole manufacturing sector. This particularly affects the comparison of 1970 data with those for 1980.
Source: The authors based on PADI.

Putting together the trends in manufacturing value-added, employment, and productivity for each of the sectors, we get the matrix shown in table 2.14. In this table, the productivity trend is positive if the gap with the US decreased, and negative if the productivity gap widened. We find that in only one sector, the "other labor-intensive," were all three positive over the 30-year period as a whole. This sector accounted for 17.9% of manufacturing value-added and 17.0% of manufacturing employment in 1998.

Food processing, the most rapidly growing manufacturing group and the one with the largest share of output and employment in 1998, experienced declining productivity relative to the U.S. This adds another concern, to those raised above, about the problematic nature of this sector as the country's growth engine. Natural resource processing gained in value-added share and in relative productivity, but did not expand employment. Non-ferrous metals, the only other group with increasing employment, experienced declining share and lost much of its tremendous productivity advantage relative to the U.S. The basic labor-intensive industries and the metal/machinery group declined on all three counts. Overall, in the late 1990s, 59.3% of manufacturing value-added and 65.5% of manufacturing employment were in groups whose productivity had declined relative to the U.S.

Table 2.14 Value Added, Employment, and Labor Productivity Trends by Manufacturing Group: Direction of Change, 1970-1998/99

Group	Value-added share		Employment share		Relative productivity	
	Direction of change	Share in 1999	Direction of change	Share in 1998	Direction of change	% of U.S. in 1998
AG	+	32.8	+	33.2	-	30.0
NR	+	22.6	No chg	17.6	+	41.6
LA1	-	4.6	-	12.9	-	25.0
LA2	+	18.1	+	17.0	+	45.8
MM	-	12.5	-	15.7	-	20.3
CO	-	9.4	+	3.7	-	130.9

The poor relative productivity performance of most of the manufacturing groups is a rather startling outcome. One of the central expectations of the reforms was that liberalization of the economy would increase competitive pressures and therefore induce greater efficiency, most significantly in the formerly heavily protected manufacturing sector. We have seen that import competition did indeed increase, especially for the core "Stage 1" ISI firms in the LA1 group. Yet the productivity performance of this sector was the weakest of all the manufacturing groups except non-ferrous metals. And overall, the decline in relative international productivity of four of the six manufacturing groups is a disappointing outcome. This is especially the case since some degree of productivity growth might have been expected even without the reforms. In a study of twenty-seven manufacturing industries in seven Latin American countries over the 1970-98 period, Paus, *et al.* (2001) found that the rate of productivity growth in an industry was strongly and significantly correlated with the rate of productivity growth of its U.S. counterpart.

Despite this poor showing of Chilean manufacturing productivity in relation to the U.S., the shift out of manufacturing had a negative effect on the Chilean economy. As figure 2.6 shows, since 1978 manufacturing productivity has been higher than the ratio of GDP to economically active population, (actual employment data are not available for sectors like agriculture) and it has also shown a much more dynamic behavior.[8] Sector shift has resulted in a lower performance of productivity and productivity growth for the whole economy.

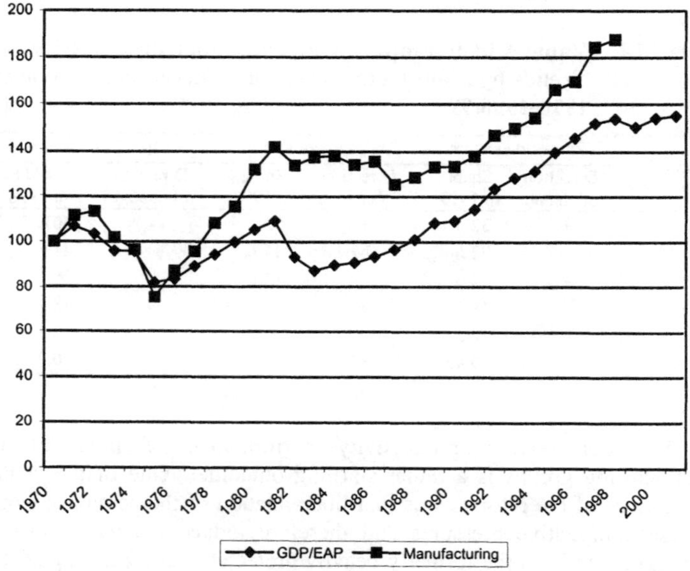

Source: PADI database and Chilean National Accounts.

Figure 2.6 GDP per Economically Active Population and Manufacturing Productivity (1970=100)

Conclusion

In some respects the outcomes of the reforms have been consistent with expectations. In some other important respects, however, they have not. On the one hand, as expected, there has been a significant reallocation of resources from importables to exportables sectors (primary, NR, AG, LA2 up; manufacturing, MM, LA1 down). This shift was especially marked in the period immediately after reform implementation, with a sharp decline in manufacturing share relative to that of the primary and service sectors,

8 We should remember, however, that the PADI database does not include microfirms, which have a much lower productivity than the manufacturing average (Stallings and Peres, 2000).

and within manufacturing, a shift to resource-based industries. On a less positive note, although the change of the National Accounts base in 1985 makes it difficult to reach a definitive conclusion, it does appear that over the three decades as a whole there has been a continued process of de-industrialization. The deterioration of manufacturing share after 1985, during a high growth period, is particularly remarkable. Nevertheless, within that sector, some groups have been able to maintain or recover their competitiveness – especially those industries involved in the processing of Chile's natural resources.

Manufacturing labor productivity did increase overall, as anticipated, and it grew faster than for the rest of the economy. However, the rate of productivity growth has been low for some industry groups, and the international frontier has moved faster. Not only does the gap continue to be large for all groups, it has even increased for most of them. This is one of the most unexpected and disappointing outcomes.

This case of economic growth without industrialization and with poor relative productivity growth runs very much against the real lesson of the East Asian miracle, which is that manufacturing growth (and manufacturing productivity growth) is a condition for development. Chile's economic reforms were able, after a difficult adjustment period, to generate a decade of rapid economic growth, but it is not clear that the underlying economic structure has developed in such a way as to provide a strong foundation for the continued development of the economy.

References

Benavente, José Miguel, Gustavo Crespi, Jorge Katz and Giovanni Stumpo, 1997. "New Problems and Opportunities for Development in Latin America", *Oxford Economic Papers*, 25, 3.

Bielschowsky, Ricardo and Giovanni Stumpo, 1995. "Transnational and Structural Changes in Industry in Argentina, Brazil,Chile and Mexico, *CEPAL Review*, 55.

CEPAL, 1992. *El Comercio de Manufacturas de América Latina* (Santiago, Chile).

Cimoli, Mario and Michele di Maio, 2002. "Technological Gaps, De-Industrialization and Catching-Up: Is the Chilean Case Still a Paradox?" Centre for Research on Innovation and Internationalization Processes (CESPRI), Milan.

ECLAC, various years. Statistical Yearbook for Latin America and the Caribbean (Santiago, Chile).

ECLAC, 2000, 2001. Preliminary Overview of the Economies of Latin America and the Caribbean (Santiago, Chile).

ECLAC, 2002. *Panorama Social de América Latina 2001-2002*, (Santiago, Chile).

IDB, 2001. "Latin America's Labor Force: Between Two Worlds," in *Latin American Economic Policies*, Third Quarter (Washington, D.C.).

INE, 2002. *Compendio Estadístico* (Santiago, Chile).

Katz, Jorge and Giovanni Stumpo, 2001. "Regímenes sectoriales, productividad y competitividad internacional", *Revista de la CEPAL*, 75, December.

Moguillansky, Graciela, 1999. *La inversión en Chile: el fin de un ciclo en expansión?* (Santiago, Chile: CEPAL).

Morley, Samuel, Roberto Machado, and Stefano Pettinato, 1999. "Indexes of Structural Reform in Latin America, *Serie Reformas Económicas 12,* CEPAL.

Paus, Eva, Nola Reinhardt, and Michael Robinson, 2001. "Trade Liberalization and Productivity Growth in Latin American Manufacturing," paper presented at the meetings of the Western Economics Association International, San Francisco, CA, July 4-8.

Pavcnik, Nina, 2000. "Trade Liberalization, Exit, and Productivity Improvements: Evidence from Chilean Plants," *NBER Working Paper 7852* (August).

Reinhardt, Nola and Wilson Peres, 2000, "Latin America's New Economic Model: Micro Responses and Economic Restructuring", in W. Peres and N. Reinhardt (editors), *The Microeconomics of the New Economic Model in Latin America*, World Development, Special Issue, September.

Stumpo, Giovanni 2000. "I sogni del giaguaro: riforme economiche, ristrutturazione produttiva e strategie imprenditoriali in Cile", in Andrea Goldstein (editor), *America Latina: Prospettive e opportunitá negli anni 2000: dalla stabilizzazione alla crescita?*, Istituto per gli Studi di Politica Internazionale (ISPI), Milan.

UNESCAP, 1997, 1998. *Economic and Social Survey of Asia and the Pacific* (Bangkok, UN Economic and Social Commission for Asia and the Pacific).

UNIDO, 1981. *World Industry in 1980* (UN: New York).

Wilkie, James, ed., 2001. *Statistical Abstract of Latin America* (University of California, Los Angeles).

World Bank, 1998. *World Development Report.*

3 Toward a Modern State in Chile: Institutions, Governance, and Market Regulation

Eduardo Saavedra and Raimundo Soto

Introduction

Over the last decades, Chile has introduced major structural changes in infrastructure and human capital accumulation that have given the private sector priority in goods and services provision. Partly motivated by the severe crisis of the early 1980s and partly by the phenomenal success of the economies of the South East of Asia, Chile is in the path, albeit hesitantly, towards the development of a market economy.

The first step in that direction has been taken already. After sustained efforts, the country has reached macroeconomic stability levels that would have been unthinkable just twenty years ago, when inflation, unemployment and high fiscal and current account deficits constituted the economic ailments of Chile. Nevertheless, this turn of the economic situation has not been the result of only the stabilization process. In addition, there have been substantial changes in the incentives system for the economic agents that were the result of privatizing state-owned companies, liberalizing markets, opening up the economy to international trade and reducing subsidies to private companies.

To a great extent, Chile's institutional structure is still incompatible with an efficient operation of the very same markets the reforms were meant to create. The absence of deep reforms in the State's management, in the administration of the Judiciary and in the working of regulatory agencies does not guarantee that the Chilean economy may reach the high growth rates needed to pull the country out of its still developing condition.

Second generation reforms for the Latin American countries have been very much talked about in order to complement the first liberalizing reforms that Chile implemented two decades ago. However, we understand there has not been a clear systematization of what those second generation reforms are, what they mean in terms of complementing first generation reforms and, most importantly, what economic aims such reforms pursue.

This chapter discusses and systematizes the kind of reforms that should be introduced and the aims that should be pursued. We understand the ruling principle of these reforms to be the fact that sustained economic growth demands a healthy microeconomy; that is to say, the incentives and regulatory structure for the involved agents should be implemented to reach the maximum potentialities in the technical and allocation efficiency that the free operation of the markets imply. It is of particular interest in this context that the government generates the most appropriate mechanisms to stimulate competition and, were this not possible, to design regulatory mechanisms to emulate its results.

To ensure progress in the direction of a State that regulates and defends competition, Chile should perfect its regulatory framework and modernize the regulatory entities in those industries with monopolistic features; it should make progress in the defense of consumer rights and of the individuals; it should strengthen the entities in charge of assuring market competition and it should update the Judiciary by granting it the capacity to settle the disputes that are typical of a market economy. This means that the role of the State as the provider of goods and services should be reconsidered as well as the way in which its actions may affect the implementation of the incentives and punishments system in which the economic agents operate.

The purpose of this chapter is not to introduce a modernization plan. On the contrary, the discussion is focused on the main aspects of economic and institutional modernization of the State with respect to the needed redesign of institutions designed to regulate, to control and to facilitate a fair market performance and competition as well as to ensure the implementation of governance mechanisms to make the changes viable. This analysis may be limited and should be complemented with the kind of reforms needed for the country's economic growth, which are not considered in this work: these reforms would include upgrading employment supply (investment in human capital) and its association with institutional health and education, the expansion of the country's infrastructure, environmental and natural resources protection, and others. Further, macroeconomic growth aspects have not been included, such as the saving-investment process.

The organization of this chapter is as follows; in the next section, the motivation for the analysis is elaborated. Section three is about the need to change the role of the State in a market economy like in Chile. Sections four and five deal with the two crucial aspects of second generation reforms that constitute the core of this paper, the modernization of the regulatory regime and support of competition, and the reform of the Judiciary and defense of citizens and consumers. The conclusion will comprise section six.

The Role of the Chilean Government in a Globalized World

The market liberalization reforms Chile introduced over the last quarter century generated sustained growth for about 15 years; however, the slowdown signs over the first years of the 21st century are easily perceived. It has become evident that the benefits that occurred after the first generation reforms may come to a standstill if effective measures to solve the bottleneck problems of growth and, therefore, of the country's economic progress, are not undertaken.[1]

In this chapter, three basic principles, which are clearly contentious, serve as the framework for the analysis that follows. They are:

(1) The Chilean economy in future will be developed on the basis of a market system as a mechanism of resources allocation and, therefore, the institutional structure that the country should enjoy will have to find the way for this mechanism to be as efficient as possible and for the adverse effects of its failures to be averted or reduced.
(2) The economy will increasingly be inserted in a globalized economic system, which implies that Chile will have to develop the ability to benefit from the new system and the capacity to defend themselves from the eventual problems that globalization may bring about.
(3) World economic development will take place in an increasingly dynamic context where change will be the most typical element in the interaction between economic agents, industries and countries. Thus, the favored strategies should promote creativity, entrepreneurial capacity and the ability to adapt to them.

Following such principles, the purpose of this chapter should be to generate discussion of a rather broad set of problems concerning the functioning of the economy and the institutional conditions of the State, which implies a thorough analysis that would go beyond this work. This is

[1] This paper is concerned especially with the institutional bottlenecks that hinder prolonged economic growth, while those aspects that might eventually have an incidence in other dimensions of the economic development process are not dealt with. This is, no doubt, a subjective choice based on the widely accepted notion that economic growth constitutes a necessary though not sufficient pre-condition for economic development.

why we have concentrated on the problem areas which we believe are determining for future economic growth. Figure 3.1 shows the interaction between globalization, markets and the role of the State.

From an economic standpoint, the growth problem is largely determined by the insertion of the region's countries in the world economy. Such insertion will have major effects on the formation of individual preferences, to the extent that consumption patterns, the appreciation of creative leisure, working habits and other aspects will change.[2] Additionally, such growth should modify the demand structure of goods and services in relation to the elasticity of the introduction of goods, with "luxury" goods filling an ever larger slot in the baskets of the different social classes. As a consequence of globalization, not much can be done to affect the demand of goods except for the first liberalizing measures: fiscal, monetary and foreign policies consistent with a health macroeconomy.

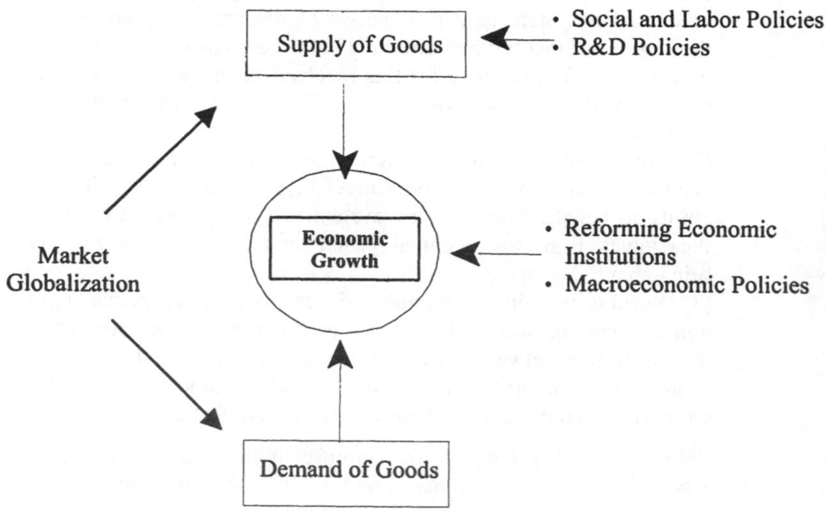

Figure 3.1 Globalization, Markets, and the Role of the State

[2] There is a wide literature regarding the effects of globalization on other aspects of the citizens' life, such as culture, identity, and so on. See for instance Brunner (1995) and Larraín (2001) for futher discussion.

The demand of goods and services also reflect the effects of globalization. The globalization conditions pose for Chilean producers a major challenge to reach the productivity and efficiency levels of those in international markets. Such challenges are not only technological but, most importantly, related to the idea that globalization will demand ever increasing levels of creativity, negotiating skills and adaptation to changes and working habits in order to offer high quality products and productive processes. This is the reason why the Chilean government is extremely concerned with advancing the reform of education, health, and social welfare.

Bearing in mind this multifaceted challenges imposed by globalization, three state-level functions in the countries of the region have been identified that may turn into major bottlenecks to adequately respond to the challenge. The functions of concern are: structure, management and administration of the public sector (the State's role) in a market economy; governance structure and mechanisms in the regulatory entities; and, the operation of the Judiciary system and the defense of citizens and consumers.

We suggest that the first function cited above, the structure, management and administration of the public sector, poses a severe threat to economic development. There is significant heterogeneity today in the level of efficiency of the different units of the public sector; while in some of them directives are clear and high performance efficacy has been reached, in others, management is highly bureaucratic and administration is disorderly with high inefficiency levels and political interference. Also, the State's entrepreneurial spirit is still debatable especially given the fact that they still control a significant percentage of the GDP, indicating further opportunities for first generation reforms.

With respect to the institutional condition and governance of the regulatory entities, reforms are needed whenever a greater participation of the private sector has been reached in typical state activities such as telecommunications, electricity, and transport. Rapid privatization often preceded the design of the regulatory framework, which may have been thought out hurriedly, with little experience and not much care. In brief, privatization was carried out without the corresponding considerations with respect to market failures inherent to the industries involved, especially when the potentially competitive market activities coexisted with those in monopolistic markets.

The weak institutional condition is also strongly present in the organizations in charge of defending and supporting free market competition. The institutions are still very much inclined to punish inappropriate conduct but have spent little time with implementing mechanisms to avoid such conduct. In other words, it is necessary that the institutions established for the defense of free competition modify their role in favor of supporting competition.

Chile shows major deficiencies in the institutional weaknesses associated with settling disputes between parties, typical of all market economies. On the one hand, the Judiciary is one of the most backward in Latin America, where procedures are still very similar to those in colonial times. Many members of the judiciary lack an economic background necessary to comprehend the issues and, worse still, they seem to be far detached from being able to assess their work and, therefore, are not very much concerned with settling disputes promptly and efficiently. A similar case can be observed with respect to the bodies for the defense of consumers and persons; legislation is outdated and permissive with practices that are detrimental to the social acceptance of the free market model that has been implemented.[3]

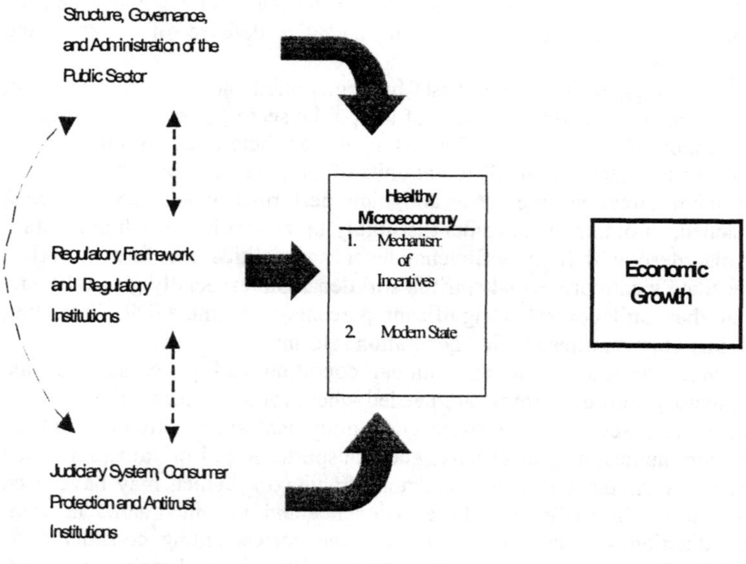

Figure 3.2 The Working of a Modern Economic Institutional System

---

[3] Since written the first draft of this paper, the Chilean government has implemented several reforms that attempt to solve the problems mentioned in this work. Some of them are: the introduction of payment incentives schemes in public officers, the reform to electricity, consumer, and antitrust acts (all of them enacted during 2003 and 2004), and several other initiatives still under legislative discussion.

In summary, figure 3.2 shows the need to enjoy an institutional structure in accordance with a regulator competition-supporter State that acts along with a Judiciary system and institutions for the defense of citizens and consumers. It is of interest to lay stress on the importance of institutional changes and on their effects on economic growth by means of what is called a healthy microeconomy.

Modernization of the State: General Aspects

Over the last three decades, substantial structural changes have been made that have given the private sector greater prominence in the provision of goods and services, in developing infrastructure and in human capital accumulation. However, the institutional structure of Chile's economy, especially its state apparatus, to a large extent happens to be incompatible with an efficient operation of the very same markets that the reforms were meant to create.

Most authors agree that the State in Latin America, at least traditionally, reached its nadir in the 1990s (Boeninger, 1999; Burki *et al.*, 1999). Historically, the State in Chile has developed a so-called "bureaucratic culture", characterized by institutional features that indicate, on the one hand, severe administrative, structural and organizational problems and, on the other, the undeniable need to implement profound changes.[4]

The State apparatus in Chile is characterized by bureaucratic excesses and rigid procedures; this results in an exasperating slow pace to respond to social needs. It is rightly perceived that management is oriented to conforming to routine procedures and that solutions are based only on expanding the use of inputs ("more of the same"), while obtaining results is not regarded as relevant. In this context, public action is typically explained in terms of bureaucratic dynamics, of following a career, and of short-term political imperatives, not in terms of the interest in solving the population's problems.

There may be genuine interest in improving the population's living standards, but it is not unusual to have efforts wasted because too many of the institutions involved are in charge of the same issues without coordination, because there is no consistency or clearly defined public policy objectives and, more sadly still, because the implementation of

---

[4] The State in Chile, as in the whole Latin America, derives its centralist conception, according to some historians, from a combination of (1) acceptance of vertical authority promoted by a conservative Catholic Church; (2) profound inequalities in social relations; (3) high concentration of wealth; (4) low educational levels and (5) marginalizing indigenous groups from national politics (Domínguez, 1994).

public plans does not respond to the most elementary constraints of the reality around (such as the so-called "white elephants"). In the worst of cases, the State does not seek the common good and it acts in the name of interest groups, political parties or social classes, developing state policies oriented to getting adherence and followers. The causes of the State's inefficiency are, then, many, inclusive of historical, cultural, economic and legal factors. In our approach, we have concentrated on the economic and institutional determinants, although the conclusions that can be derived from a legal or political analysis are no less important.

From an economic standpoint, the origin of the State's inefficiency and inefficacy is to be found in the absence of proper incentives and regulation mechanisms in public organizations as well as in private cases. Chile is not alone here since the whole of Latin America is known for the absence or generalized weakness of the public administration evaluation mechanisms to assess private or organizational achievements and to punish indolence, inefficiency and lack of endeavor to attain the assigned objectives. The absence of accountability or personal responsibility is the result. Furthermore, the State in Chile has traditionally paid little attention to public opinion; thus, tax payers do not stand the chance of getting informed concerning the destiny given to their taxes or, to find the way to best use them, or recall public officers who are inept or corrupt.

To some extent, the reason for the lack of accountability and recall lies in the restriction of resources that prevent the development of proper mechanisms. Nevertheless, it must be acknowledged that, rather than the limited funds, the institutional restrictions imposed on the State are far more important.

On the one hand, inefficiency in the implementation of public resources is due to the labor overprotection enjoyed by public officers. Very often, officers enjoy labor tenure, their income is related to fixed salary schemes and negotiated collectively, and they get promoted on the basis of seniority. This situation is not linked to the kind of efforts generally needed to obtain rewards; thus, workers become discouraged to make efforts which are not appreciated while the opportunism of those who do their least seems to be welcomed. On the other hand, there is no "public manager" in public organizations, as there is in private enterprises, commissioned by owners and responsible to them, to obtain given social benefits from the assigned resources.[5]

Updating the structure of the public sector is a manifold area that involves privatization, restructuring organizations and functions, decentralizing, updating information systems and training personnel, among other needs. A thorough analysis of this situation is not the

---

[5] As mentioned, some incentive mechanisms and a newer, formal, open, and transparent process of hiring public managers/officers were implemented during 2003. Although this reform will not solve the problem, it is a enormous step in the right direction. See details of this reform in Valdés-Prieto (2003).

pretense in this section; rather, focusing attention on a possible reordering of the State with a view to developing market economies in the region, with increasing private participation levels in the provision of goods and services and with a greater consumer participation in policy making is the purpose.

In his classic study of goods and services provision, Oates (1972) mentions the three basic objectives of the State: stabilization, resources allocation and distribution of wealth. In this paper, we concentrate on the last two as they constitute the most important objectives in Chile at the present time. Nevertheless, we have disaggregated resources allocation into three categories: the provision of ordinary goods and services, the provision of public goods and services, and the design of the regulatory framework. The three aspects related to resource allocation along with redistribution mechanisms and equal access make up the first part of our analysis.

Table 3.1 Scope of the State and Private Participation

	Decision Making Process	Management	Incentive Mechanisms
Provision of normal goods and services	Private	Private	Private
Provision of public goods and services	State	Private	Both
Design of Regulatory Framework	State	State	Both
Income Distribution and Opportunities	Both	State	Both

In the next section, the functions of the State have been classified into three different levels: decision making (deciding how much and for whom to produce), management (how to produce), and the incentives mechanism plan and performance assessment (which the production rules are).[6] Table 3.1 shows the double entry matrix with both analyses, which will serve as guidance. In each box, we provide our interpretations, which are the consequence of the analysis that follows next.

After the military *coup d'etat* in 1973, Chile conducted the important process of privatizing many of the state-owned enterprises. Nonetheless, the State is still present in economic areas linked to mining, the energy sector and basic services, among others. Even admitting that State

[6] It is pertinent to mention that Chile has the lowest level of corruption indicators in Latin America and one of the lowest in the world (ranks 18-20 out of 145 countries in 2003). If this were not the case, another crucial topic in the reform of the State should be the controlling of corruption.

ownership in itself is not necessarily inappropriate, historical experience suggests that privatizing and granting concessions seem to allow a better management of the resources, less extended corruption and greater efficiency without causing serious market distortions.

It must be pointed out that there is general awareness in Chile that the State offers no advantages in the decision making process related to production and investment levels and in providing goods and services where no externalities or particular production conditions are be found (e.g., economies of scale). The idea that the State should coordinate or plan market development, that it should administer better than the private sector or that it should offer more efficient incentives mechanisms for resources allocation has been abandoned. On the contrary, it is the public sector that increasingly seeks to incorporate incentives systems that partly replicate the private sector mechanisms. This is why the first row in table 3.1 shows that it is possible and advisable to grant the provision of ordinary goods and services to the private sector and allow the latter to decide on what, how and for whom to produce, and also allow it to find the most convenient incentives and control mechanisms within the legal framework of the different societies concerned.

Regarding the provision of public goods and services, there is no consensus over the need or convenience of divesting public companies in these markets. Many authors maintain that state ownership is justified in terms of market imperfections such as natural monopolies and public goods. In such cases, it is said, privatization would lead to a goods and services provision level below optimum and, by and large, would lead the private sector to enjoy monopolistic benefits. There is no empirical evidence to support the assertion that when the State operates monopolistically, the proper production level is assured. On the contrary, there is substantial proof that many public companies are highly inefficient and that the monopolistic benefits are appropriated by the executive officers or the employees in the form of high salaries and fringe benefits (Galal *et al.*, 1989).

The privatization experience in Chile in public utilities shows that private ownership may reduce prices and provide incentives to invest. However, this experience also shows that the privatization of utilities demand a carefully designed regulatory framework free of ambiguities, with legal and regulatory entities willing to enforce the terms and conditions of privatization or concession contracts. Moreover, during the 1990s Chile started to develop markets where the private sector operates and, in many cases, finance companies that provide goods and services, such as highways, ports and airports franchising. The Chilean state continues to be responsible for determining the provision levels, which is made possible through private companies with the assistance of subsidies or franchising mechanisms.

A widespread justification for the maintenance of some state-owned companies is that they play a strategic political role, such as by media (newspapers and television) and military or war related companies. Their social role must be admitted, but the evaluation of the extent to which they are strategic for social development and of the extent to which they may prove useful to perpetuate spheres of power in the hands of privileged classes or power groups must be conducted carefully. For instance, the arguments in favor of state monopolies based on military strategic reasons, those which formerly explained the development of war industries, have lost ground with economic liberalization and globalization. Currently, the destiny of taxes for national defense is being debated because, on the one hand, the perception is that the need for defense has diminished in Latin America; on the other hand, such use of taxes greatly reflect the military negotiating power rather than Chile's need of defense.

Similarly, the need to maintain a state bank in Chile has been its role in regional development, especially in the areas lagging behind progress where private capital markets cannot support productive activities. The less developed sectors, such as rural and small business, certainly demand the substantial support of the rest of society to integrate them more equitably in the process of economic growth. This suggests assistance that should be well targeted, particularly access to loans and to technical aid, and not necessarily directed to expanding state enterprises in the areas.

As a consequence, it should be pointed out that although the State may divest public goods and services provision, the responsibility for the decision on which goods and services are provided and who will provide them cannot be referred to the private sector. Given the presence of market failures, centralized coordination of the provision levels is required in order to obtain a social optimum from the allocation of resources.

A third objective of the State is to provide operation rules for the economic agents and also to provide the mechanisms to adapt, update and upgrade such rules. Such governance as a State function has been recently changed in many economies in Latin America as a result of the openness processes and market liberalization implemented over the last 25 years. However, because it has been the pioneer in introducing liberalization policies and because of the dogmatism with which such policies were conducted, Chile is still lagging behind institutional reforms compared with other countries whose divestiture processes took place later.

Certainly, we are dealing with an area where decision making is a public responsibility exclusively. The private sector may participate with regulation improvement proposals, as is the case in Chile, but the mechanisms used for such proposals must be transparent and efficient, without the margin for the regulating agent to be captured by the regulated enterprises. Similarly, the administration of the bodies that dictate the regulations and panel procedures must belong to the State, given the need to protect the collective good above individual or group interests, an issue to be dealt later in this chapter.

A less developed area that may play a very important role in the future is a more direct consumer participation in the results and incentives control of public decisions. The centralist characteristic of the state administration has traditionally led to little consumer participation in the decisions of the state-owned enterprises and bodies. As has been already remarked, this situation means the neglect on the part of state officers when having to comply with their social function as well as the disappointment of users concerning the capacity of the State to resolve problems. It has recently been proposed that public hearings be organized to discuss and fix public tariffs or service conditions, with the participation of consumers together with the enterprises and regulation representatives. It would certainly improve accountability of the regulating agents and also improve consumer welfare. The right to recall must be exercised responsibly; it has been seldom resorted to, with bureaucratic complications, so that a major reconsideration of it must be made to turn it efficient.

Regarding income and opportunities distribution, Chile's unequal income distribution is perhaps one of the major challenges confronting this country in the 21st century. Initially, the interest of public policies would be to guarantee universal access to the benefits a market economy offers and to the duties it demands. Nevertheless, it must be admitted that there are substantial distortions and constraints that actually prevent equal access that, to a large extent, explain the active policy participation of the State.

There are two kinds of policies to reduce inequality and guarantee equal opportunities. On the one hand, drawing on Tiebout (1956) and Oates (1972), there has been a strong school of thought that suggests that the allocation of resources is economically efficient in providing local goods and services when it has been divested and the decision made at local level. On the other hand, there still are a wide scope for policies aim to reduce poverty and unequal opportunities at the central level.

Whatever the decentralization level chosen, decision making will be a mixed function. The State should centrally retain those redistribution proposals that because of externalities or of economies of scale are of national scope, or those in which there is no capacity to pay at all (assistance).

Toward a Modern Regulatory Institutional Framing and Defense of Competition

Mention has already been made of the private sector participation in sectors with natural monopoly characteristics in Chile during the final quarter of the last century, especially in gas, energy, water and telecommunications. With adequate regulation, it should bring about increased internal efficiency in those companies (productive efficiency) and should also offer benefits to consumers, as the literature in the field has underlined.[7] Nevertheless, as some authors have shown, the term "adequate regulation" happens to be a chimera in many such sectors; severe efficiency problems in the allocation of resources have arisen when control was tightened over the market regulated monopoly that was expected to perform more competitively.[8] The question we now mean to address is how far can we go with an institutional development proposal capable of guaranteeing a balanced development of the advantages of productive and internal efficiency of the private sector in the public utility services area, together with the adequate competition support and consumer defense in those sectors?

Competition Regulator and Supporter Institutional Structure

Following the rich empirical evidence available, it has become clear that all those market segments with monopolistic characteristics and operated by private enterprises must be regulated. Then, it is assumed that the disadvantages of regulation, measured in terms of direct and indirect costs, are fewer than the advantages with respect to the social benefits they bring about. In this sense, and from a practical standpoint, we rule out as irrelevant the existence of challenging markets in basic services.

Market regulation though is not problem-free. The theoretical and empirical literature on monopoly regulation of public services remarks that the information asymmetries between the regulated firms and the regulators mean a serious constraint to reach allocation efficiency in these markets. The information asymmetries originate in the greater and closer knowledge of the technologies used and of the market conditions enjoyed by the monopolists. As a result of such information asymmetries, "informational rent" is derived and strategic behavior is encouraged by the economic agents.

In sectors with natural monopoly characteristics, the problem is exacerbated by the degree to which public utility services are vertically related to potentially competitive markets; such is the case of the fixed telephone network and mobile telephone, long distance calling and data transmission, electricity distribution with (potentially) competitive generation and marketing segments, the products to transport natural gas and corresponding extraction and marketing. These vertical relations between monopolistic markets and competitive markets allow the market

---

[7] A very good summary of such experiences can be found in Newbery (1999).

[8] See for instance Basañes *et al.* (2001) and Bitrán *et al.* (1999), who are critical of the poor regulatory framework for basic services in Chile.

power of these firms on regulated markets to be used to obtain abnormal benefits in potentially competitive markets.

In principle, the way to reduce informational rents consists of establishing and implementing regulatory frameworks that provide clear solid rules from a technical point of view. Additionally, it is necessary for the regulatory agents to have trained staff to demand compliance with the rules and, in case problems arise, to count on a panel of legal experts capable of settling the matter between the individual parties and, or between the involved party and the State in an open expeditious way. A further point is that the regulatory frameworks be capable of modifying and adapting to the economic changes that inevitably occur. The problem that arises is how to ensure that the changes in regulation are not anti-efficiency, and that they do not generate rent for the monopolist or not allow the political capture of the regulator.

In practice, in many developing countries, there are many constraints that prevent regulators from inhibiting rent seeking in those sectors where private firms operate in monopolistic conditions. This is mainly due to three reasons: our regulatory entities are technically weak to enforce the existing regulations; the regulatory framework is in many cases incomplete or is the source of great ambiguities; regulation is particularly complex occasionally, from the technical point of view.

Regulatory Entities Technical Capacity Weaknesses

As is the case all over Latin America, the first constraint for regulatory entities in Chile is the limited technical capacity offered by the regulatory agents. This technical weakness is due to three main reasons: no independence from political power, no independent budgeting and low salaries.

With respect to the *no independence from political power*, basic services regulation authorities in Chile are officers who enjoy the total confidence of the President of the Republic, who can decide whether they can stay in office, without following clear procedures to support the decision. Lobbying is, then, made possible, and the regulatory bodies may be inhibited concerning the implementation of required technical measures that are politically costly.

As far as the lack of independent budgeting is concerned, in Chile, the national budget is the source of funds of the regulatory entities and, therefore, they operate within the institutional framework of the public sector. As discussed in the previous section, the incentives plan for the public sector shows severe constraints that do not allow it to function efficiently (rigidity, bureaucracy). In only a few countries, like Argentina and Brazil, the regulatory entities are financed with specifically created taxes or with the proceeds generated by private exploitation rights in regulated markets. However, such a possibility has not been proposed seriously for implementation in Chile.

Finally, the salary scheme for public officers is not consistent with the maintenance and training of the staff's technical capacity. The empirical evidence of this problem is clear: the remunerations in the public sector are below those in the regulated industry, which favors regulatory capture and the corruption of the regulatory entities. Secondly, there are very few incentives that foster specialized training among the staff and the development of a career within the regulatory entities. Both conditions deter the best young professionals from exploring jobs with the regulatory agency; consequently, they are generally captured by the private sector.

Incompletion and Ambiguities of the Regulatory Framework

The second serious regulation problem in virtually all developing countries is that the regulatory framework is, in many cases, highly incomplete and or ambiguous. The institutional or contractual structure ruling relations between the regulator and the firm does not predict all the possible contingencies of operating the sector, or imparts political guidelines which are inconsistent. The existence of ambiguities in any kind of regulation is usually the result of both the complexity of the phenomenon dealt with and the incapacity to predict and anticipate potential conflicts derived from regulating in a poor information context. The presence of ambiguities or the absence of definitions in regulating generally causes opportunistic conduct on the part of both the regulated enterprise and the State institutions.

Tangible examples of ambiguities within the regulatory framework of basic services have arisen over the last years in different countries in Latin America. In Chile's energy sector, for example, the absence of definition of the responsibilities when a period of drought occurred made the crisis worse and, first in a long time, led to rationing of consumption, which might have been avoided. In telecommunications, the authority has had to constantly create regulations to prevent local telephone companies from wielding their monopolistic power in other markets (long distance calling, Internet, etc.). The fishing activity overexploitation in some coastal countries has caused long negotiations over the imposition of constraints to make the sector's development sustainable. The opportunistic conduct in some road construction concessions may reduce the government's credibility, which in turn may produced suboptimum investments.[9]

[9] As mentioned again, recent legal modifications tend to reduce some ambiguities in these regulatory frameworks. Two examples are the following. In the electricity sector, firms are clear regarding their responsibilities in providing energy during drought (reform implemented in 1999), they know their transmission tariffs and that private arbitrators are going to settle any disputes among them (both reform implemented in 2004). The second example is how the government settle lobbying into the fishery sector, where a 10 years

Regulatory Complexity and Incentives Regulation

A third problem occurring not only in developing countries is the fact that regulation may prove especially complex from a technical point of view; there is no consensus with respect to the best possible regulatory regime. Regulation is often confronted with economic and technical problems for which there are no theoretical or practical solutions (for example, electricity transmission rates).

Additionally, technological progress often causes substantial changes in market operation and renders the former regulation obsolete. Even the technological changes may defy the very definition of what constitutes "a market" regulated by an authority. Two examples may be useful: one of them is found in telecommunications, where mobile telephone's boom and cheap prices have made it a closer substitute for land-based telephones. In turn, this puts the regulator in a difficult position to decide which market is relevant for the regulation of fixed telephones; in the other instance, more importance will be given in the medium term to investment cost reduction and network operation, which will make electricity distributors request authorization to offer telephone service (and vice-versa). The regulator will have to face network integration and competition conflicts between economic sectors.

Certainly, there are no simple solutions or prevention of these problems. What must be demanded of regulation is the capacity to face complexities with mechanisms capable of supplying an appropriate consensus-based solution within a reasonable period, and, also, if regulation mistakes are found, to provide effective mechanisms to correct them. Unfortunately, very often the regulation mechanisms are not easily modified.

There is still a lot to be learned although regulatory problems have been widely debated at the moment of establishing the regulatory institutional structure. Most problems are in sectors whose regulatory framework was designed in the 1980s. For example, the regulation of Chile's energy sector, a pioneer in allowing competition for generation at that time, has remarkably lagged behind and has raised severe operational problems, with conflicts and growing litigation in the sector.

However, some reforms introducing competition in other sectors are remarkably positive. For example, Telecommunications regulation in Chile, quite precarious initially, has evolved toward establishing better and more effective local telephone regulation regimes. More significantly yet, the government made a great effort to implement a long distance multi-carrier system that brought about a major increase of the sector's competition and competitiveness and has reduced rates to the benefit of

---

operating act was enacted in 2001 in order to make clear the operation of the sector for a decade before enacting a new definitive act for this sector, to be operative in 2011.

consumers.[10] Similarly, the opening up of public bids for road construction and the privatization of water companies have incorporated the experience of the previously privatized sectors to correct possible mistakes and to avoid the opportunistic conduct of the regulated enterprises (Basañes *et al.*, 2001).

Notwithstanding this learning process, there is still much that remains to be done to update the regulatory institutional conditions in Chile. Not only is it necessary to give the regulatory entities technical and financial capacity but also they must receive the minimum required directives to ensure economic and political independence with respect to their environment. It is additionally necessary to allow them to identify and resolve ambiguities, to increase transparency in administrative procedures, to go forward with incentives regulation mechanisms, and to reach economies of scope in regulation, in competition support and in the defense and information to consumers. Although a thorough treatment of the mentioned directives is not the pretense, the last introduced elements will be further dealt with.

Regulatory Entities Independence

The regulatory organizations must be given independence from political power and from the regulated sectors themselves. This presupposes deep changes when defining the regulatory institutional conditions of the basic services in Chile, whose minimum directives should at least guarantee:

Separating the regulatory entities according to the economic activities. For various reasons, it is advisable not to centralize regulation in a sole entity. First, the regulation of the different sectors (energy, gas, telecommunications, others) is highly heterogeneous from the point of view of the technical, economic and, particularly, the development level of each sector. Secondly, this would make accountability of the corresponding superintendents easier. Thirdly, the regulated enterprises and the political parties would be less motivated to capture a very powerful regulator. Finally, the interruption of regulation activities of sectors that for political reasons or other circumstances are less appealing than other activities would be diminished.[11]

Regulatory entities economically and hierarchically independent of ministries. It is essential that political authorities, and their activities concerning the sector's development and competitiveness, be separated

---

[10] Bitrán *et al.* (1999).

[11] It is important to remark that this separation of regulatory entities that not prevent for create the figure of a supraregulator of utilities, however this position should be think as a person whose aim is beyond any technical regulation, more precisely this person should be in charge of balance power with private holdings operating in more than one utility sector.

from the role of regulator with respect to the regulatory function the latter exercises. This eliminates the political dependence of regulators, avoids the opportunistic conduct of the government with aims other than the long-term development of the sector and reduces the political capture motivation; the regulators' technical capacity and the implementation of more efficient mechanisms is made operative, from the point of view of the incentives and career-making chances with these entities.

Allowing the President of the Republic the ability to appoint and to remove superintendents, but in both cases using a transparent process. This measure, implemented in many developed countries, would keep the rank of regulators as officers who enjoy the President's confidence, but it would allow more transparency in their appointment and evaluation. This requires clearly established procedures for their appointment and their removal (proven negligence, regulatory capture, others).

Strengthening of the Regulatory Entities

The institutional capacity of the regulating agents must be strengthened so that they can solve ambiguities efficiently within the regulatory framework of the basic services. Not much has been done to identify them and, thus, change norms and regulations. Unfortunately, it is only when opportunistic conduct appears that the mentioned ambiguities also appear. Three minimum necessary though insufficient changes to improve this situation are:

To provide regulators and comptroller agents with the human and financial resources that could allow them to perform their function on equal conditions as the basic services companies under their supervision. An interesting aspect to analyze is the possibility for the regulatory agent to be partly financed with taxes on the regulated enterprises themselves, with some clear objective mechanism as, for example, being paid for the job they do. Although this is the way used in very few countries in Latin America, the experience of the regulatory agents in Argentina (ENRE and ENERGAS) has been clearly successful.

To go further with the implementation of dispute settling mechanisms of conflicts occurring outside current legal proceedings and with the enforcement of the solutions contributed with by private arbitrage may prove convenient in the short run. The electricity act enacted in March 2004 certainly is in this direction, whose example should be followed at least in the telecommunications and water and sewage sector.

To study how to adapt to the regulatory framework, with reference to the significant policies in each individual sector, should, in the medium term, be centered on the ministries, not on the regulatory organizations. The latter should only provide support to the technical work done by ministries; they should not become involved in fostering the deep changes in the norms ruling the sector they themselves regulate. The regulatory agencies would then become technical bodies only; the political discussions inherent in the transformations in the regulatory structure could, then, be avoided. On the other hand, the strengthening of the regulatory institutions would reduce the existing ambiguities within the regulatory framework and also the underlying opportunistic conduct entailed in them.

Transparency of the Regulatory Process

The regulatory entities procedures must be updated to have transparency in the regulation process. This suggestion points in the direction of helping with the profound changes that imply the regulators' independence. An indirect way to achieve the independence of the regulatory entities is to reform the procedures they are ruled by in order to make them transparent. Some minimum requirements in this direction are:

The demand to back up the decisions made by regulators and comptrollers. For example, it is desirable that the methods the regulator follows to make decisions, particularly tariffs decisions, could be replicated by third parties, especially independent academicians; the regulators should have the obligation to substantiate their assumptions and judgments in written form.

The adoption of a comprehensive administrative procedure applicable whenever the regulator makes a decision. Apart from helping to reach transparency in the decisions, this could foster public participation in the process because it would allow those who were interested to have the opportunity of having a say in public and of becoming involved in the decision making process.

The open supply of regulatory activity information. This could be accomplished by publishing Internet pages that, by offering all the information available, would thus do away with third party entry barrier to access information.

Implementation of regulatory accounting in basic services. This systematization of information can help with system transparency, with the memory preservation. By doing so, it can generate stability in the procedures used and in the rules of the game for the regulated enterprises themselves.

The procedural changes suggested should enhance the prospects of making the regulator accountable in the hope that it will help to control administrative acts by binding them to minimum procedural standards. Similarly, and closely related, is the need to create, along with the procedural reform, a system to allow those affected to present claims in case the transparency rules may have been trespassed. This issue is dealt with further in the next section.

Incentives Mechanisms

For regulation to be successful, the means used must be improved. Regulation should be direct; this means a regulation is applied and non compliance with it is punished. Indirect regulation seems to be better: the inclusion of market elements in regulation. The aim is to modify the incentives so that the agents' interest lies in "complying" with the regulation. This approach enjoys certain advantages concerning regulation costs. Both kinds of regulation are necessary, but different legal bodies might change many direct regulations and displace them with others that are more indirect or with incentives.

As an example, more competition in telecommunications has allowed local telephone companies to enter different market segments, the interest of the new firms being to capture clients with more important demands. Because of the rigid legislation, the incumbent cannot react to greater competition by offering alternative plans as quickly as an efficient operator would be expected to do, especially given the months it takes to obtain authorization from the regulator to make the offer. In terms of incentives, what may appear as self-evident is to authorize alternative plan offers by the regulator and always maintain the regulated tariffs option, while, *ex-post*, ensuring that these practices are neither discriminatory nor predatory.[12]

Best Use of Economies of Scope in Sectoral Regulation

Finally, the governance structure must be redefined in order to make the best use of economies of scope and to enhance the interaction between the regulator role and the competition supporter role. The responsibility for the defense of competition belongs typically to other public entities: *Fiscalía Nacional Económica* (the Chilean equivalent to the Department of Justice in USA) and the Antitrust Commissions (currently the Competition Court, a special court in charge to settle disputes on this regard). The responsibility for the defense of consumers rests with SERNAC (Consumer National Agency).

However, the problems concerning basic services present high specificity and are complex to resolve. Experience has shown that involving these entities may cause severe problems, in particular regarding co-regulation of utilities. It is extremely important to clearly define the

---

[12] In fact, Telefonica obtained the right to offer flexible plans to its subscribers in local telephony from the Antitrust Commission (currently, Competition Court) in 2003. However, such flexibility requires Telefonica to obtain a permit from the regulator before implementing any alternative plan.

role of each institution, to separate duties and avoid inconsistencies in regulation, and to enhance communication among them in order to facilitate their working.

Bottlenecks in the Promotion and Defense of Competition

Establishing modern regulatory institutional conditions in a market economy open to a globalized world demands an institutional structure for the defense of competition to complement it in order to reach the aim of supporting competition. Therefore, it is necessary to have commissions and a legal system in charge of watching over competition in markets involving oligopoly (or potentially competitive); especially, the markets related to regulated basic services.[13]

It has proven advantageous to separate functions: fact finding and investigating unfair practices on the one hand; making legal and other decisions, on the other. In the first case in Chile, the work is done through the *Fiscalía Nacional Económica*; the legal work is in charge of the Antitrust Commissions (from now on, indistinctly Competition Court). Within this institutional structure, the antitrust commissions function like the courts of the judicial power system and they should be, in theory, independent of any other public office. The *Fiscalía* was thought of as a public service branch with its own separate budget and staff; in Chile, it is directly dependent on the President of the Republic.

Although, in Chile, the courts have clearly decided in favor of competition in the markets, we believe various problems restrict their scope. They are:

The aims of the antitrust commissions are often not clear or are poorly defined. The objectives the commission members follow to make their evaluation vary immensely, from commissions whose task is to defend competition to those whose responsibility is to defend consumer rights, market development, or other aims. This is the reason why, even in the same country, similar unfair practices have been judged following different criteria.

Insufficient professionalism of the commissions. The first restrictive factor is to work exclusively according to the sense of responsibility the commission members may have; they obtain no remuneration for the job done, do not have advisors to support their decisions and cannot neglect their private activities to entirely devote themselves to this one. Usually,

---

[13] Most of these problems were solved upon the creation of the Competition Court, which replaced the Antitrust Commissions. The new law was enacted at the end of 2003 and the first draft of this article was used as a discussion paper for implementing such a reform. See Saavedra (2003) for further details of this legal reform.

this implies that the time left available to comply with this duty is very limited and often confined to attending commission meetings only.

Commission integration has not been organized to allow the most qualified members to be part of it. Experts are ever more needed because the economy evolution is accompanied by increasingly complex strategic business activities. The integration of the commissions may affect and be affected by the interpretation of the legislation related to the defense of competition. For example, emphasis on punishing conduct contrary to competition, where concrete evidence of such conducts is fundamental, should demand the presence of a legally trained professional. On the other hand, the stress on *defending competition* should be associated with the need of specialists in market organization (economics).

In many cases, the commissions are not independent of political power, especially the government. This is a particularly delicate aspect when considering possible conflicts between the Antitrust Commissions and State organizations such as state-owned companies, superintendent offices, and regulatory entities, among others.

Antitrust Commissions have not been properly defined in terms of the relations with the Judiciary. Such Commissions in Chile are part and are not part of the judicial power pyramid. It is not clear how the Supreme Court is going to revise judgments made by the Antitrust Resolution Commission, what adds uncertainty to do business in Chile because the scarce preparation on economic grounds that the member of the Supreme Court have.

Antitrust commissions overlap with regulatory entities. Almost all over the Latin American countries with an institutional framing for the defense of competition, little attention has been paid to the fact that the antitrust commissions have become co-regulators of the system. Many of the decisions made by the administrative authorities have been rejected by the firms affected by such measures, thus paving the way to the kind of opportunistic conduct that ends up partly sidestepping regulation. Administrative decisions delay strategy has been widely used by companies in the energy and telecommunications sectors in Chile during the 1990s and more recently.

The Fiscalía Nacional Económica has economic constraints for hiring the number of appropriate well-paid staff that would be needed; additionally, neither are there funds enough to commission studies or hire specialists in the diverse issues involved. This situation has been partially resolved with the Reform DL 211, in 1998.

In the light of the information contributed, it is relevant to comprehensively revise the institutional framing for the defense of competition, including the aims of the institutions and their structure, their integration and the faculties of both the antitrust commissions and of the regulatory entities. The result of this comprehensive revision will help to determine with greater certainty what aspects of each of the institutional framing elements must be strengthened.

Clarifying the Aims of the Legislation for the Defense of Competition

The priority in updating the institutional framing for the defense of competition is to clearly define the aims of the legislation. This is particularly valid in a context in which the option has been not to define the criminal conducts themselves. Along with the strengthening of the traditional role in the regulation of unfair practices, it should be expected that:

Commissions and regulators defend competition. With reference to basic services, deregulation of potentially competitive markets should be supported.

Antitrust commissions become organizations of consultancy and permanent discussion for regulatory entities. Nevertheless, to be able to play this critical role, it is necessary to make the commissions more independent of the Executive Power.

The Antitrust Resolution Commission with Full Time Members

To have a more professional Antitrust Resolution Commission by having full time commissioners (judges) is a necessary condition for recruiting professionals trained on industrial organization; moreover, this should be the main activity for these commissioners. By doing so, uncertainty about judgments and delays on resolution would be reduced.

Resources should be made available to find the appropriate professionals who could accept and dedicate themselves to a full time commitment. Special provisions should be considered not to allow the pursuit of other activities, except perhaps for part time academic activities, during the time the commission member remains in the position. Similarly, there should also be explicit provisions not to allow certain activities to be performed after leaving this position.

Redefining the Appointment Mechanisms of the Commission Members

Redefining the appointment mechanisms of members seeks to help the members be independent of political power as well as of the Judiciary system. The demands imposed by modernization and the development of the Chilean economy toward an institutional framing for the defense of competition require corresponding resources and personnel. A step forward is the training of professionals with a greater degree of specialization and elimination of the hazards of the present appointment system.

The main obstacle to appoint the most appropriate candidates to occupy public administration positions is perhaps the dependency on vested interest groups. To help improve the situation, profound changes must be introduced in the appointment procedures:

Essential changes in the selection of members by ad-hoc committees not directly dependent on the executive power. The selection of the candidates must be transparent. It is advisable that the selection board should enjoy the corresponding qualifications and not be linked to other State branches; also, citizens should be able to have the opportunity to participate in this selection process and there should be the possibility to implement an enquiry system.

Changes in the commission members selection and appointment procedures. The aim of the procedure to appoint these members is to select the most qualified individuals to occupy the position, which is not an easy task since "qualification" cannot be testified by third parties.[14] The application process should be simple in formalities, with ex-post information examination; it should be left to the interested parties; substantive requirements should be demanded, like publications on related issues in prestigious academic journals, experience in antitrust cases, and others; transparency in the process should be improved by making the application process equal the public selection rank, and making the candidates' qualifications and background publicly available.

Limiting Review of the Commission Decisions

The review of the commission decisions should be limited while, at the same time, the formal protection of the commissions by the judicial power should be maintained. Although the decisions made by the commissions should be subject to control by the Judiciary, such control should be exercised over formal errors the members may have generated, not over the fundamental content in the decisions.

Improved relations with the Judiciary system may help to avoid the main risk concerning the appointed commissions; that is to say, the little concern with the procedures and due process of law other than those followed by commissions (which occurs when the defense of competition is not within the control of the judicial power). Similarly, not being part of the Judiciary prevents the possible inappropriate uses of legal appeals by preventing complex technical matters being dealt with by members not skilled effecting these areas (a situation that takes place when the commissions remain part of the judicial power structure).

Referral of the Competition Defense Decisions to the Regulatory Entities

---

[14] Some aspects of this discussion have been taken from Galetovic and Sanhueza (2002).

The power of the commissions that decide on regulations affecting free competition should be limited. They may become co-regulating agents of the decisions made by the administrative authority.

One way to avoid such possibility is to have the regulatory entities resort to the mentioned commissions for non-binding advice concerning the sector's issues. This is the way the administrative authority may count on a significant opinion on the matter while free competition would not become the guiding principle of the management regulation function. The institutional deficiencies relating to a matter under administrative law (see the next section) could be weakened and the above situation might quickly turn into a functional equivalent to substitute for the failures of the system.

Justice Modernization and the Defense of Consumers and Persons

What is the appropriate role and the minimum expected of a modernized Judiciary system more in accordance with a market economy? These are the questions to be addressed in this section. We also discuss the institutional requirements for the defense of persons with respect to the State and the defense of consumers in relation to private enterprises.

One of the fundamental components for market economy operation is an independent, reliable judicial power that can settle increasingly complex technical matters. Unluckily, both the legal proceedings applicable in economic issues and the commission members' capacity to resolve these problems prove quite inadequate in Chile as well as all over Latin America.

The judicial power system acknowledges the conflicting nature of the economic issues, but antitrust commissions and arbitration systems have been created to deal with them. However, a substantial portion of the disputes, sooner or later, is channeled out to the central Judiciary (especially to the Courts of Appeal and the Supreme Court), where the economic disputes receive treatment similar to other legal cases. The major constraints found in Chile's judicial power system are the very low procedural efficiency, the judges' poor general economic background, the absence of specific commissions to treat highly technical issues or the absence of courts for contentious administrative cases. These constraints increase the direct and indirect litigation costs: it is rather difficult to predict the decisions to be made by judges, while a social and individual fair treatment of the cases is not guaranteed.

Some authors go further and point out that a system based on Roman Law, mostly in force all over Latin America, tends to inhibit the technological innovation process and the entrepreneurial spirit that constitutes the essence of the market system, imposing too many restraints on the private sector, which can only act according to law. By contrast, Common Law is more flexible and only punishes what is not permitted, which is stimulating for the introduction of innovations (White, 1997).

Bottlenecks in the Judiciary

The Chilean judicial power system is not efficient in settling disputes because the different procedural stages take a great deal of time. There is no systematic quantitative analysis available concerning penal procedures, but different studies have shown that even the most expeditious procedures are considerably slow in Chile, even compared with those in other countries of Latin America which, it is said, enjoy lower institutional standards. Table 3.2 summarizes the length of civil procedures in some of the Latin American countries selected.

The data in table 3.2 are consistent with other studies for Chile, where the summary civil procedures last approximately an average of 2 years and 5 months (Cerda, 1993); the duration of contentious-administrative procedures related to alimony, visitation rights and custody reach on average one year and 2 months in the initial instance stage only (Universidad Diego Portales, 1994).

Table 3.2 Duration of Ordinary Civil Procedures
(two instances)

Country	**Duration**
Argentina	More than 2 years
Chile	**2 years and 9 months**
Colombia	2 years and 9 months
Costa Rica	10 months
Paraguay	More than 2 years
Perú	4 years and 6 months
Uruguay	8 months

Source: Martínez (1999)

Similarly, in cases brought to the Antitrust Commission for unfair practices in Chile's energy sector, it was estimated that the average duration of the trials in the years between 1989 and 1997 reached 2 years and 8 months, not including the Appeals to the Supreme Court, where treatment and final decision took a similar time (Basañes *et al.*, 2001). This poor legal performance in Chile demonstrates the need for modernizing the Judiciary system, both in its procedures and in its structure. To such end, three changes should be introduced:

(1) To implement or strengthen reforms to civil and penal procedures to make them more expeditious and reliable to the parties involved. These improvements are complementary to the proposal for the creation of special commissions.
(2) General and professional training of legal officers, and retraining of those who hold office; specific economic training for judges.
(3) Creation of special commissions to settle highly technical economic matters, and to resolve problems or disputes derived from deeds or omissions committed by the State to the detriment of individuals. Next we refer to the last two changes mentioned above.

As explained by Vargas (1999), when dealing with penal procedural reforms taking place in Chile, the present procedures applicable virtually all over the countries in the region and in most cases are the ordinary procedures followed for simple criminal offenses.

These are the procedures that have been followed since the Inquisition days, according to which the interest of the State in punishing crime is above the rights of the individuals. The system, then, proves inefficient for the defense of the accused and considerably affects the corresponding individual rights. Transparency is not present and judges rarely get directly involved in the cases, which ultimately results in generalized unfairness and legal administration inefficacy. Finally, in this system, the judge investigates and passes sentence, thus giving rise to serious conflicts of interests related to the situation of the judges in the administration of justice.[15]

It will be essential to introduce procedural reforms for civil actions in Chile, and also to go deeper into the penal procedural reforms under way since the end of the 1990s. These reforms need to focus on the implementation of oral, public, more simple and improved procedures; that is to say, procedures entirely different from the procedures for civil cases that are in force in Chile today. Whenever pertinent, before and during the proceedings, the parties involved should be encouraged to accept mediation with the assistance of a judge or of a mediator external to the judicial power system. This would diminish the workload and would reorient the focus of the system from being a punishing agent to making amends for the damage caused.

The main advantages of procedural reforms supported by mediation would be upgraded legal services and the potential for the poorer sectors of the economy to gain access to the services. This would improve procedures and would offer more efficiency, access and transparency while, at the same time, the system could become more productive.

---

[15] See Dewatripont and Tirole (1999) for a formal treatment on the separation of tasks between a judge and the parties in conflict.

These kinds of reforms require well trained judges and legal professionals familiar with economic issues, something that is not very common. Very few judges have received an appropriate background in economics nor have they been trained to deal with economic issues. These gaps in formal academic training to analyze economic issues raise two major issues:

The considerable high degree of economic-related matters litigated in Chile. Very often, bureaucracy or the absence of competent decision-making power on the part of the judges delays procedures which otherwise would be shorter. The experts' reports may frequently exhibit little impartiality in this matter; they may even offer no substantive contribution to the resolution of the case.

The judges tend to make decisions based exclusively on evidence derived from unlawful activities. In the economic field, concrete evidence of unfair practices is hard to find; for example, proving predatory practices is virtually impossible except when those who perpetrated them are extremely careless. However, it is possible to punish circumstances in which there exists the suspicion of the unfair practices. Even though by law the judges may interpret and enforce law following presumptions, the latter demand the judge be highly professionally competent and have wide experience. A judge contrary to taking risks will probably concentrate on tangible evidence to avoid incurring in legal errors.

The first issue, delay in resolving cases, is occasionally solved by the parties involved with the assistance of independent arbitration. This is common practice in Chile and in Argentina to settle disputes in regulated industries. Even though arbitrators have intervened in settling important disputes, especially those in the public utility services, they are not empowered to hold binding arbitration (for both parties), which considerably restraints their effect. Consequently, consideration should be given to the possibility of developing an arbitration system that carries with it the threat of punishment for failure to follow through with the agreements.

However, the most important need is for judges with knowledge of economic issues and with decision-making power based on the analysis of the conditions that allow opportunistic conducts. Chile's judicial power system should include a permanent educational program in economic and legal matters; as noted earlier, profound changes in procedures should also be made. Finally, the creation of special commissions for economic issues and, in particular, for issues where the State is one of the parties involved is becoming ever more necessary, a topic that will be addressed next.

Regarding the creation of special commissions in the judiciary, the need to establish them is not related solely to economic matters. There are not many cases in the Latin American judiciary with such characteristics; there is none of the sort in Chile. Consequently, it is possible to think of having economic commissions, contentious-administrative commissions perhaps, like those already functioning in Argentina, France or Spain, or with a more comprehensive scope, to deal with different economic issues, with or without the presence of the State.[16]

Having special economic commissions would mean an improved justice administration, quicker procedures and more efficiency, access and transparency in the functioning of the Judiciary system as legal decisions related to influential groups could be made independently, helping to prevent corruption within the judiciary itself. In practical terms, these advantages would be the direct consequence of two separate innovations to be introduced in the mentioned special commissions:

In civil economic cases: the courts have become overburdened with basic services payment or interpretation of contracts between private parties, mainly oral public procedures stripped of formalities would make the system work more quickly. For example, over 60% of civil and penal actions are related to matters not requiring the intervention of a judge; only the bureaucratic procedures, such as in aggressive collection causes (excluding the trial itself), making inheritance effective, reassigning legal budgets, miners' demonstrations, and others, could be required.

More complex cases: these would demand a closer more profound analysis of the corresponding sources and implications. Consequently, specially trained staff should be hired to support the judges in these matters, thus allowing the latter to have a more comprehensive view of the dispute to be settled.

There would be three potential economic quantifiable gains from such changes. First, time saving for the system users, which could be significant in the more complex cases since they generally involve hiring professionals of high alternative cost and the interests at stake are enormous. Secondly, reduction in the number of cases that could be referred to the courts of appeal, a direct consequence of better assessed and better made decisions in the first instance. Finally, the market system credibility, since the state would be subject to legal scrutiny in administrative acts affecting persons, especially in the case of regulation of basic services.

Consumer Rights and Defense Bodies

---

[16]There have been proposals already. The government of Chile, through Comisión de Modernización de la Institucionalidad Reguladora del Estado (Committee for the Modernization of the State Regulator Institutional Framework) in 1998 suggested the creation of national economic commissions, which would represent only an instance for further appeal in matters related to competition and basic services. Unfortunately, this idea has only been partially included in the draft for the creation of fiscal commissions.

We believe it is also possible to introduce the Ombudsman in Chile. Although in Chile this office has recently been opened (2002), it has not been thought out in accordance with a regulator institutional framework; rather, an organization parallel to the state, open to society as a whole and independent of political pressure groups, with the main aim of defending people before political power abuses. We, at least, feel sure it is not an entity meant to defend people from deeds or omissions of the State related to the type of litigation occurring in the regulated public utility services.

The Servicio Nacional del Consumidor (SERNAC) [Consumer Defense Agency] should be made stronger. This is the office in charge of informing the consumers and, eventually, defending them from abuses by the business sector. A side discussion is the introduction of novel instruments to award people the possibility to defend themselves in cases where the whole population may be affected, like, for example, incorporating class action suits, widely known in the United States, to our judicature. This could make the elimination of barriers possible, for people to have access to a better and more efficient administration of justice.

It is important to mention that the recent modification to the consumers protection act (enacted in July 2004) incorporates the idea of class actions suits through the notion of consumers' *fuzzy* rights, but in a narrower sense than that used in the United States.

Conclusions

Chile, with its liberalization reforms of the final quarter of the 20th Century, is heading toward the development of a market economy. Substantial structural transformations were introduced that granted the private sector greater predominance in the provision of goods and services, in infrastructure development and in human capital accumulation. In part of the 1980s and the 1990s, the country enjoyed high sustained growth that, we believe, is the result of the mentioned reforms implementation.

The institutional structure of Chile's economy, the state apparatus most particularly, is incompatible with the efficient functioning of the market that the reforms were meant to open. The absence of profound changes in State administration, in the administration of justice and in the regulatory agencies and competition institutions does not guarantee the Chilean economy can reach the high sustained growth rates needed to lead the country to full economic development.

The root of the efficiency and efficacy problem in the functioning of the State is to be found in the absence of adequate incentives and regulation mechanisms for persons and for public entities. There is generalized weakness in the public administration evaluation mechanisms that should praise individual and corporate achievements, and punish indolence, inefficiency and the little effort to obtain the desired objectives. Instead, little individual accountability responsibility is the result. Furthermore, the State in Chile has traditionally acknowledged little weight to public opinion; tax payers stand poor chances of obtaining information related to the destiny given to their taxes or of having a say in their application, or of recalling inefficient corrupt public officers.

Chile must also respond to the challenge of implementing regulatory frameworks and competition defense bodies to reap the benefits of market liberalization and privatization of state-owned enterprises. In practice, there are numerous constraints that prevent regulators from inhibiting rent seeking in sectors where private firms operate in monopolistic conditions. There are three reasons to account for this situation: our regulatory entities are technically weak to enforce the existing regulation; the regulatory framework is not complete and may be the source of ambiguities that give rise to opportunism; occasionally, regulation is particularly complex, from a technical point of view.

The regulatory entities must be independent of political power and of the regulated sectors, which presupposes profound changes to the institutional framing of basic services. The regulatory organizations' institutional power must be strengthened to be able to efficiently resolve the ambiguities within the basic services regulatory framework. Not much has been done to identify them and thus modify the norms and regulations. Unfortunately, it is only when opportunistic conducts appear that such ambiguities come to the surface.

The means to achieve regulation must be perfected. Currently, the focus is on direct regulation, in which a regulation is implemented and then punishment applied if it is not compliance. Indirect regulation appears to be better; that is to say, the introduction of market elements in regulation. The purpose is to improve incentives so that the agents themselves develop an interest in compliance.

Governance structure must be redefined to benefit from economies of scope between the role of regulator and that of competition defense. The responsibility for defending consumer rights and competition typically belongs to Antitrust Commissions; educating and informing consumers is virtually non existent given the SERNAC institutional weakness.

Chile's performance in legal matters points to the need for a significant updating of both the procedures and the structure of the judicial power system. To reduce the present weaknesses, the following changes are needed. First, implementing or strengthening reforms to civil and penal procedures to make them more expeditious and reliable to the parties involved (including special commissions for economic cases); secondly, professional education of the judicial power officers and the retraining of those currently active as civil servants, with particular emphasis on training judges in specific economic matters; and thirdly, setting special commissions to resolve highly technical economic issues or settle litigation derived from deeds or omissions by the State to the detriment of persons.

Finally, we should note that the future development of Chile requires attention to corruption, a problem that is widespread in most Latin American countries. This scourge causes substantial direct costs in the political, economic and social spheres that diminish, if not inhibit, the gains from structural reforms, privatization and market openness to private sector participation. Any reform to the role of the State, in management, structure, regulation and competition bodies or the Judiciary system, will ultimately be unsuccessful in the presence of high corruption rates.

References

Basañes, F., E. Saavedra and R. Soto (2001) "Post-Contractual Renegotiations and Disputes in Chile," in F. Basañes and R. Willig (eds.) *Second Generation Reforms in Infrastructure Services*, Inter-American Development Bank.

Bitrán, E., A. Estache, J. L. Guasch and P. Serra (1999) "Privatizing and Regulating Chile's Utilities, 1974-2000: Successes, Failures, and Outstandings Challenges," in G. Perry and D. Leipziger (eds.) *Chile: Recent Policy Lessons and Emerging Challenges*, World Bank Institute Development Studies.

Boeninger, E. (1991) "El Papel del Estado en Latinoamérica," in R. Lüders and Luis Rubio (eds.) *Estado y Economía en America Latina: Por un Gobierno Efectivo en la Epoca Actual*, CINDE.

Brunner, J.J. (1995) "Notes on Modernity and Postmodernity in Latin American Culture," in J. Beverley, J. Oviedo, and M. Ahorna eds. *The Postmodernism Debate in Latin America*, Duke University Press.

Burki, S.J., G. Perry, and W. Dillinger (1999) *Beyond The Center: Decentralizing The State*, The World Bank.

Cerda, C. (1993) "Duración del Procedimiento Sumario en los Juzgados de Santiago." Proyecto Fondecyt N° 1920509, 1992.

Dewatripont, M. and Tirole, J. (1999) "Advocates," *Journal of Political Economy* 107, 1-39.

Domínguez, J. (1994) *Authoritarian and Democratic Regimes in Latin America.* New York: Garland Pub.

Galal, A., L. Jones, P. Tandon, and I. Vogelsang (1994) *Welfare Consequences of Selling Public Enterprises: An Empirical Analysis*, Oxford University Press.

Galetovic, A. and R. Sanhueza (2002) "Regulación de Servicios Públicos: ¿Hacia Dónde Debemos Ir?," *Revista de Estudios Públicos* 85, 101-136.

Larraín, J. (2001) "Cultura Chilena en los Noventa," *Persona y Sociedad* 15, 93-106.

Martínez, N.H. (1999) "De los Diez Pecados de la Reforma Judicial y Algunos Anatemas," in R. Lüders and Luis Rubio eds. op. cit.

Newbery, D. (1999) *Privatization, Restucturig, and Regulation of Network Utilities*. Cambridge, MIT Press.

Oates, W. (1972) *Fiscal Federalism*. New York, Harcourt-Brace-Jovanovich.

Saavedra, E. (2003) "Promoción de la Competencia en Chile: Reflexiones a la Luz de las Recientes Modificaciones Legales," in *Día de la Competencia*, edited by the Fiscalía Nacional Económica, Chile.

Tiebout, C. (1956) "A Pure Theory of Local Public Goods," *Journal of Political Economy* 64, 416-24.

Universidad Diego Portales (1994) "Duración de los Procedimientos Contenciosos en los Juzgados de Menores del Area Metropolitana," mimeo Servicio Nacional de la Mujer.

Valdés-Prieto, S. (2003) "Contratos y Remuneraciones de Altos Directivos Públicos," in *Revista de Estudios Públicos* 89, 279-411.

Vargas, J.E. (1999) "La Modernización de la Justicia Criminal Chilena," in *Perspectivas en Política, Economía y Gestión* 2, 1-22.

White, M. (1997) "Legal Practice and Economic Adaptation," Mimeo White & Associates.

Part II

Sectoral Analysis

4 Trade Reforms and Manufacturing Industry in Chile*

Roberto Alvarez and J. Rodrigo Fuentes

Introduction and Motivation

The big changes in both political spectrum and economic conception experienced by the Chilean economy in the 1960s and 1970s have attracted the interest of economists as well as political scientists. From the pure economic point of view, after the Great Depression of the 1930s, and following the strategy of most of the countries in the world, the Chilean economy became less outward oriented through the introduction of several barriers to international trade. This gathered even more strength after Prebich's ideas about economic development and international trade in the 1950s.

These policies reached their peak in the early 1970s under the government of President Salvador Allende, who was supported by a coalition of left political parties. Under his government from 1970 to 1973, not only the economy became almost closed but also the idea of resource allocation by the market was completely abandoned. Most private firms were nationalized, and price and interest rate controls were introduced.

After the military coup in 1973, the new team reversed several of these measures in almost six years, introducing what may be the largest structural change in Chile's economic history. The actions taken by the military administration were severely criticized by politicians and economists that opposed the new government. Criticism was based on the idea that the new model of development would push the economy towards

* We are grateful for the useful discussions with Antonio Escandón, Ricardo Vicuña and the participants in the XXXVII Anual Meeting of the Asociación Argentina de Economía Política. The views and conclusions presented in the paper are exclusively those of the authors and do not necessarily reflect the position of the Central Bank of Chile or of the Board members.

becoming a primary product exporter, thus very vulnerable to the fluctuations of the international market. Also, it was argued that the new policies would undermine the industrial sector and therefore the Chilean economy would never be able to join the group of more developed countries.

Regarding the Chilean industry, several articles have explored the impact of trade liberalization on productivity growth, but methodological problems leave open the question about whether outward orientation has a positive impact on productivity. The theoretical trade literature provides conflicting predictions about the impact of liberalization on productivity. Both groups, inward and outward oriented policy advocates, expect higher rates of productivity growth in manufacturing as a result of their respective opposite policies (Pack, 1988). Much of the empirical evidence has focused on this topic for developing countries, but the evidence is not yet conclusive.[1]

The goal of this chapter is to present another look at the large structural changes in the 1970s and 1980s in the Chilean economy and their effects on the manufacturing sector, from a long-term perspective. One of the issues to be addressed is the hypothesis that Chile became a less industrialized economy, because of the abrupt trade reform in the 1970s.[2] Our approach is to analyze how the manufacturing industry performed during and after these reforms, and what were the losses and gains of the process. Is this a story of just losses? Do we have a weak industrial sector? Today, we have the benefit of a longer-run perspective that can provide additional insights on this topic.

The methodology used is the following. First, prior work is reviewed that addresses the relationship between trade and productivity in the Chilean manufacturing industry. Secondly, we provide our own estimates of technological progress and technical efficiency indices. The difference with previous studies is that now we can assess the effect of trade liberalization on both variables over a longer time span. Thirdly, we analyze changes in productivity over time and across sectors, and its link to trade liberalization.

The chapter continues as follows. The next section describes in more detail the structural changes in the Chilean economy during the 1970s and 1980s. In particular, the trade reform and the exchange rate policy of the late seventies had the greatest impact on the manufacturing sector. Using this as background, the third part examines the manufacturing industry to provide a sense of the magnitude of these changes. The fourth section offers a brief review of the empirical studies concerning the relationship between trade liberalization and manufacturing industry performance.

---

[1] For a survey of theoretical arguments and empirical evidence, see Rodrick (1995).

[2] See for example Ffrench-Davis and Saez (1995).

Then, the fifth section, using plant-level data, estimates productivity changes in the post trade liberalization period. The chapter ends with some concluding remarks.

The Structural Change of the 1970s

The reforms of the 1970s and 1980s have been the object of numerous studies. Among the most comprehensive ones, it is worth singling out Edwards and Edwards (1987) and the book edited by Bosworth, *et al.* (1993). These reforms were deep and drastic; they resulted in a big shift in the development strategy that had prevailed in Chile since the 1940s.

Chile did not escape the ideas of inward oriented development that were common around the world after the Great Depression.[3] This inward oriented strategy was accompanied by proactive industrial policies and an increasing share of the government in the economy, through the creation of state owned enterprises. The manufacturing industry was protected with high tariffs, non-tariff barriers and multiple exchange rates. All this happened between 1940 and 1970, with a failed attempt to reverse this trend between 1959 and 1961.

In 1970, a newly elected government deepened the inward oriented policy and government intervention. Before the military coup of 1973, the Chilean economy could be characterized fairly as a closed economy (high barriers to trade and to capital movements)[3] with strong government intervention, price and interest rate controls, a large fiscal deficit and high inflation. Moreover, during the 1970-1973 period, the government nationalized an important number of private companies.

Among the trade protection measures, it is worth mentioning that in 1973 there was a high dispersion in import tariffs, ranging from 0% to 750%, with an average nominal tariff equal to 105% and a mode of 90%. Half the tariffs were above 80% and only 4% of the tariff positions had rates below 25% (see Corbo, 1985). There was also import prohibition for 187 tariff positions, a 90-day import deposit requirement of 10,000% over the CIF value, plus some other discretionary actions that could be taken by the Central Bank.

Immediately after the military coup, Chile moved toward a market economy. The most meaningful policies were price liberalization (including interest rates), the abrupt reduction of the fiscal deficit through reduced government spending and the privatization of state-owned enterprise. Among the reforms of the first ten years of the military administration, it is worth mentioning trade and capital liberalization, a

[3] In fact, Chile was one of the countries with the highest degree of trade distortions in the world. See Edwards (1994) and the references therein.

new pension fund system and new rules for the operation of the capital market.

Table 4.1 Effective Rate of Protection 1974-1979

Sectors	1974	1975	1976	1977	1978	1979
Food	161	105	48	28	16	12
Beverage	203	119	47	32	19	13
Tobacco	114	68	29	19	11	11
Textile	239	138	74	49	28	14
Apparel and Footwear	264	164	71	48	27	14
Leather	181	98	46	36	21	13
Wood Products	157	93	45	28	16	15
Furniture, except Metal	95	58	28	17	11	11
Paper and Pulp	184	114	62	37	22	17
Printing	140	75	40	32	20	12
Chemical Products	80	53	45	24	16	13
Plastic	80	53	45	24	16	13
Petroleum and Coal	265	101	17	0	12	13
Glass, Pottery and Non Metallic	128	87	55	32	20	14
Basic Metals	127	86	64	38	25	17
Metallic Products	147	101	77	52	27	15
Electrical and Non Electrical	96	72	58	35	19	13
Manufacturing Industry (Average	156.5	93.2	50.1	31.2	19.2	13.5
Agriculture	30	27	19	11	10	10
Mining	7	18	24	17	13	14
Non Tradable	-30	-19	-11	-7	-4	-3

Source: Aedo and Lagos (1984)

Perhaps the deepest reform conducted over that period, and closely related to our study, was trade liberalization. In less than six years, almost all the trade restrictions were lifted. By June 1979, all the non-tariff barriers (NTBs) were eliminated and an across the board 10% tariff was imposed. Table 4.1 shows the evolution of the effective rate of protection (ERP) during that period. Two features are important to highlight from table 4.1. The first one is the high ERP enjoyed by the manufacturing industry in 1974, compared to other sectors in the economy. Thus, the trade liberalization introduced a big change in relative prices in favor of agriculture, mining and non-tradable goods. The second important characteristic concerns the high ERP dispersion across the manufacturing sectors at the beginning of the period and the fact that there were almost no differences at the end of the period. These large changes in relative prices affected the allocation of resources within the economy.

In addition to the relative price shifts described above, the exchange rate policy also played a significant role in the resources allocation. In an effort to control inflation, in June 1979 the economic authority decided to peg the exchange rate, a move that coincided with the completion of the first trade liberalization process. However, the low speed of convergence between domestic and international inflation rates (because of wage indexation) and capital inflows (as a result of the external financial liberalization), the peso experienced a large real appreciation[4]. This result, combined with wage indexation based on past inflation, introduced an even larger loss in competitiveness by the tradable sector. Corbo and Sanchez (1985) referred to this episode as a "second and more intensive trade liberalization."

A lack of external funding plus low world economic growth rates induced a deep recession in 1982. Wage rigidities hindered the necessary adjustments in the labor market, so the government decided to devaluate the peso in 1982, after two years of fixed exchange rates. After several devaluations and a short episode with flexible exchange rates, Chile adopted a crawling peg system.

Given the situation at the time, the government decided to modify the trade policy by increasing tariffs from 10 to 20% in 1983 and to 35% in 1984 (always across the board). Additional tariffs were imposed for electronic goods and automobiles, and a price band for certain crops (wheat, sugar and oil seed). Somehow, the idea of equal tariffs for all goods was left behind.

In 1985 a second trade liberalization process was implemented. Tariffs were reduced from 35 to 20% and to 15% in 1988. Finally, in 1991, a newly elected government implemented a further tariff reduction to 11% and established free trade agreements with several countries, whereby tariff differences were again introduced according to origin and type of good, but now at a much lower level.

The History of the Manufacturing Industry in Numbers

As stated above, the large changes in relative prices introduced important changes in resource allocation across sectors. The share of the manufacturing industry in GDP diminished, but less dramatically than many authors have argued.[5] The base year of the national accounts was changed in 1986, making it difficult to compare figures before and after that year, even in current prices. For instance, in 1985 (a year that is common to both national account systems), there is a difference of 5.2 percentage points between the 1977 series compared to the 1986 one. To construct a more consistent series of manufacturing valued added over

[4] See Edwards (1989) and Le Fort (1988) for empirical evidence on the real exchange rate behavior over that period.

[5] For instance Ffrench-Davis and Saez (1995) mentioned that the share of the manufacturing industry in 1989 was way below the 1960-1969 average. This conclusion cannot be drawn from figure 3.1, below.

GDP, we interpolated the series using the relative prices estimated with the input-output matrix of 1986.[6] The new series appears in figure 4.1.

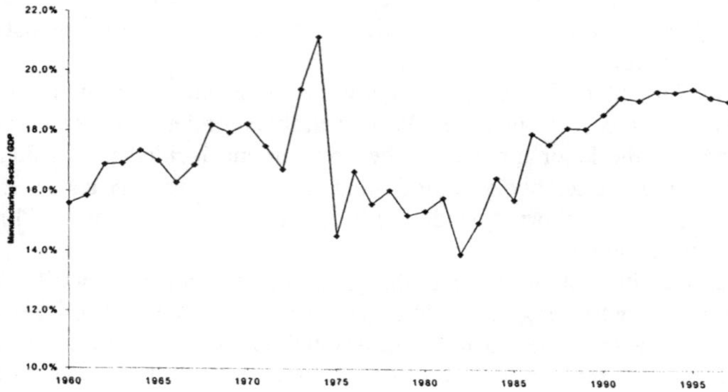

Source: Central Bank of Chile; authors' calculations

Figure 4.1 Share of the Manufacturing Sector in GDP

The average share in the 1960s was equal to 17.0% while in the 1975-1985 period, the figure was down to only 15.4%. After 1987, the manufacturing sector increased very fast, mainly due to a higher real exchange rate. Although the real exchange rate peaked in 1990, to decline after that, the manufacturing sector still grew faster than the rest of the economy. As section five of the chapter will show, this growth was driven mainly by productivity increases. Moreover, the 1986-1999 average is similar to the rate in the 1960s, but with a more competitive industry, as will be seen below.

In exports, the manufacturing sector also reveals an interesting behavior. In 1970, Chile was mainly a copper exporter, and even today, this is by far its most important exported product; however, the weight of copper in total exports has decreased while manufacturing exports have increased as a share of total exports. By the end of the 1990s the share of manufacturing in total exports was almost three times as high as in 1970 and almost four times with respect to 1960 (see figures 4.2 and 4.3). It is important to consider that between 1960 and 1989 total exports increased from 490 million to 8.19 billion US dollars. Unfortunately, because of an

[6] We did the same exercise using the 1977 relative prices, and the conclusion does not change, what changes is the level of the share but in all periods. We agree that this is not a first best methodology, but it is more accurate than compared shares in nominal terms under different National Account systems.

export classification problem, the figures after 1990 are not strictly comparable with those in figure 4.2. That comparison is shown in a different graph below. As can be seen, the significance of the manufacturing industry increases even further, outperforming the mining sector in 1999.

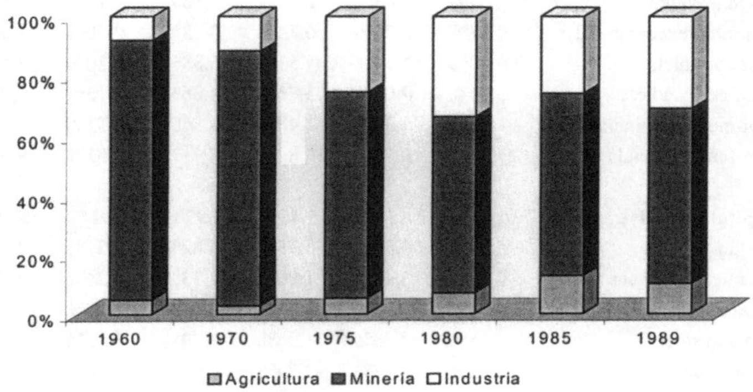

Figure 4.2 Exports by Sectors over Total Exports 1960-1989

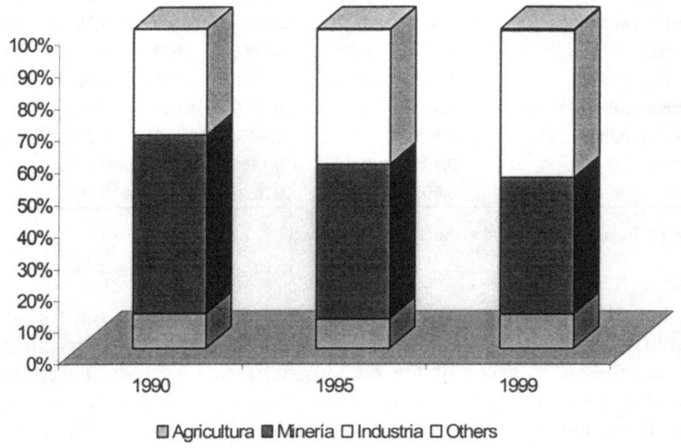

Figure 4.3 Exports by Sectors over Total Exports 1990-1999

Table 4.2 Value Added Distribution Across Sectors

Sectors	1974	1979	1982	1986	1990	1994
Natural Resources Intensive	**52.31%**	**49.99%**	**57.66%**	**58.60%**	**59.10%**	**56.40%**
Food	11.66%	18.04%	19.66%	18.93%	18.54%	20.93%
Tobacco	3.01%	3.80%	4.77%	4.32%	3.25%	3.54%
Wood products	1.37%	3.68%	2.91%	2.58%	3.18%	3.82%
Furniture, except metal	0.27%	0.76%	0.70%	0.58%	0.70%	1.00%
Paper products	3.10%	4.54%	4.53%	6.88%	6.20%	7.49%
Petroleum and coal	3.61%	4.09%	5.76%	4.06%	5.15%	6.23%
Non-metallic minerals	1.31%	2.30%	2.48%	2.86%	2.53%	3.70%
Non-ferrous metals	27.98%	12.79%	16.86%	18.41%	19.55%	9.68%
Capital Intensive	**36.19%**	**31.34%**	**25.46%**	**25.97%**	**25.91%**	**25.16%**
Textile	5.73%	5.39%	3.79%	4.82%	4.21%	3.19%
Chemical products	3.25%	3.48%	1.90%	2.33%	3.24%	3.77%
Other chemicals	4.39%	6.22%	7.77%	6.23%	6.94%	7.66%
Iron and steel	8.38%	4.03%	3.96%	4.79%	3.29%	2.55%
Metal products	3.85%	4.38%	3.74%	3.67%	4.46%	4.45%
No-electrical machinery	2.21%	2.18%	1.75%	1.56%	0.53%	0.63%
Electrical machinery	3.58%	2.28%	1.20%	1.48%	1.45%	1.23%
Transport equipment	4.80%	3.38%	1.36%	1.08%	1.80%	1.69%
Labor Intensive	**11.49%**	**18.67%**	**16.88%**	**15.43%**	**14.99%**	**18.44%**
Beverages	3.37%	5.19%	5.77%	4.26%	4.15%	5.15%
Clothing and footwear	2.68%	4.42%	3.82%	3.30%	3.55%	4.19%
Leather	0.75%	0.78%	0.50%	1.62%	0.52%	0.47%
Printing	1.49%	3.95%	3.74%	2.49%	2.92%	3.47%
Rubber products	1.31%	1.35%	0.98%	1.05%	0.86%	1.10%
Plastic products	0.81%	1.70%	1.44%	1.80%	2.27%	3.16%
Pottery	0.48%	0.46%	0.11%	0.21%	0.11%	0.16%
Glass	0.60%	0.81%	0.52%	0.70%	0.60%	0.73%

Sources: Fuentes (1995) and authors' calculations.

In light of the evidence presented herein, the so-called deindustrialization process is doubtful, to say the least. However, there are still arguments in favor of the deindustrialization process, based on the idea that the development of the manufacturing industry is intensive in natural resources. Considering the standard Heckscher-Ohlin-Vaneck model of international trade, a country that opens to trade would tend to specialize in those goods that use more intensively the most abundant factor, which is the case of Chile with natural resources. Nevertheless, it is important to point out that the evidence concerning natural resource abundance, as a barrier for growth is not over yet. In a seminal paper

Sachs and Warner (1995) argued that natural resources abundant economies grow slower than the rest of the world. However Leite and Weidmann (1999) and Lederman and Maloney (2002) have challenged this idea using different types of arguments.

Table 4.2 shows the value-added distribution across sectors of the manufacturing industry. The table reveals how sectors more closely associated with natural resources and labor intensive activities increase their importance, in terms of total value added, in the manufacturing industry. Conversely, those sectors that are more capital intensive account for one fourth of the total value added, which is lower than their share in 1974. This evidence considers the important change in resource allocation after the trade reform. It is no surprise, however, considering that in 1972 Chile could be classified as relatively abundant in minerals, land and literate non professional workers, and relatively scarce in capital and illiterate workers (Leamer, 1984). On top of this, Chile exhibited highly distorted relative prices, as shown in the previous section.

Previous Studies in Productivity and Efficiency in the Chilean Manufacturing Industry

Several empirical studies have focused on the link between trade liberalization and productivity growth in the Chilean economy. It has been argued that higher productivity growth is expected when the economy reduces its trade barriers. Arguments have been provided to explain this positive link between trade liberalization and productivity growth. The first one relates to the expected increases in technical efficiency once the domestic industry is forced to compete in the international markets. In protected sectors, the absence of competition discourages efficient production because firms can enjoy monopolistic power. Hence, trade liberalization is assumed to contribute to an increase in efficiency.

Other authors argue that, in developing countries, trade liberalization would increase the rate of technological progress mainly for two reasons. First, more integrated developing economies have advantages to absorb technological innovations generated in the advanced nations.[7] The second reason stems from the literature on foreign exchange constraints and focuses on the evidence that developing countries import capital and intermediate goods that are not very substitutable by domestic ones due to embodied technological progress. Thus, trade liberalization would allow importing these more technologically advanced goods, increasing the technological progress embodied in imported goods. The empirical evidence in Lee (1995) supports the idea that imported capital goods

---

7 A model based on this idea of "learning by looking" is developed in Edwards (1992).

contribute positively to economic growth, particularly in developing countries.

Corbo and Sánchez (1985) carried out one of the first empirical studies in this area using a special survey on manufacturing firms after trade liberalization. They found that, due to increasing import competition, the surveyed firms closed down their inefficient plants and reduced production lines. They also strived to increase efficiency by expanding investment and reducing their labor force.

In a more systematic approach, Tybout *et al.* (1991) analyzed the hypotheses related to the link between trade liberalization and efficiency. Using cross- sectional data for the manufacturing industry, they estimated industry-specific technical efficiency indices for 1967, when the economy was highly protected, and for 1979, when trade had been liberalized. Their findings reveal little evidence about efficiency improvements between pre and post liberalization years. Of the 21 sectors analyzed, only 9 showed an increment in technical efficiency, and barely 10 had improved their scale efficiency. Although overall industry efficiency did not improve significantly between both periods, industries with larger reductions in protection were found to achieve the highest increments in efficiency.

Two similar papers have studied the same issue, but over a longer time period. Marshall (1992) estimated industry-specific efficiency indices for the 1979-1986 period. She found that efficiency and productivity tended to increase between 1974 and 1979, but to decrease between 1979 and 1986. This behavior would be strongly related to the changes in tariffs that occurred in both periods. In fact, between 1974 and 1979 the average tariff was reduced from 57 to 10%, but between 1979 and 1986 it was raised to 20%.[8]

Liu (1993) focused on plant-specific efficiency during the same period. The results in his paper, consistent with Marshall (1992), suggest a negative relationship between efficiency and protection. A distinctive feature of this article is the evidence presented on the performance of different groups of firms. Liu distinguished among surviving, entering, and exiting plants and he searched for differences in the evolution of efficiency within these three groups. His results indicate that entrants had higher efficiency than exiting plants, but lower than surviving ones. However, efficiency was almost always increasing in entrants, but slightly decreasing in surviving plants. Then, he concluded that the competitive pressure of trade liberalization forced less efficient producers to shut down, generating positive effects on aggregate efficiency.

Some other authors have approached this issue using a different methodology. Fuentes (1995), applying growth accounting methodology to aggregate data at the three-digit level of ISIC, reports changes in productivity growth after trade liberalization in manufacturing sectors.

---

[8] During this second period, the tariff reached a maximum of 35% in 1984

Consistent with the hypotheses mentioned above, his results show that trade liberalization was accompanied by huge increments in labor productivity and total factor productivity for almost every sector in the manufacturing industry, in the 1974-1979 period.

Liu and Tybout (1996) estimated separate total factor productivity and efficiency indices for manufacturing plants. Although their objective was to analyze the role of entry and exit on aggregate productivity, their estimates are highly consistent with the above-cited studies. Between 1979 and 1986, total factor productivity and efficiency were negatively correlated with protection.

More recently, Pavcnik (2002) undertook a critical review of the econometric approach used in these studies. Her contribution, using plant-level data for the same period of the other studies, is to correct the estimates of production function parameters by the presence of selection bias and simultaneity, obtaining a more consistent measurement of total factor productivity. After that, she carried out a regression analysis between firm productivity and outward orientation of the industries, separating among non-tradable, exportable, and import-competing sectors. In general, she found that plants in the exportable and import-competing sectors were more productive than plants in the non-tradable sector. The changes over time in productivity are not very consistent with expected results. Although the productivity differentials between firms in the non-tradable and import-competing sectors increased from 1981 through 1986, the same is not valid for plants in the exporting sector.

Consistently with the international experience, the evidence for Chile has not been conclusive about the relationship between trade liberalization and productivity.[9] There are several shortcomings in the cited studies. First, more often than not, the empirical analysis covers a relatively short time span. Although a great part of trade liberalization was carried out between 1974 and 1979, this was reversed after the 1982-83 crisis. We argue that a longer time period is needed, to allow for firms to adjust to the new economic conditions. Also, a long-run analysis is preferable in order to make inferences that are not distorted by the severe 1982-1983 crisis.

Secondly, to our knowledge, there have been no studies about productivity growth in the Chilean manufacturing industry that estimate jointly efficiency and technological progress indices. Past literature has either focused on total factor productivity, or estimated technical efficiency. Theoretically, total factor productivity involves these two elements. Higher production may be achieved by increasing the technical efficiency (reaching the maximum output given the inputs) or improving the production technology (producing more with the same inputs).

---

[9] For a critical survey of this literature and the international evidence, see Deraniyagala and Fine (2001).

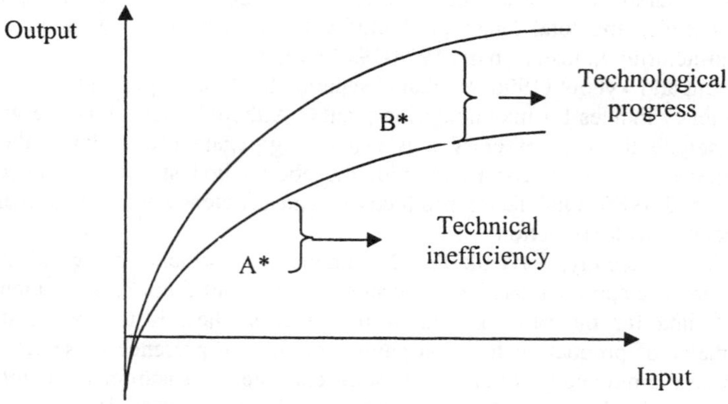

Figure 4.4 Efficiency and Technological Progress

Figure 4.4 illustrates both concepts. If attention is focused only on productivity defined as technological progress, assuming that firms are always efficient, changes in productivity will be equivalent to the vertical distance between two different production functions. On the other hand, if the focus is only on technical efficiency, the correct measure is the distance between an actual production point and the corresponding level of output in the production frontier. Changes in efficiency over time are measured by looking at how much closer the firm is to the frontier in point *A* versus *B*. In the empirical analyses carried out in Chile until now, there is no distinction between both elements.

A third shortcoming of these studies, that is also a limitation for this one, concerns the data. Neither of them has a direct measurement of outward orientation at the plant level. Actually, in Pavcnik (2002) the differences in international exposure are determined at the industry level and used in the total factor productivity regressions at the plant level. For example, if there were benefits from competing in the international markets, one would expect that in a same sector, exporter firms would be more productive than non-exporters.[10] These productivity differentials have received little attention in Chilean exporter firms.

---

10 Many recent empirical studies document the existence of productivity differentials between exporter and non-exporters. See Bernard and Jensen (1999) for evidence of this in the United States.

Productivity and Technical Efficiency: Evidence at the Plant Level

The empirical approach in this chapter contributes to the previous analysis in three ways. First, in the next section, we estimate joint indices of technological progress and technical efficiency. Hence, we can distinguish the effect of trade liberalization on both variables. Secondly, we have used a longer time period than similar studies. Thirdly, we analyze changes in productivity over time and across sectors, and their link to trade liberalization. The data are obtained on an annual basis from the nationwide survey on manufacturing establishments (ENIA) conducted by the National Institute of Statistics (INE), for the period from 1979 to 1994.

Methodological and Measurement Issues

Following recent developments in the measurement of productivity, a stochastic frontier production function was estimated to decompose total factor productivity into technical progress and changes in technical efficiency.[11] The stochastic frontiers methodology was developed by Aigner *et al.* (1977) and Meeusen and Van den Broeck (1977), and it has been used to obtain efficient production frontiers that represent the maximum level of output that can be reached with a given specific quantity of inputs. The most efficient firms will be those that are closest to this frontier.

A stochastic frontier production function is defined by:

$$Y_{it} = F(X_{it};\beta)\exp(e_{it}) \tag{4.1}$$

and

$$e_{it} = v_{it} - u_{it} \tag{4.2}$$

where Y is the output of the ith firm ($i = 1,\ldots, n$) in the tth period of time ($t = 1,\ldots, T$); F is the production frontier and X is a vector of inputs. The error term, e_{it}, is divided into two random components: v_{it} is the traditional error term, independent and identically distributed as $N(0,\sigma_v^2)$, and u_{it} represents technical inefficiency, which is assumed to be independent and identically distributed as a positive truncated normal.

We model inefficiency as a function of the degree of protection in the economy. Our hypothesis is that a reduction in trade barriers would be associated with an increment in firms' efficiency. Also, if trade liberalization favors technological absorption from more advanced economies, we expect higher technological progress through this period. The protection level (P_t) is measured at the aggregate level and is time varying, but constant across the different sectors. This is given by:

$$P_t = (1+a_t)RER_t$$

---

[11] See Kim and Han (2001) for an application of this methodology in Korea.

where *RER* is the real exchange rate and *a* is the average tariff.

We estimate two specifications of the production function: Translog and Cobb-Douglas.[12] Then, we compute a likelihood ratio test to identify the most appropriate functional form. Every specification is estimated for 21 sectors in the manufacturing industry; in general, these sectors correspond to 3-digit ISIC industry with the exception of Food (ISIC 311). Due to its great size, we have disaggregated to the 4-digit ISIC; namely sugar products (ISIC 3113), fruits and vegetables (3114), dairy products (ISIC 3115), meat products (ISIC 3116) and bakery products (ISIC 3118).

Output is measured as value added and it has been deflated using the 4-digit SIC deflators built by Yagui (1993). These deflators were extended using the same methodology. As for employment, the survey identifies blue-collar (U) and white-collar (S) workers. A simple measurement of total employment would be to add directly both types of workers. However, since both groups have different productivity, we express labor in units of efficiency using the minimum wage as a common measure of low human capital (or productivity). Thus, employment of each type is defined by:

$$U_t^* = \frac{w_t U_t}{w_t^{Min}} \text{ and } S_t^* = \frac{w_t S_t}{w_t^{Min}} \tag{4.3}$$

Where w is mean wage in every category and w^{Min} is the minimum wage. Hence, labor used in the estimates is the sum of both kinds of workers expressed in the same units.

No direct measure of capital stock for every plant is available from the survey. In addition, investment data, which potentially could be used to estimate capital input, reveals a very erratic behavior, and not all the plants report this information in the survey. Instead, electrical energy consumption is used as a proxy for capital stock. This proxy has the advantage that it measures directly the utilization of capital stock and would capture in a best way any changes in capital utilization during business cycles. Costello (1993) mentioned other advantages for using this variable. First, it is a perfectly homogeneous of invariant quality, and lacks many of the measurement problems that are common to other methods for measuring capital utilization. Secondly, because electric energy cannot be easily stored, its consumption in a productive process corresponds exactly to the quantity used in such process. However, a disadvantage of this variable, especially in long series, is that changes in the relative prices of different types of energy induce changes in relative demand by types of capital.[13] In order to incorporate these substitution

[12] Specific details about the production function are shown in the Appendix.

[13] For example, a raise in the cost of electrical energy may provide an incentive for the replacement of machines and equipment for others that use alternative energy sources, like petroleum.

possibilities, the relative price between electric energy and petroleum is incorporated into the production function regressions.[14]

Table 4.3 Changes in Efficiency by Sector

ISIC Sector	Description	Efficiency 1979	Efficiency 1994	Change %	*t*-test	*P*-Value
3113	Sugar Products	0.56	0.62	11.0	2.69	0.008
3114	Fruits and vegetables	0.61	0.62	0.3	0.08	0.933
3115	Dairy products	0.58	0.61	6.0	0.94	0.351
3116	Meat products	0.69	0.68	-1.4	-0.52	0.604
3118	Bakery products	0.54	0.49	-8.8	-0.31	0.579
313	Beverages	0.53	0.57	8.2	1.65	0.100
321	Textiles	0.65	0.67	2.7	1.84	0.066
322	Apparel	0.67	0.70	4.5	3.40	0.000
331	Wood products	0.58	0.63	8.4	4.26	0.000
332	Furniture, except metal	0.63	0.66	4.7	1.83	0.068
341	Paper and pulp	0.58	0.69	18.7	2.25	0.028
351	Chemical products	0.66	0.63	-4.4	-1.31	0.193
352	Other chemicals	0.55	0.58	5.5	1.52	0.130
356	Plastic products	0.61	0.68	11.5	1.22	0.231
371	Iron and steel	0.65	0.64	-1.4	-0.38	0.705
372	Non-ferrous metals	0.53	0.57	7.5	0.98	0.330
381	Fabric. metal products	0.65	0.69	6.2	4.57	0.000
382	Non-electrical machinery	0.61	0.66	8.7	3.16	0.002
383	Electrical machinery	0.71	0.70	-2.3	-0.95	0.341
384	Transport equipment	0.65	0.67	4.3	1.72	0.086
385	Prof.& scient. equipmt.	0.49	0.68	38.8	3.14	0.004

Estimation Results

Efficiency

If trade liberalization had some positive effect on efficiency, a higher average efficiency would be expected in 1994 as compared to 1979. Table 4.3 shows the estimated level of efficiency and the difference in the mean between both years. According to these results, almost every sector in manufacturing industry experienced an increment in technical efficiency over the period 1979-1994. The sectors professional and scientific equipment (385), and paper and pulp (341) experienced the greatest increments in efficiency, by approximately 20%. In some other sectors, such as meat products (3116), iron and steel (371), electric machinery

[14] Technically, assuming a Cobb-Douglas functional form for the capital input, it can be proven that relative price of electricity is an independent variable in production function estimates. See the Appendix for the final functional form estimated.

(383), chemical products (351) and bakery products (3118), efficiency declined, although these changes are not statistically significant.

Table 4.4 summarizes these results. Out of the 21 industrial sectors analyzed, more than 70% experienced a significant increment in efficiency. In addition, for those industries that experienced a reduction in efficiency, the differences between both years are not statistically significant. From these estimates, it can be concluded that, along the path toward a more open economy, almost every manufacturing sector has gained in efficiency, which is consistent with the benefits associated with trade liberalization.

Table 4.4 Statistical Test Summary

H_0: Means Equality	Higher Efficiency		Lower Efficiency	
	Sectors	%	Sectors	%
Significant*	11	52.4	0	0.0
Non-significant	5	23.8	5	23.8
Total	16	76.2	5	23.8

* At 10% level of significance.

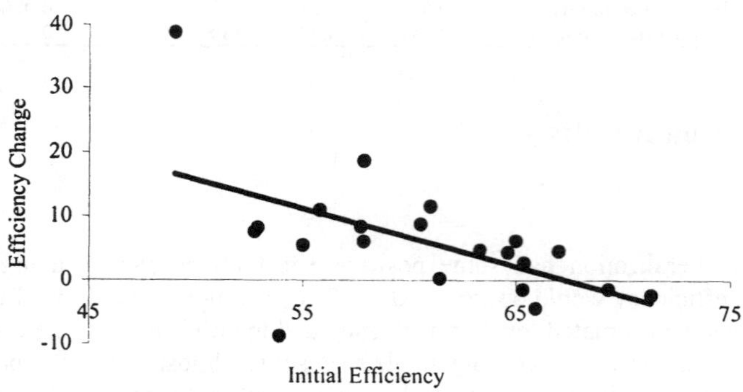

Figure 4.5 Convergence in Efficiency

Convergence in Efficiency

Given the results obtained for average efficiency by sectors, we now look at the question about the existence of convergence in efficiency. Industries closest to efficiency frontier will expectedly experience lower increments in efficiency than those that were less efficient at the beginning of the period. This is similar to the concept of β-convergence in cross-country studies about economic growth. Thus, increments in efficiency should be negatively correlated to initial efficiency. The results presented here support this idea. In figure 4.5, we plot changes in efficiency versus initial efficiency level for every industry in our sample, and a regression line between both variables. The results of this exercise indicate that changes in efficiency are negatively correlated with the initial level of efficiency, suggesting that convergence in efficiency exists across industrial sectors.

Another concern would be to verify whether there is evidence of dispersion in efficiency diminishing over time across manufacturing sectors (σ-convergence). Table 4.5 shows the results of a statistical test for changes in efficiency dispersion across industrial sectors. The null hypothesis is that the variance in 1979 is the same as in 1994 or, in other words, that the variance ratio is equal to one. It can be appreciated that in most of the manufacturing sector (19 over 21), the efficiency variance in 1994 is smaller than in 1979, although in only 8 of these sectors, the reduction in variance is statistically significant. An increment in variance is observed in only two sectors, but this is not significant. These results are summarized in table 4.6.

Table 4.5 Changes in Efficiency Variance by Sector

ISIC Sector	Description	Variance 1979 (1)	Variance 1994 (2)	Variance Ratio (2/1)	*p*-Value
3113	Sugar products	0.025	0.020	0.788	0.138
3114	Fruits and vegetables	0.021	0.015	0.714	0.045
3115	Dairy products	0.039	0.031	0.791	0.199
3116	Meat products	0.019	0.013	0.683	0.036
3118	Bakery products	0.055	0.097	1.755	0.758
313	Beverages	0.044	0.039	0.888	0.270
321	Textiles	0.020	0.019	0.941	0.271
322	Apparel	0.021	0.014	0.666	0.000
331	Wood products	0.034	0.019	0.552	0.000
332	Furniture, except metal	0.025	0.019	0.766	0.004
341	Paper and pulp	0.019	0.016	0.856	0.333
351	Chemical products	0.017	0.016	0.922	0.371
352	Other chemicals	0.034	0.029	0.874	0.183
356	Plastic products	0.029	0.028	0.944	0.411
371	Iron and steel	0.015	0.012	0.790	0.229
372	Non-ferrous metals	0.022	0.032	1.431	0.842
381	Fabricated metal products	0.025	0.013	0.527	0.000
382	No-electrical machinery	0.032	0.019	0.597	0.000
383	Electrical machinery	0.011	0.010	0.873	0.287
384	Transport equipment	0.020	0.014	0.701	0.022
385	Prof. And scientific equipment	0.039	0.027	0.695	0.231

Table 4.6 Statistical Test Summary

H_0: Variances ratio = 1	Higher Variance		Lower Variance	
	Sectors	%	Sectors	%
Significant*	0	0.0	8	38.1
Non-significant	2	9.5	11	52.4
Total	2	9.5	19	90.5

* At 10% level of significance.

Technological Progress

The evidence in this chapter suggests that during the period when the Chilean economy had increased its openness to international trade, the manufacturing industry also experienced increments in technical efficiency. Here, we discuss our results about the technological progress in this period. In Table 4.7, annual rates of technological progress for each sector are shown.

Table 4.7 Technological Progress by Sector

ISIC Sector	Description	Annual Growth Rate (%)	*t*-test
3113	Sugar products	-1.9	-0.48
3114	Fruits and vegetables	5.3	1.29
3115	Dairy products	5.7	4.04*
3116	Meat products	-3.6	-2.54*
3118	Bakery products	7.5	4.32*
313	Beverages	-2.2	-0.63
321	Textiles	1.4	1.31
322	Apparel	3.9	16.99*
331	Wood products	2.0	0.18
332	Furniture, except metal	0.1	0.13
341	Paper and pulp	-1.2	-1.02
351	Chemical products	4.9	0.78
352	Other chemicals	0.6	1.51
356	Plastic products	2.2	0.33
371	Iron and steel	-0.7	-0.55
372	Non-ferrous metals	5.8	4.72*
381	Fabricated metal products	1.1	4.79*
382	Non-electrical machinery	-0.5	-0.52
383	Electrical machinery	5.5	4.19*
384	Transport equipment	3.6	3.39*
385	Prof. and scientific equipment	-1.3	-1.58

* Significant at 5% level.

The evidence is less conclusive compared to our findings for technical efficiency. The results show that not all the sectors experienced technological progress during the period analyzed. Technological progress growth is positive and statistically significant for only seven sectors in the manufacturing industry.

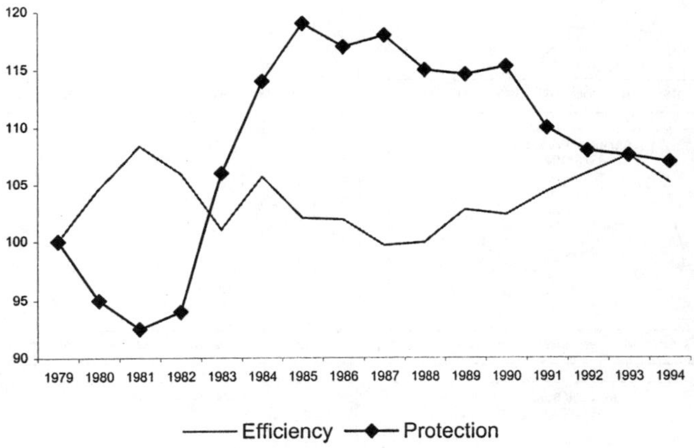

Figure 4.6 Efficiency and Protection

Efficiency and Trade Liberalization

One important question concerns the causality relationship between efficiency and trade liberalization. Although the evidence presented above supports the idea that openness has been associated with greater efficiency, causality has not been discussed. First, consider the results in figure 4.6 that plots average efficiency for the manufacturing industry and the measurement of protection used. A kind of inverse relation can be observed between these two variables. When protection was increased in the first part of the period, efficiency tended to decrease. During the second part of the period, reduction in protection was followed by an increment in efficiency.

Similar evidence regarding the evolution of technical efficiency by sectors is shown in figure 4.7. In general, in almost all the sectors efficiency increased at the beginning of the period, then declined until the mid 1980's. From there, efficiency grew slightly up to the end of the period.

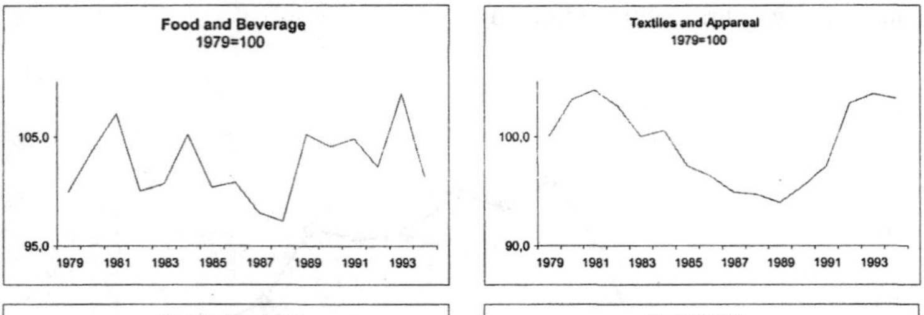

Figure 4.7 Evolution of Technical Efficiency Across Sectors

A more formal analysis is presented in table 4.8. As explained above, we include protection as an explicative variable in the estimation of inefficiency from the production frontier. The expected value of the parameter associated to protection is positive, under the hypothesis that increases (reductions) in protection generate greater (smaller) inefficiency. Our results show a positive and significant parameter in nine sectors. We can conclude that, although there is not evidence for all the sectors, trade liberalization has had a positive impact on efficiency for an important number of sectors in the Chilean manufacturing industry.

Table 4.8 Efficiency and Protection by Sector

ISIC Sector	Description	Parameter	*t*-test
3113	Sugar Products	-22.6	-7.08*
3114	Fruits and vegetables	20.1	2.35*
3115	Dairy products	-10.4	-4.93*
3116	Meat products	21.3	2.84*
3118	Bakery products	-0.5	-1.15
313	Beverages	-23.3	-1.45
321	Textiles	4.5	6.49*
322	Apparel	16.2	3.34*
331	Wood products	-18.4	-4.87*
332	Furniture, except metal	-11.6	-3.36*
341	Paper and pulp	12.1	6.48*
351	Chemical products	24.1	3.17*
352	Other chemicals	-9.9	-5.37*
356	Plastic products	11.9	1.63
371	Iron and steel	34.1	3.79*
372	Non-ferrous metals	5.1	1.25
381	Fabricated metal products	2.5	9.31*
382	Non-electrical machinery	-12.8	-3.15*
383	Electrical machinery	13.4	5.45*
384	Transport equipment	-11.0	-4.1*
385	Prof. and scientific equipment	-19.1	-1.63

* Significant at 5%

Concluding Remarks

This chapter has shown how the trade reforms in the 1970s have affected the manufacturing industry. We found no evidence of de-industrialization in Chile after the reforms, as defined by the share of the manufacturing industry in GDP and the export of manufactured products. In fact, the share of manufacturing sector of GDP increased during the 1990s, where the average was higher than the 1960s. Further, manufacturing exports surpassed mining exports in 1999. However, a case can be made that the manufacturing sector has developed based on natural resources, and therefore Chile is still exporting primary products. This is consistent with having comparative advantage in natural resources intensive industries as predicted by the standard Heckscher-Ohlin-Vaneck model. Nevertheless, it is important to point out that the controversy concerning natural resource abundance, as a barrier for growth, is not over yet.

Besides the level of the manufacturing sector production, it is important to notice the significant shifts that have occurred in the structure and level of productivity in the manufacturing industry after the trade liberalization. Specifically, our findings reveal that increases in productivity are closely associated with changes in technical efficiency for the manufacturing industry as a whole and for most manufacturing sectors. We cannot find strong evidence of technological changes in the manufacturing industry, but, given that Chile has a natural advantage in mining products, the manufacturing sector has to be highly competitive to become as important as mining in terms of exports.

References

Aedo, C. and L. Lagos (1984) "Protección Efectiva en el Sector Manufacturero," *Working Paper*, 94, Universidad Católica de Chile.

Aigner,D.J., Lovell, C.A.K. and P. Schmidt (1977) "Formulation and Estimation of Stochastic Frontier Production Function Models", *Journal of Econometrics,* 6, 21-37.

Bernard, A and J. B. Jensen (1999) "Exceptional Exporter Performance: Cause, Effect, or both?" *Journal of International Economics*, 47, 1-25.

Bosworth, B., R. Dornbusch and R. Labán (1994) *The Chilean Economy: Policy Lessons and Challenges*. Washington D.C, The Brookings Institution.

Corbo, V. (1985) "Chile Economic Policy and International Economic Relations Since 1970." In G.M. Walton (ed.) *The National Economic Policies of Chile*, Greenwich, CT, JAI Press, pp. 107-144.

Corbo, V. and J.M. Sanchez (1985) "Adjustment by Industrial Firms in Chile during 1974-1982." In Scrambling for Survival – How Firms Adjusted to the Recent Reforms in Argentina, Chile and Uruguay, *World Bank Staff Working Papers*, No 764.

Costello, D. (1993): "A Cross Country, Cross-Industry Comparison of Productivity Growth," *Journal of Political Economy,* 101, 207-222.

Deraniyagala, S. and B. Fine (2001) "New Trade Theory versus Old Trade Policy: A Continuing Enigma," *Cambridge Journal of Economics*, 25, 809-25.

Edwards, S. (1994) "Trade and Industrial Policy Reform in Latin America," *NBER Working Paper*, No 4772.

Edwards, S. (1992) "Trade Orientation, Distortions and Growth in Developing Countries," *Journal of Development Economics*, 39, 31-57.

Edwards, S. (1989) *Real Exchange Rates, Devaluation, and Adjustment: Exchange Rate Policy in Developing Countries*. Cambridge, MA, MIT Press.

Edwards, A. and S. Edwards (1987) *Monetarism and Liberalization: The Chilean Experiment*. Chicago, University of Chicago Press.

Ffrench-Davis, R. and R Saez (1995) "Comercio y Desarrollo Industrial en Chile," *Colección de Estudios de Cieplan,* 41, 67-96.

Fuentes, R. (1995): "Openness and Economic Efficiency: Evidence from de Chilean Manufacturing Industry," *Estudios de Economía*, 22, 357-387.

Kim, S. and G. Han (2001) "A Decomposition of Total Factor Productivity Growth in Korean Manufacturing Industries: A Stochastic Frontier Approach," *Journal of Productivity Analysis*, 16, 269-81.

Le Fort, G. (1988) "The Relative Price of Nontraded Goods, Absorption, and Exchange Rate Policy in Chile," FMI *Staff Papers*, 35, 336-370.

Leamer, E.E. (1984) *Source of International Comparative Advantage: Theory and Evidence*. Cambridge, MA, MIT Press.

Lederman, D. and W. Maloney (2002) "Open Questions About the Link Between Natural Resources and Economic Growth: Sachs and Warner Revisited," *Working Papers* No 141, Central Bank of Chile

Lee, J-W. (1995) "Capital Goods Imports and Long-Run Growth," *Journal of Development Economics*, 48, 91-110.

Leite, C. and J. Weidmann (1999) "Does Mother Nature Corrupt? Natural Resources, Corruption and Economic Growth," *IMF Working Paper* 99/85, International Monetary Fund.

Liu, L. (1993) "Entry-Exit, Learning, and Productivity Exchange: Evidence from Chile," *Journal of Development Economics*, 42, 217-42.

Marshall, I. (1992): "Liberalización Comercial en Chile y su Impacto sobre la Eficiencia Técnica Industrial: 1974-1986," *Colección de Estudios CIEPLAN*, No 135, 201-245.

Meeusen W. and J. van den Broeck (1977) "Efficiency Estimation from Cobb-Douglas Production Functions with Composed Error," *International Economic Review*, 18, 435-444.

Pack, H. (1988) "Industralization and Trade," In H. Chenery and T.N. Srinivasan (eds.) *Handbook of Development Economics,* Vol. I, Amsterdam, North Holland, pp. 333-380.

Pavcnik, N. (2002) "Trade Liberalization, Exit, and Productivity Improvement: Evidence from Chilean Plants," *Review of Economic Studies*, 69, 245-276.

Rodrik, D. (1995): "Trade and Industrial Policy Reform," In J. Behrman and T.N. Srinivasan (eds.) *Handbook of Development Economics,* Vol. III, Amsterdam, North Holland, pp. 2925-2982.

Tybout. J., De Melo, J. y V. Corbo (1991): "The Effects of Trade Reforms on Scale and Technical Efficiency: New Evidence from Chile," *Journal of International Economics*, 31, 231-250.

Yagui, E. (1993): "Un Deflactor para la Encuesta Nacional Industrial Anual (Base 1989=100)," *Revista de Estadística y Economía*, 6, 129-63.

Appendix: Functional Form of the Production Function

Two alternative functional forms of the production function were estimated: (A1) Translog, and (A2) Cobb-Douglas. These can be expressed respectively as:

$$\log Y_{it} = \beta_0 + \beta_1 t + \beta_2 t^2 + \beta_3 \log L_{it} + \beta_4 t \log l_{it} + \beta_5 \log K_{it} + \beta_6 t \log K_{it} + \beta_7 (\log L_{it})^2 + \beta_8 (\log K_{it})^2 + \beta_9 \log L_{it} \log K_{it} + \varepsilon_{it} \quad \text{(A1)}$$

$$\log Y_{it} = \beta_0 + \beta_1 t + \beta_2 LogL_{it} + \beta_3 LogK_{it} + \varepsilon_{it} \quad \text{(A2)}$$

where i represents the plant, t the time, Y the value added, L the corrected employment, K the capital services, and ε is the previously defined error term.

We suppose that services of capital (K) can be approximated by a combination of electric energy consumption (E) and petroleum (M). Using a Cobb-Douglas function, we can write an expression for capital services as:

$$K = E^{\lambda} M^{1-\lambda} \quad \text{(A3)}$$

The first order condition establishes that the firm will combine energy and petroleum according to the ratio of marginal productivity and relative prices of these types of energy.

$$\frac{\lambda M}{(1-\lambda)E} = \frac{P_E}{P_M} \quad \text{(A4)}$$

Substituting (A4) in (A3) and taking logs, K can be expressed as a function of electric energy consumption (E) and the price ratio of energy and petroleum $p = P_E / P_M$:

$$\log K = (1-\lambda)\log\left[(1-\lambda)/\lambda\right] + \log E + (1-\lambda)\log p \quad \text{(A5)}$$

Substituting (A5) in (A1) and (A2), both production functions are given by *Translog*:

$$\log Y_{it} = \alpha_0 + \alpha_1 t + \alpha_2 t^2 + \alpha_3 \log L_{it} + \alpha_4 t \log L_{it} + \alpha_5 \log E_{it} + \alpha_6 t \log E_{it} + \alpha_7 \log p_t + \alpha_8 t \log p_t + \alpha_9 (\log L_{it})^2 + \alpha_{10} (\log E_{it})^2 + \alpha_{11} (\log p_t)^2 + \alpha_{12} \log L_{it} \log E_{it} + \alpha_{13} \log L_{it} \log p_t + \alpha_{14} \log E_{it} \log p_t + \varepsilon_{it} \quad \text{(A6)}$$

Cobb-Douglas:

$$\log Y_{it} = \alpha_0 + \alpha_1 t + \alpha_2 LogL_{it} + \alpha_3 LogE_{it} + \alpha_4 Logp_t + \alpha_5 \log E_{it} \log p_t + \varepsilon_{it} \quad \text{(A7)}$$

5 Chile's Export Structure, 1970-1996

Nola Reinhardt

> I'm in agreement with free trade. But it's like a wave in the sea. If you don't know how to ride it, it will swallow you. If you know how, you can ride it, and enjoy it.[1]

Introduction

Chile has been a leader in trade liberalization in the Latin American region. Its strong export growth record since the mid-1980s has led observers to call it Latin America's economic "tiger." The implication is that it has been following in the footsteps of the East and Southeast Asian tigers in successfully implementing an export-led growth strategy.

Chile's economic growth, especially in the decade from 1985-1995, was extremely strong by Latin American standards, as table 5.1 demonstrates. While GNP per capita grew at an anemic average annual rate of only 0.3% in the Latin America and Caribbean (LAC) region, and only 0.8% globally, it grew at a remarkable 6.1% rate in Chile. This was close to the average for the fast-growing East Asia and Pacific (EAP) region, and it placed Chile in the top nine fastest-growing countries in the world during this decade.[2] Chile's economic boom was closely tied to an export boom, with exports increasing from US $4.7 billion average in 1986-1987 to US $16 billion average in 1996-1997 (IMF, 2000), before declining due to the Asian financial crisis. As table 5.1 shows, Chilean export growth between 1985 and 1996 approached that of the EAP region and was strong by global standards.

---

[1] Efrain Perez, President, Costa Rican Association of Export Producers (Breslin, 1996, p. 23).

[2] Out of 133 reported in World Bank, 1997, Table 1.

Nevertheless, a close examination of the Chilean experience reveals that it differs in a number of fundamental ways from that of the Asian economies. It is by now fairly well-known that the Chilean approach has been closer to the neoliberal model of the laissez-faire open economy than was the case in East Asia.[3] While pursuing the growth of exports, the Asian governments continued to protect industries established under the previous import-substitution regimes. By contrast, the rapid opening of the Chilean economy (or "shock treatment") in the 1970s under the military government of General Pinochet effectively destroyed much of Chile's existing industry.[4] In the Asian cases, the basis for new export success was created through a wide array of government interventions in favor of new export activities. The Chilean government, on the other hand, adhered fairly strictly to the neoliberal doctrine of non-intervention in the 1970s, becoming directly supportive of export activities only after the economic crisis of the early 1980s.

Table 5.1 Chile's Boom Period, 1985-1996

Country	GNP per Capita, 1995 ($)	Average annual growth, GNP/Capita, 1985-95 (%)	Exports 1996 (million $)	Average Annual Export Growth, 1985-96 (%)
Chile	4,160	6.1	18,709	15.8
LAC	3,320	0.3	297,959[a]	11.2[a]
EAP	800	7.2	718,498[b]	17.1[b]
World	4,880	0.8	6,689,040	12.3

a Total for Argentina, Bolivia, Brazil, Chile, Colombia, Costa Rica, Dominican Republic, Ecuador, El Salvador, Guatemala, Haiti, Honduras, Jamaica, Mexico, Nicaragua, Panama, Paraguay, Peru, Trinidad and Tobago, Uruguay, Venezuela. Growth rate excluding Mexico was only 9%.

b Total for China, Indonesia, Malaysia, Papua New Guinea, Philippines, Republic of Korea, Singapore, Thailand.

Sources: Calculated from World Bank, *World Development Report*, (1987, 1997, 1998/99).

---

3 A review of the policies of the East Asian and Southeast Asian countries is beyond the scope of this paper, but these policies have been widely discussed in the literature (see, for example, Chowdhury and Islam, 1993; Alam, 1989; Hughes, 1988; Yang, 1994; White, 1988; Biggs and Levy, 1991; Wade, 1990; Ariff and Hill, 1985; Amsden, 1989).

4 According to Gwynne (1986, p.36), manufacturing output fell at an average annual rate of 1.4% between 1973 and 1978. Gatica Barros (1989, Ch. 2) documents the process of 'deindustrialization' that followed, with industrial bankruptcies far exceeding the historical norm in Chile after 1978. The most severely affected sectors were clothing, machinery, transport equipment, and scientific equipment.

It is less well known that the outcomes in Chile have also differed in key respects from those in East Asia. As this chapter shows, while Chile's export and output growth rates have led the Latin American region, the character of that growth has differed significantly from the nature of the export-led growth experience of Asia. The strong export performance of the Asian countries – both the East Asian "NICs" and, more recently, the "second-tier" Southeast Asian countries – has been based on growth in manufactured exports, while Chile's recent export growth has been based heavily on unprocessed and simply processed natural resources. We demonstrate the extent of this difference here, using a classification system that distinguishes between these resource-based goods and goods with a higher degree of processing. This classification system is applied to export data from the UN Commodity Trade Statistics (COMTRADE) Database for the period from 1970 to 1996.

Observers regularly point to the increasing weight of manufactures – and within manufactures, of those with greater skill and technology content – in the export profiles of the East Asian countries as a key factor in their economic success. This movement up the "export ladder" (Pearson, 1994) reflected changes in their factor endowments, as capital, skills and technological capabilities expanded. By contrast, the much lower share of manufactured exports in the Chilean case may signify potential problems in the continued economic growth of this Latin American "tiger." As described below, the export strategy of many Chilean firms has been based primarily on the cost advantages associated with existing factor endowments of raw materials and unskilled labor. While trade opening has indeed led, after a costly period of adjustment, to static gains from resource reallocation, the long-run dynamic implications of this structural adjustment are open to question. In particular, after twenty-five years of neoliberal policies in Chile there is still little evidence of the development of international competitiveness based on enhanced skill and technological capabilities.

This growth pattern has raised important questions about the sustainability of Chile's export-led growth. Indeed, even before the 1998 downturn, observers had voiced concern about Chile's growth "peaking." Rising currency values and real wage increases in excess of productivity gains threatened Chile's competitive position in its major exports, without the economy having established the basis for continued export growth in new areas of competitive advantage. This weakness is suggested here through a review of the competitiveness strategies of leading export firms.

The next section examines the development of Chile's export structure from the early 1970s through the rapid growth period of 1986-1996. The following section compares this to the export development of the Asian countries, as well as to other Latin American countries, and considers the implications of these different trajectories. The next section examines the competitive strategies of firms in Chile's principal export sectors, and the final section demonstrates some of the weaknesses of these strategies.

The Development of Chile's Export Profile under the Reforms

The resource-rich Chilean economy has long depended on primary exports. In 1970, ores and minerals accounted for 85% of the country's exports. As we will show, although the dominance of mining has lessened since then, natural-resource based products overall still account for the lion's share of the country's exports. In order to see this more clearly, we classify Chile's exports into five categories: mineral (MIN), primary (PRIM), semi-manufactures (SEMI), manufactures (MFR), and other (OTHER).[5] The category of semi-manufactures includes simply processed natural-resource based products such as fishmeal, prepared fish, chipwood, wood pulp, preserved fruits and vegetables, wine, vegetable oils, etc., that are often included under the category of primary products in export classification schemes, but under manufactures in industrial classification schemes based on ISIC codes. Separating out these products from the primary and manufactured categories here gives us a more accurate picture of the development of Chile's comparative advantage in international trade.

The depth and rapidity of the reform effort in Chile can be seen from the reform indexes developed by Morley *et al.* (1999). Their overall reform index is a composite of five areas of reform: trade, financial, capital account, privatization, and tax. On a scale of 0 (lowest effort) to 1, Chile's overall index rose from 0.316 in 1973 to 0.576 in 1975, and continued to rise to 0.788 in 1981. By way of comparison, the average overall index for seventeen Latin American countries rose from 0.464 in 1973 to only 0.560 in 1981. Trade liberalization was pursued most aggressively in Chile; this index rose from 0.280 in 1973 to 0.685 in 1975, and continued to rise to 0.974 by 1979.

In the first decade after the implementation of economic reforms in Chile, the country's overall economic performance was erratic. The reforms themselves were implemented in a setting of severe economic crisis. The immediate effect of the policies was several years of recession, with GDP per capita falling by 14.3% in 1975 alone. Although economic growth resumed thereafter and continued for the rest of the decade, GDP growth was an anemic average annual rate of 1.4% for the 1974-81 period

---

[5] The classification scheme used here draws on CEPAL, 1992. A detailed description of this classification system and its derivation is provided in Reinhardt, 1997.

(Ffrench-Davis, 2002). Nevertheless, Chile's total exports grew at a respectable annual average rate of 14% over the decade (table 5.2).[6] All categories of exports except minerals experienced rapid growth.

Table 5.2 Export Growth Rates,* 1970-1996

PERIOD	TOTAL EXPORTS	PRIM	MIN	SEMI	MFR	OTHER
1970-80	14.0	18.9	9.6	28.4	24.7	34.3
1980-86	-2.4	3.5	-6.5	-.5	-2.7	6.7
1986-96	14.3	16.1	11.1	14.3	21.7	21.2

*Average annual percent change.
Source: Calculated from UN Commodity Trade Statistics Database (COMTRADE).

Table 5.3 provides a more detailed breakdown of Chile's export performance, showing Chile's leading exports (export share over 1.5%) in each of four years: 1970, 1980, 1993, and 1996. Ores and minerals were the only leading exports in 1970, accounting for 85% of total exports, but they fell to 64% of 1980 exports. Two primary products, fresh fruit and rough wood, emerged as leading exports in this decade. The strongest growth in the 1970s was registered by semi-manufactures, several of which also emerged as leading exports: fishmeal, wood pulp, and shaped wood.

This rapid growth of Chilean exports was not simply the result of trade liberalization, rather, it was the fruition of decades of development of the Chilean fishing, fruit, and forestry sectors. The roots of this development lay in the pre-Pinochet era, in a series of government initiatives that nurtured the development of producers in these sectors (CEPAL, 1986; Gomez and Echenique, 1988; Jarvis, 1991; Ffrench-Davis and Munoz, 1992; CEPAL, 1995; Pietrobelli, 1995; Casaburi, 1999). Several decades of inward-oriented industrialization in Chile had also contributed to the development of a small core of dynamic local entrepreneurs in the agro/fisheries/forestry sectors.[7]

In the 1970s, these sectors were initially protected from the shock treatment applied to the manufacturing sector, with agricultural price regulation continuing and special subsidies remaining in effect for the forestry sector (Palma Arancibia, 1995; Gwynne, 1993; Pietrobelli, 1995). Currency devaluation created incentives for expansion of primary and

---

[6] According to Ffrench-Davis (2002, p. 165), this was due in large part to excess export capacity and to cost reductions through substitution of cheaper imported inputs.

[7] See chapter 8 in this volume for the development of entrepreneurs in agriculture

semiprocessed exports, which grew both absolutely and as a share of the total. Over the course of the decade, however, the laissez-faire approach was increasingly applied to the primary sector: state support for technology development was virtually eliminated, as were inputs subsidies such as subsidized credit and exemptions and tax discounts on imported inputs (Palma Aracibia, 1995). At the same time, the sharp appreciation of the currency in the late 1970s hurt many exporters.

Table 5.3 Chile's Leading Exports,* 1970-1996

Export/SITC (Rev. 1)	Category	1996 Value (US$ '000)	Percent of Exports				Average Annual Growth 1986-96
			1970	1980	1993	1996	
MINING							
Copper/682	MIN	4,401,010	76.9*	43.8*	29.2*	29.4*	11.2
Copper ore/2831	PRIM	1,881,500	2.3*	5.1*	9.2*	12.6*	21.8
Gold, non-monetary/971	OTHER	427,612	N.A.	N.A.	2.6*	2.8*	N.A.
Inorg chems/ oxides/513	SEMI	131,629	0.8	2.5*	0.6	0.9	12.3
Iron ore/281	PRIM	147,561	5.8*	3.5*	1.2	1.0	5.2
Silver/plat/681	MIN	153,046	0.0	2.6*	0.9	1.0	8.4
Other metals (molyb)/689	MIN	3,460	0.2	5.7*	0.0	0.0	4.6
FORESTRY							
Sulphate wood pulp/2517	SEMI	764,354	1.3	4.3*	5.2*	5.1*	14.7
Shaped wood/ 243	SEMI	332,530	0.1	3.0*	2.1*	2.2*	16.1
Wood mfrs/63	SEMI	280,526	0.0	0.1	2.2*	1.9*	33.4
Paper/64	SEMI	238,238	1.2	1.2	1.6*	1.6*	14.5
Rough wood/242	PRIM	116,119	0.0	1.6*	1.7*	0.8	9.4
FISHING							
Fresh/froz fish/ shellfish/031	PRIM	860,485	0.5	1.4	6.1*	5.7*	24.5
Fishmeal/0814	SEMI	612,650	1.3	5.0*	4.0*	4.1*	6.7
Prep'd fish/032	SEMI	182,408	0.2	0.5	1.9*	1.2	9.3
FRUIT							
Fresh fruit/051	PRIM	1,007,729	1.0	3.1*	7.5*	6.7*	7.6
Dried/preserved fruit /052,053	SEMI	356,651	0.2	0.5	2.2*	2.4*	21.5
Wine/1121	SEMI	294,372	0.1	0.5	1.·	2.0*	36.3
Leading exports	----	11,457,657	85.0	80.2	75.5	76.5	

*Leading exports: export share greater than 1.5%.

Sources: Calculated from UN COMTRADE Database; UNECLAC *Statistical Yearbook*, 1994; UN *Yearbook of International Trade Statistics*, 1975, 1985, 1995.

In 1981 and 1982, as the debt crisis spread throughout Latin America, Chile's success evaporated. GDP per capita fell by 14.5% in 1982, the largest annual decline since the Great Depression and the largest economic collapse in all of Latin America. The data in table 5.2 show the collapse of trade in the first half of the 1980s; growth of all exports except primary products was interrupted in this period. The crisis of the early 1980s led to important modifications in economic policy, including a rise in tariff rates and re-regulation of the banking sector. The overall reform index fell to a low of 0.646 in 1984, and the trade index to a low of 0.835 in 1985. At the same time, exporters benefited from the abandonment of the fixed exchange rate in favor of automatic currency devaluations, which resulted in a 32% decrease in the real exchange rate between 1984 and 1986 (IMF, 1999).

After 1984, the Pinochet government further deviated from its laissez-faire approach of the latter 1970s by implementing export-promotion policies that provided a much-needed stimulus to the primary-export sectors, measures that mainly benefited domestic entrepreneurs. These measures included export tax reductions, drawbacks for non-traditional exports, and special credit programs (UNECLAC, 1992; Barham *et al.*, 1992; Taylor, 1993; Gwyne, 1993; Pietrobelli, 1995). The agricultural sector was especially targeted in the 1984-86 Three Year Plan, which emphasized credit and technical assistance for small producers (Palma Arancibia, 1995). Taylor (1993) goes so far as to argue that "Chile's 'miracle' was very much a state-bourgeoisie joint affair." An important role was also played by Fundacion Chile (the Chile Foundation), a non-profit agency created with mixed public-private funding, in supporting local entrepreneurial development, particularly in the fruit, vegetable, and fish industries (Huss, 1991).

With these measures, the overall export growth rate in the 1986-96 period returned to the 1970s level. There was some difference in the performance of the subcategories in this period, with semi-manufactures only recovering to half of their previous growth rate. Despite the rapid overall growth of manufactures, none had yet emerged as a leading export. The most important export sector in 1996 continued to be copper mining (copper ore, copper, copper oxides). The other leading product groups were the natural-resource based sectors of forestry (logs, sawnwood, chipwood and other wood manufactures, pulp, paper), fishing (fresh fish, chilled/frozen fish, prepared fish, fishmeal), and fruit cultivation (apples, grapes, raisins, wine). The growth rate of these exports varied widely in the 1986-96 period, as table 5.3 shows, with a number of products posting gains considerably above the average for all exports.

Another indicator of the evolution of Chile's export profile is the export specialization ratio, or ESR, also referred to as the revealed comparative advantage index. This measure compares the share of a product in a country's exports to the share of that product in world trade. A ratio greater than 1.00 indicates that the country has above-average specialization in that product. The same approach can be used to examine a country's specialization in broad groups of products, such as the five categories defined here, by comparing the share of that export group in the country's exports to the share of that export group in world trade. This approach was used to calculate ESRs for the five export categories, using OECD import shares as the measure of world trade.

Table 5.4 Chile's Export Specialization Ratios, 1970-1993

Year	PRIM	MIN	SEMI	MFR	OTHER
1970	0.61	16.84	0.36	0.04	0.06
1971	0.92	19.32	0.57	0.04	0.00
1980	0.71	16.38	1.14	0.11	0.38
1981	0.90	18.72	1.17	0.11	0.16
1986	1.72	18.42	1.43	0.07	0.55
1987	2.29	15.54	1.48	0.08	0.50
1992	2.45	16.21	1.61	0.12	0.67
1993	2.55	16.21	1.68	0.15	0.67

Source: Calculated from United Nations COMTRADE database.

The results in table 5.4 show clearly that Chile has international specialization in minerals, primary products, and semi-manufactures. Although the ESR for mineral exports has declined slightly from the early 1980s, it remains very high. The specialization ratios for primary products and semi-manufactures have steadily increased, with semi-manufactures emerging as specialization products by the early 1980s, and primary products even more strongly by the mid-1980s. The ESR for manufactures has been erratic, rising in the 1970s, falling in the early 1980s, and then rising again since the mid-1980s, but remains very low. The ESR for the "other" category has risen steadily, primarily due to increased non-monetary gold exports, but remains below 1.00.

Chile's Export Profile in Comparative Perspective

Chile's pattern of export development rooted in natural-resource-intensive exports is quite unlike that of the Asian countries that Chile has supposedly emulated. This can be seen in figure 5.1, which compares the development of Chile's export profile since 1970-71 to that of the East

Asian NICs,[8] and to that of the "second-tier" East Asian countries, the ASEAN-4. The exports of each country were classified into the five categories listed above. We can see in figure 5.1 that the natural resource categories played a very small role in the export-led growth of the resource-poor East Asian NICs. In 1970-71, within a decade of the initiation of their export-promotion policies, mineral and primary exports accounted for only 16.9% of their export total, and semi-manufactures, or simply processed natural-resource-based goods, for another 19.1%. By 1992-93, manufactures accounted for most - 85.1% - of the export total.

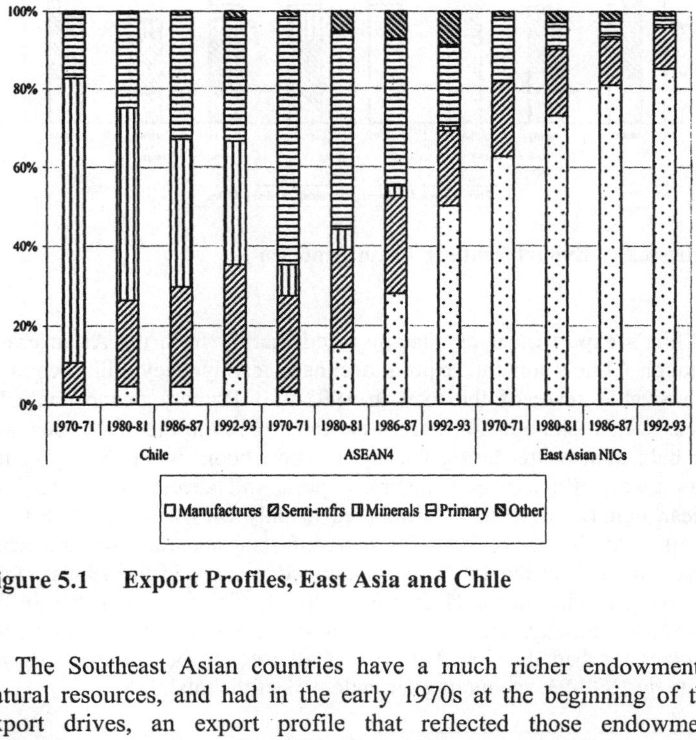

Figure 5.1 Export Profiles, East Asia and Chile

The Southeast Asian countries have a much richer endowment of natural resources, and had in the early 1970s at the beginning of their export drives, an export profile that reflected those endowments. Manufactures were a scant 3.2% of their exports in 1972-73. Chile's export profile in 1970-71 was similar to that of the ASEAN-4, in the sense that primary and mineral exports dominated the export picture. Over the next twenty years, the weight of natural-resource based sectors decreased

---

8 The East Asian NICs included in figure 5.1 are South Korea, Hong Kong, and Singapore. The export profile of Taiwan has developed along similar lines, but statistics for Taiwan are not included in the COMTRADE database.

sharply in the ASEAN countries. By 1992-93, manufactured exports dominated their export profiles, accounting overall for 50.3% of total exports. The export profile of these countries in 1992-1993 was moving in the direction of the East Asian NICs in 1970-71.[9]

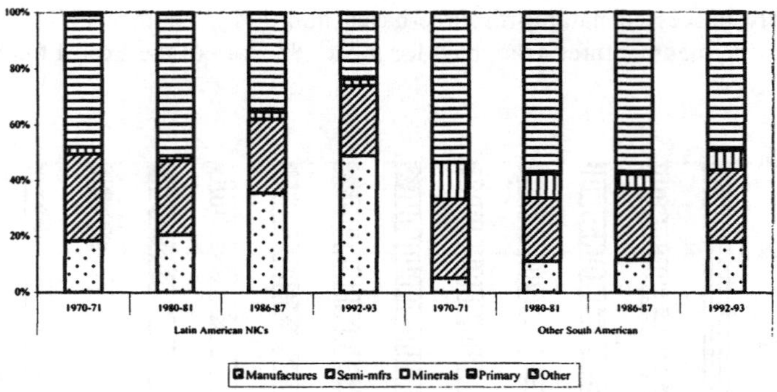

Figure 5.2 Export Profiles, Latin America

Chile's export trajectory has diverged sharply from the Asian cases. Although Chile's mineral exports declined steadily, they still accounted for a sizable share of the total in 1992-93. Primary exports actually increased their share in Chile from the early 1970s to the mid 1980s, and then held their share during the latest export boom while falling in the Asian cases. Primary and mineral exports still accounted for 63% of Chilean exports in 1992-93, compared to only 21.9% of the ASEAN-4 exports. At the same time, the share of semi-manufactures increased sharply in Chile in the 1970s and continued to grow in the 1980s, while decreasing steadily in the NICs and declining after the mid-1980s in the ASEAN-4. Finally, after two decades of economic opening in Chile, manufactures had developed only a small role in the country's export profile by 1992-93, accounting for under 9% of the total.[10]

---

[9] In the cases of the two leading Southeast Asian countries, Malaysia and Thailand, manufactures accounted respectively for 63% and 65% of their exports in 1992-93, giving them an export profile almost identical to that of the East Asian NICs in 1970-71 (Reinhardt, 1997).

[10] These data show clearly the usefulness of the classification system employed here, since these findings contrast sharply with a number of more positive recent assessments of Chile's manufactured export success that do not distinguish between semi-manufactures and manufactures. According to Chilean Central Bank

The development of Chile's export structure differs also from that of the rest of the Latin American region, as figure 5.2 shows. In the case of the three largest Latin American economies (Argentina, Brazil, and Mexico), manufactures had become the largest export category in 1992-93, accounting for 49% of the total, while natural resource based exports had steadily declined in share. Their export trajectory is similar to that of the Southeast Asian nations, and quite unlike that of Chile. The export trajectory of the other South American countries is closer to Chile's in terms of the continued large weight of primary and mineral exports combined. However, the rest of South America on average had more than double the manufactured export share of Chile in 1992-93, Ecuador being the only country with a smaller share.

What are the implications of Chile's unique export path for the country's economic future? While many developing countries have experienced short-lived commodity-export booms, there is compelling evidence that sustained economic growth is generally accompanied by a structural shift of economic activity from primary to secondary activities, with an accompanying shift in the structure of exports (see, for example, Syrquin and Chenery, 1989). Recent econometric studies have demonstrated that technology-based exports add significantly to a country's economic growth compared to primary commodity based exports (IDB 2001; World Economic Forum, 2002). This is exemplified by the rapid economic growth of the East Asian NICs accompanying their movement up the export ladder (UNIDO, 1986; Pearson, 1994). In an open-economy model driven by factor endowments, this change in the factor basis of exports presumably reflects a growing endowment of capital, skill, and technological capabilities. Similarly, the lack of structural change in a country's exports reflects a lack of development of enhanced factor endowments. Indeed, this presumed connection between export profile and resource endowments is the theoretical basis for the revealed comparative advantage index.

Chile's export profile suggests that its export success has been based on low resource and labor costs, rather than on the development of enhanced factor endowments. The problem with this type of export boom is that its very success often undermines continued growth, as production costs are pulled up by emerging resource scarcities and Dutch Disease effects. Within a decade of their export success, the East Asian NICs were experiencing declining international competitiveness in their labor-intensive exports due to rising wages. A similar problem has afflicted many developing countries with booming labor-intensive agricultural exports, in addition to the problem of rising land prices. The history of the

---

figures, for example, manufactures accounted for 38% of exports in 1991 and 44% in 1998 (Banco Central de Chile, various years).

Latin American countries in the nineteenth century is replete with short-lived commodity export booms.

In the Chilean case, there were already some signs of emerging difficulties before the late-1990s Asian crisis downturn. As table 5.5 shows, between 1990 and 1998 there was a steady increase in real wages and an appreciation of the currency. While these factors meant a significant improvement in the standard of living, they, in combination with rising resource costs discussed in more detail below, have weakened Chilean competitiveness in many products. Despite the strong copper prices that prevailed over much of the period, peaking at a high level in 1995, the country experienced a persistent current account deficit as imports grew rapidly.

Table 5.5 Emerging Difficulties in the 1990s

Period	1990	1991	1992	1993	1994	1995	1996	1997	1998
Wages & salaries	100.0	128.0	154.0	......	......	......	......	......	......
Hourly wages (1995 = 100)	......	......	......	84	89	100	115	125	135
Consumer prices	52	64	74	83	92	100	107	114	120
Real effective exchange rate	82.3	84.5	89.5	91.6	94.3	100	103.4	113.1	111.1
Current account (mill US$)	-485	-99	-958	-2554	-1585	-1350	-3510	-3728	-4139

Source: IMF *International Financial Statistics Yearbook*, December 2000.

A common response to this set of problems is devaluation accompanied by wage repression, such as occurred throughout Asia in the late 1990s. This approach may restore a country's competitiveness in the short run, but at the expense of the standard of living of the labor force. A more desirable response to rising costs is for exporters to increase productivity, either through continual cost-saving technological change in existing exports, or through a change in the productive structure to higher value-added products, that is, through process or product innovation. This upgrading in turn depends on the development of new factor endowments: expanded capital resources, entrepreneurial, managerial, and labor force skills, and technological capabilities. Ultimately, continued export growth itself depends on these changes in the character of a country's comparative advantage. In the following section, leading export sectors are examined for evidence of the development of dynamic competitive capacity through product or process innovation.

Dynamic Competitive Development in Chile's Leading Export Sectors

The first step to moving up to a higher rung on the export ladder can be to move up within the existing rung. For example, Chilean exporters may have been moving to higher-value-added products within the resource-based sectors, and thus developing the skill and technological capabilities that could support a future move up the ladder should that become necessary. The data on Chile's exports show a mixed record in this regard.[11] There has been some movement into the higher value-added end of some product groups. However, Chilean exports overall remain concentrated in the lower value-added end of the product spectrum, where competitiveness is based mainly on low costs for natural resource inputs and/or low labor costs.

Copper mining and its derivatives is one example of this mixed picture. On the positive side, within the category of copper alloys (SITC 682) the lower value-added unrefined copper exports decreased in volume and value after 1986, while refined and worked copper exports increased sharply in volume and value. Unrefined copper exports accounted for only 8.7% of the category in 1993, down from 29.6% in 1970. Another higher-value-added copper derivative, inorganic copper bases (SITC 51369), also increased markedly over the period. On the other hand, the lowest value-added product, copper ore (SITC 28311), classified as a primary product, grew steadily as a share of exports both in the 1970's export boom and in the late 1980s boom.

The wood industry, Chile's second-largest export earner, has also attracted significant investment, most of it external. The performance of this sector presents a similarly varied picture. The pulp and paper sector has performed well. The pulp industry, Chile's leading industrial exporter (SITC 251), has experienced a strong product upgrading. During the earlier 1970's export spurt, both lower value-added unbleached pulp and higher value-added bleached pulp exports increased. In the post 1986 export boom, however, unbleached cellulose exports decreased in volume and value, while bleached cellulose exports rose sharply in volume and value. Bleached pulp exports accounted for 81% of Chile's pulp exports in 1992-93, up from 59% in 1986-87.

The related paper industry (SITC 64), too, underwent some product upgrading according to the export data. Newsprint, the lowest value-added category, remained Chile's principal paper export, accounting for 49% of paper exports in 1993, but had declined in relative importance

---

[11] Unless otherwise indicated, all export data in this discussion comes from the COMTRADE database. The export categories used here are the Standard International Trade Classification (SITC) Revision 1 codes (see UN, 1961).

during the export boom. Newsprint exports had suffered a decline in volume and value over the 1970s, falling from 64% of paper exports in 1970 to only 48% in 1981, but then surged in volume and value to reach a high of 86% of paper exports in 1987. Subsequently, the value of newsprint exports declined due to volume decreases and price declines, while higher value-added paper exports increased both absolutely and as a share of this category. Nevertheless, these exports have had a difficult time penetrating markets outside of Latin America, which absorbed 90% of their value in 1992 (Arze and Svensson, 1997).

Aside from pulp and paper, the data for other sectors of the wood industry show less favorable developments. The basic category, wood exports (SITC 24), steadily increased in value from the early 1970s. However, the most rapid rate of growth was in the low value-added rough wood category (SITC 242 - PRIM), mainly saw/veneer logs, compared to the higher value-added shaped wood category (SITC 243, SEMI). While increasing in absolute value, shaped wood exports fell from 99.9% of the wood category in 1970-71, to an average of 72% in 1980-81, to an average of 62% in 1992-93.

The next category up the ladder of wood products, wood manufactures (SITC 63, SEMI), shows a similar pattern of growth in the lower value added products. Products in this category range from the low value-added chipwood (SITC 63183), to higher value-added products such as veneers and wood mouldings (in the SITC 631 category), and boxes, domestic wood manufactures, tool handles, spindles, etc (in the SITC 632 category). While wood manufactures have been one of Chile's fastest growing exports in the recent period (see table 5.3), figure 5.3 graphically demonstrates the dominance of chipwood in this growth. This low value-added export, which accounted for less than 1% of wood manufactures exports in the 1970s, made up 49% of this category in 1986-87, and 73% in 1992-93. This reflects substantial investments by Japanese companies, with most woodchip exports (94% in 1992) destined for that country (and Svensson, 1997).[12]

The next step up the ladder of wood products, entering the manufactures category, is furniture (SITC 82, MFR). Chile rapidly increased its furniture exports after 1986, due to the efforts of a dynamic sector of small and medium enterprises (Messner, 1993). Nevertheless, these exports still accounted for only 0.3% of the total in 1996. The slowing of growth in furniture exports reflects the low quality of human and capital resources in this sector, making it difficult to compete in

[12] Gwynne (1993, p. 164) points out that 'there seems. .. to be an inverse relationship between the rate of export growth and the amount of value-added. Countries with which high export growth is recorded [East Asia] specialise in low value-added imports from Chile, while countries importing higher value-added forest products from Chile [Europe, Latin America] seem to have static demand.'

international markets where design and quality are of paramount importance (and Svensson, 1997).

The fruit and fishing industries, Chile's other dynamic export sectors, show similar patterns of dominance by the lower value-added products. In 1996, as table 5.3 shows, unprocessed fish and shellfish accounted for 52% of the fisheries exports, and fresh fruit accounted for 61% of the fruit products exports.

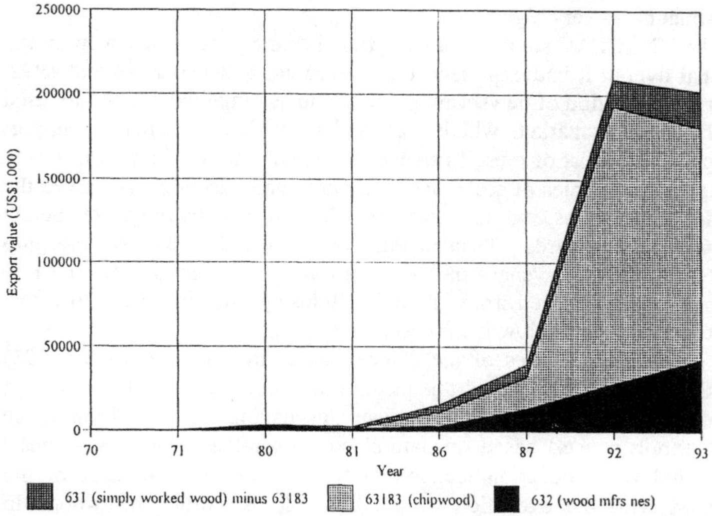

Source: Calculated from UN Commodity Trade Statistics Database (COMTRADE), SITC Revision 1, division 63.

Figure 5.3 Chilean Manufactured Wood Exports, 1970-1993

The evidence thus suggests that within the resource-based sectors, there was limited movement into higher-value-added product lines during Chile's export boom. Let us consider a second possibility, namely, that Chilean exporters were increasing value-added through the development of new technological capacity in existing export activities. Considerable attention has focused on Chile's wood-processing industry, believed by many to be the leading sector of the new economy. A UNECLAC study (CEPAL, 1995) generally found the pulp and paper industry to be technologically dynamic and internationally competitive, although this conclusion was mainly based on the pulp rather than the paper sector. The increase in Chile's bleached cellulose exports was due principally to the opening of three new pulp factories in 1991-1992. According to the

UNECLAC study, all six factories in Chile (owned by four companies) were or were becoming state-of-the art producers, incorporating the latest in technological advances in production processes and in automatic control systems. They each employed between 300 and 450 workers, many of them skilled. Data from 1990 showed that the older long-fiber plants enjoyed a solid cost advantage compared to their main global competitors. However, their competitiveness was due to low wood costs, low labor costs, and low finance charges on their mainly amortized capital. The competitiveness of the newer plants is less clear, since their investment was very high.

The UNECLAC study was more critical of the paper industry, pointing out that overall it had experienced slow growth between 1988 and 1992. With the exception of newsprint, paper products remained heavily focused on the internal market, where they had been facing increasing import competition. Most of these firms were of small and medium size, unable to capture economies of scale, and using antiquated technology. Even the newsprint factories, while large by Chilean standards, were below international standards. Data in this study show that, as with the pulp plants, the competitiveness of the newsprint plants was due to low raw materials costs, derived from internal cellulose production using low-cost Chilean wood, and to low labor costs.

Two detailed studies of the Chilean wood industry, Messner (1993) and Svensson (1997) extend this critique to most sectors of the industry; Svensson (1997) describes the industry as having "passed through the 'easy export-phase,' based on natural cost advantages and low wages." They find the production technology to be "obsolete" in most of the industry, with the exception of the big pulp, sawmill, and woodchip factories. Messner (1993) questions whether many Chilean firms have taken the necessary steps to retain their international competitiveness in the long run. Successful exporters had developed marketing competence, and many firms had introduced modern technology. However, Messner points out that most of these firms still based their competitiveness on Chile's low wages and abundant timber resources, what he calls the 'factor-driven phase' of international competitiveness, with limited potential for long-term success.

Messner (1993) argues that long-term competitiveness requires more than mere capital investments. Rather, it requires moving into an "investment-driven" phase of development characterized by a process of technological learning to develop "manufacturing competence." According to Messner, "....it is evident from the technical problems (adaptation problems, incompetent maintenance, parts of the production apparatus at a standstill) encountered particularly - but not only - in technologically more complex branches of production (furniture, boards) that manufacturing competence and the technological level of production are still low" (emphasis in original). In the board industry, "...the operating and maintenance personnel clearly do not yet have sufficient industrial manufacturing competence or technological know-how for the (imported) equipment ... to be used as it should be" (Messner, 1993, pp. 42-43). Svensson concurs that the skill level of workers in the wood industry is still "limited."

The introduction of new technology, then, does not necessarily mean that the firm's labor force has attained mastery of this technology. According to a growing body of research on the development of technological capacity, the achievement of technological competence does not come about in a passive "learning by doing" manner, but rather requires investments in human capital.[13] While the UNECLAC study documented the hours of employee training in the five largest pulp and paper firms, and Messner agrees that the "dynamic exporting enterprises attach more importance to the training of their employees than the traditional, inward-oriented firms," he goes on to argue that much of this training was unsystematic and not supported by organizational changes within the firm or outside of the firm (the "meso" level) to facilitate the learning process (Messner, 1993, pp. 37, 43-44). While there existed what he calls islands of efficiency in this industry, Messner concludes that "(t)he dynamic Chilean entrepreneurs have so far been particularly neglectful of the primacy of technology, technological competence and the organization of work as determinants of sustainable competitiveness and of the fundamental importance of the productivity of labour as an indicator of economic efficiency...They are thus more interested in safeguarding existing competitive advantages than in creating new ones."

This analysis echoes conclusions reached by other authors with respect to the forestry industry, and regarding Chilean industry overall. Gwynne (1993) argues that the emphasis of forestry exporters was on resource rather than product development: "Their technological thrust has been concerned with improving the quality of their resource in silviculture rather than in developing high value-added forest products or related machinery." Pietrobelli's (1995) comprehensive study of Chilean export performance documents the low level of development of technological capability on the part of Chilean exporters, and the persistence of natural resource endowments as the source of Chilean comparative advantage. Other observers note that the tendency of Chilean firms has often been to focus on marketing rather than the shop floor when facing competitive pressures, which some attribute to the emphasis on commercial rather than technological training of management personnel (Alcorta and Peres, 1995).

---

[13] (See Nelson, 1993; Lall, 1992; Porter, 1990; Fajnzylber, 1990, 1991; Cooper, 1994; Bradford, 1994; Pietrobelli, 1993, 1995; Alcorta and Peres, 1995; Buitelaar and van Dijck, 1996; Bruton, 1998.)

Table 5.6 Chilean Industry Classified by Wages and Productivity, 1991

	BELOW AVG WAGES (<US$5,477)		ABOVE AVG WAGES (>US$5,477)	
	PRODUCT	#WKRS / VA	PRODUCT	#WKRS / VA
BELOW AVG PRODUCTIVITY<US$30956	FRUIT&VEG PROC'G	15,621/$90.7m	NON-ELEC. MACH.	8,922/$126.2m
	FISH CANNING	17,221/$151.8m	PRINTING & PUBL.	8,990/$271.3m
	BAKERY PRODS	7,006/$123.5m	OTHERS	16,754/$347.2m
	KNITTING MILLS	6,325/$81.5m		
	FURNITURE	5,264/$59.1m	TOTAL	34,666/$744.9m
	FOOTWEAR	11,883/$138.5m		
	APPAREL	18,033/$195.7m		
	SAWMILLS	16,558/$258.5m		
	SPINNING/WEAVING	18,321/$261.8m		
	ANIMAL FEEDS	1,178/$30.6m		
	MEAT SLAUGHT.	9,726/$258.6m		
	MISC.PLASTIC	11,241/$183.4m		
	PAPERBOARD CONT.	2,972/$63.4m		
	COCOA&CHOCOLAT	3,922/$73.7m		
	STRUC.METAL PROD	7,498/$125.3m		
	MOTOR VEHICLES	3,941/$87.3m		
	FABR.METAL	10,315/$183.8m		
	OTHERS	20,513/$278.8m		
	TOTAL	187,538/$2,747 m		
	28.9% OF MFG. VALUE-ADDED 61.0% OF MFG.EMPLOYMENT		7.8% OF TOTAL MFG VALUE-ADDED 11.3% OF TOTAL MFG EMPLOYMENT	
	QUADRANT I		**QUADRANT II**	
ABOVE AVG PRODUCTIVITY >30956	**QUADRANT III**		**QUADRANT IV**	
	3.0% OF TOTAL MFG. VALUE-ADDED 2.3% OF TOTAL MFG EMPLOYMENT		60.2% OF TOTAL MFG VALUE-ADDED 25.4% OF TOTAL MFG EMPLOYMENT	
	WINE	3,523/$112.3m	DAIRY	6,755/$220.2m
	PAPER/BOARD ARTC.	2,102/$116,2m	OTHER FOODS	4,425/$173.2m
	OTHERS	1,460/$54.7m	ANIM /VEG.OILS	10,580/$380.4m
			MALT & LIQUORS	2,003/$119.6m
	TOTAL	7,085/$283.2m	IRON & STEEL	7,540/$283.0m
			OTHER CHEM	3,242/$143.4m
			PULP & PAPER	5,422/$471.8m
			SOAP	5,485/$297,4m
			SOFT DRINKS	4,531/$203,6m
			DRUGS & MEDS	5,919/$248,5m
			TOBACCO	703/$440.4m
			IND'L CHEM.	2,772/$241.1m
			NON FER METAL	8,608/$1,521.m
			CEMENT/LIME/PLSTR	1,526/$153.9m
			PETROL REF'G.	1,284/$550.2m
			OTHERS	7,353/$277.5m
			TOTAL	78,148/$5,726m

Source: United Nations Industrial Development Organization INDSTAT4 database 1995.

The concentration of Chile's exports in low-productivity/low-wage products can be seen in table 5.6. The UN Industrial Development Organization's INDSTAT4 database, which provides wage, value-added, and employment data for 1991 manufactures classified according to the Standard Industrial Classification (ISIC) system at the 4-digit level, was used for these calculations.[14] Industries in each quadrant are presented in order from lowest to highest wages in 1991. Chile's main exports are indicated in bold.

The products in Quadrant I have below-average productivity and below-average wages, and are in general unskilled-labor intensive. They dominate Chile's manufacturing employment, but contribute only 29% of overall manufacturing value-added. Chile's main industrial exports are concentrated in Quadrant I. The products in Quadrant II also have below-average productivity, but have above-average wages. These are products that rely more heavily on skilled labor, but may lack productivity-enhancing capital investments. The products in Quadrant III have below-average wages, but above-average productivity. In general, these products combine capital with unskilled labor. Neither Quadrant II nor Quadrant III products make significant contributions to Chilean manufacturing employment or value-added. One of Chile's leading exports, wine, is in Quadrant III, reflecting its capital-intensity but heavy reliance on unskilled labor.

Finally, Quadrant IV products have above-average productivity and above-average wages. These are products that rely more heavily on capital, skills, and technology than Chile's other industries. They are the most important manufacturing group in terms of value-added, and also make a significant contribution to Chilean manufacturing employment. Of Chile's leading exports, only non-ferrous metals and pulp and paper are in Quadrant IV. Indeed, this quadrant's large share of manufacturing value-added is due in large part to non-ferrous metals, which alone accounts for 27% of the quadrant's value-added. These data show that, while investments in wine, pulp, and copper give these industries above-average productivity (but not, in the case of wine, above-average wages), Chile's other exports remain low-productivity, low-wage activities despite their rapid export growth.

---

[14] Because of differences between the SITC and the ISIC classification systems, it was not possible to directly match all of Chile's leading exports to their ISIC counterparts. Nevertheless, most of Chile's leading manufactured and semimanufactured exports are included in table 5.6. Unfortunately, there is no comparable data for primary products. While there has apparently been considerable investment in new technology in fresh fruit and farm-raised fish production (Friedland, 1997), the effect of this on relative wages and productivity could not be assessed here.

Threats to Chile's Static Comparative Advantage

At the same time as many Chilean exporters have continued to rely heavily on cost-based advantages, these advantages have come under attack by a combination of internal and external pressures. While export diversification has reduced Chile's dependence on copper, unprocessed or simply processed natural resource-based goods continue to dominate Chile's exports. Commodities are vulnerable to severe price fluctuations. Chile's exports have not been immune to these problems, as we can see from table 5.7, which presents indices of unit value for a number of Chile's leading resource-based exports. While some of these products have exhibited only mild price fluctuations after the inflationary years of the 1970s, in other cases the fluctuations in unit value have been severe.

In the case of chipwood, unit value fell by 22% from 1986 to 1987, then recovered. Copper and cellulose values have exhibited the greatest variation. They collapsed in the early 1980s. Copper values recovered in the late 1980s only to drop again in 1993. They then rose to a new high in 1995, dipped in 1996, recovered briefly in early 1997, and then collapsed again. The price of copper fell by 30% between July and December of 1997 (Lucchetti, 1997), and high-grade copper July futures were trading at a ten-year low of 73.6 cents per pound. By 1999 they had fallen to a 30-year low of 61 cents per pound (Torres, 2000). They recovered to 83 cents per pound in 2000, but in 2001, a 2.5% drop in copper consumption caused prices to collapse again, to 68.3 cents a pound (WSJ, 2001). Cellulose prices recovered from 1987 up to 1989, and then collapsed again after that. The price of bleached cellulose fell from US$787 per ton in 1989 to US$352 in 1993 (CEPAL, 1995, p. 44). The data in table 5.7 show a drop of 25% in unit value in just one year, from 1992 to 1993. The roller coaster ride continued with sharp increases in the next two years, and then a steep fall in 1996. More recently, pulp prices fell by over 14% in the first two months of 1998 (Asia Pulse, 1998a).

Cellulose prices have tended historically to be cyclical, with high prices stimulating investment in new large-scale facilities, which then drive prices down sharply when they come on line (CEPAL, 1995). Industry experts agree that the pulp market is the most volatile sector of the paper industry - a weakness that has recently led industry giant Kimberly-Clark to divest itself of three pulp mills in order to transfer resources into more profitable consumer products (Pulp and Paper Week, March 3-7, 1997a). Chilean exporters, however, remain concentrated in the volatile low end of the paper industry. While the present slump in cellulose prices may be cyclical, the increasing use of recycled paper in the industrial countries, combined with new investments being undertaken in other low-cost countries such as China, Indonesia, Malaysia, and

Thailand, may keep cellulose prices depressed for the foreseeable future (CEPAL, 1995; Pulp and Paper Week, March 3-7, 1997b; Asia Pulse, 1998a).

Table 5.7 Unit Value and Unit Value Indices,[a] Selected Chilean Exports, 1970 to 1996

Commodity	SITC.1	1970	1971	1980	1981	1986	1987	1992	1993	1994	1995	1996
Unrefined Copper	68211	1,321 (66)	1,028 (51)	2,002 (100)	1,615 (81)	1,243 (62)	1,512 (76)	2,117 (106)	1,805 (90)	2,126 (106)	2,899 (145)	2,310 (115)
Refined Copper	68212	1,451 (67)	1,073 (50)	2,164 (100)	1,739 (80)	1,337 (62)	1,578 (73)	2,258 (104)	1,913 (88)	2,194 (101)	2,943 (136)	2,323 (107)
Unbleached Cellulose	25171	151 (37)	144 (35)	412 (100)	369 (90)	287 (70)	411 (100)	393 (95)	312 (76)	387 (94)	709 (172)	391 (95)
Bleached Cellulose	25172	162 (31)	165 (32)	523 (100)	490 (94)	369 (71)	533 (102)	453 (87)	341 (65)	471 (90)	796 (152)	476 (91)
Newsprint	6411	123 (25)	132 (27)	484 (100)	504 (104)	393 (82)	476 (98)	509 (105)	483 (100)	510 (105)	817 (169)	709 (146)
Chipwood	63183	--	--	52 (100)	--	50 (96)	39 (75)	51 (98)	54 (104)	54 (104)	57 (110)	59 (113)
Fish	031	1,142 (95)	1,679 (139)	1,204 (100)	1,422 (118)	1,866 (155)	1,852 (154)	3,605 (299)	3,545 (294)	3,687 (306)	4,177 (347)	3,798 (315)
Fishmeal	0814	150 (33)	151 (33)	453 (100)	464 (102)	293 (65)	338 (75)	670 (148)	530 (117)	506 (112)	620 (137)	754 (166)
Fresh fruit	051	194 (40)	209 (43)	485 (100)	533 (110)	719 (148)	516 (106)	624 (129)	584 (120)	614 (127)	638 (132)	698 (144)
Wine	1121	(N.A.)	(N.A.)	784 (100)	911 (116)	1,116 (142)	762 (97)	1,358 (173)	1,339 (171)	1,213 (155)	1,277 (163)	1,444 (184)
IUVA[b] (% chg)		49	51	100	99	95	96	134	123 (-8.8)	130 (6.0)	166 (27.8)	148 (-11.2)
IUVB[b] (% chg)		65	50	100	82	65	76	109	93 (-14.6)	106 (13.8)	141 (33.2)	114 (-19.4)
IUVC[b] (%chg)		78	57	100	80	60	67	101	91 (-8.9)	99 (8.9)	129 (29.6)	109 (-15.1)

[a] Unit value in US dollars per metric ton; figure in parentheses is unit value index, base year = 1980.

[b]IUVA = average unit value index; IUVB = unit value index weighted by base year share of ten exports; IUVC = unit value index weighted by current year share of ten exports; figure in parentheses is percent change from previous year.

Source: Calculated from "value" and "quantity" data, UN Commodity Trade Statistics database (COMTRADE) and UN *Yearbook of International Trade Statistics*, various years.

The Chilean fruit industry has also faced external problems, including increased competition from other Latin American exporters and continued protectionist policies in importing developed countries, including strong non-tariff barriers (Palma Aracibia, 1995). Nevertheless, Chilean fruit and wine exports have exhibited strong growth (table 5.3), and the unit value of fresh fruit and wine exports have generally been above their 1980 value, although exhibiting considerable price variability. Wine has been a particularly bright spot in Chile's export picture, but industry experts caution that the long lead times in viticulture can lead to large price corrections when new fields begin production. The exponential growth of Chilean wine exports in recent years has been matched by that of Australian wine exports (Asia Pulse, 1998b).

Fresh fish and shellfish values have had the strongest showing of all Chile's leading exports, rising sharply and consistently since the early 1980s. Fishmeal unit value has also been higher in the 1990s, but has been extremely variable.

While individual prices have been subject to gyrations, one important question is whether Chile's export diversification has reduced the fluctuations in overall export earnings due to price swings. This effect was measured by comparing three indices of unit value. The first index, IUVA, is the simple average of the indices for each commodity (base year = 1980), showing us the change in average export earnings if each commodity's share of exports was the same. This, of course, is not the case: we need to adjust for export shares. The second index, IUVB, weights the unit value of each commodity by its share in the base year:

$$IUVB = \sum_i UV_{it} w_{iB} / \sum_i UV_{iB} w_{iB}$$

where UV_{it} is the unit value of commodity i in year t, B is the base year (1980), and w_{iB} is the export share of commodity i in year B. IUVB reveals the change in average export earnings due to price changes alone, holding the composition of exports constant at the base year level. The third index, IUVC, allows both price and export share to change. It compares the unit value of each commodity weighted by its current export share, to the base year weighted unit value:

$$IUVC = \sum_i UV_{it} w_{it} / \sum_i UV_{iB} w_{iB} .$$

This index shows us the actual change in average unit value given the change in the composition and price of exports.

Table 5.7 presents the results of the calculations for the ten commodities listed. Chile's average earnings per unit of these commodities, measured by IUVA, rose sharply in the 1970s, dipped slightly in the 1980s, and rose strongly in the 1990s. If the export share of each commodity had remained constant at the 1980 level, as measured by IUVB, the average export earnings for these commodities would have been significantly lower in the 1980s due to the large weight attached to falling copper prices. The rise in the 1990s would also have been considerably smaller, even during the 1995 copper price peak, as copper prices rose less than some of Chile's other exports.

However, the relative weights of these exports changed considerably over this period, with the share of copper falling relative to other exports. Comparing IUVC to IUVB, we can see that the changing composition of exports actually lowered average export earnings even further. This is because the overall export share of lower-value exports increased relative to higher unit-value copper. Indeed, the trade-weighted average unit value of Chile's exports in 1993 and 1994 were actually below their 1980 level, with Chile's higher export earnings in those years therefore due to increased export volume.[15]

Although the peak earnings in the 1990s were lower due to copper's lower share, yearly fluctuations were moderated by the shift away from copper: the annual change in IUVC from 1992 to 1996 was lower in every year than the annual change in IUVB. However, these findings must be interpreted with caution, as it is evident that annual fluctuations in IUVC were still considerable in the 1990s. Indeed, the sharp fall in average unit value in 1996, due primarily to decreased copper prices, caused the country's total exports to *fall* in that year, from US $15.5 billion in 1995 to US $15.0 billion in 1996.

While Chile's natural-resource based exports have become more diversified, they have also become increasingly reliant on the Asian market. By 1997, just four Asian countries, Japan, China, South Korea and Taiwan, accounted for 29.7% of Chile's exports. The Asian financial crisis had a severe impact on the Chilean economy, as exports to these four countries fell by 34% in 1998 (calculated from Banco Central de Chile, 1999).

Internal cost considerations have exacerbated the difficulties arising from external market conditions, as table 5.5 revealed. After over a decade of depressed real wages, the Chilean labor force began after the late 1980s to see a historic recovery of their incomes due to tightening labor markets. At the same time, Chile's currency appreciated with respect to its main trading partners. While currency appreciation benefited Chilean consumers, it compounded exporters' problems due to rising wages. The ILO (1995) found that Chile's rising currency value had completely offset overall net productivity gains. All the Chilean cellulose plants were negatively affected after 1990 by the combination of rising real wages and appreciating currency, as were the newsprint plants. Friedland (1996) argues that 'the steady appreciation of the peso in recent years has already virtually killed off traditional high-employment industries such as textiles and footwear and, depending on weather conditions elsewhere, periodically threatens the global competitiveness of such important Chilean exports as fruit and wine.'

These problems were masked to some extent by the strength of Chile's mining sector. As is evident from tables 5.3 and 5.7, high copper prices contributed to a surge in copper export earnings in the mid-1990s. The

---

[15] This does not, of course, tell us anything about factor productivity. The changing composition of exports may have enabled Chile to produce a greater total value of exports at lower resource cost.

collapse of copper prices in the late 1990s, however, revealed the continued vulnerability of Chile's export-led economy.

Some observers expect the strong currency to be a permanent feature of the Chilean economy, due both to its export success and to the reduction in its foreign debt (Palma Aracibia, 1995). However, the data in table 5.5 show that the appreciation of the currency between 1990 and 1998 occurred despite current account deficits in every year. It was the continued inflow of foreign capital that kept Chile's currency strong in the 1990s. The good news is that much of this investment has taken the form of direct foreign investment, which may increase Chile's productive capacity in the future. The bad news is that the strong currency weakens export competitiveness in the interim, making productivity increases all the more vital.

Other sectors are facing environmental challenges that compound the above difficulties. One of the most affected sectors is the fishing industry, which has confronted serious overfishing problems (Barham *et al.*, 1992; Meller *et al.*, 1996 Schurman, 1996). Despite the strong prices for fresh fish, exports of prepared fish products grew slowly in the 1986-96 period (table 5.3). Overfishing sharply raised production costs in the late 1980s, leading the government to begin comprehensive regulation of the industry with the 1991 Fisheries Law (Thorpe and Aguilar Ibarra, 2000). Environmental problems have also affected agricultural producers, who have faced soil pollution due to pesticide use and irrigation (Barham *et al.*, 1992). Addressing these problems may push up Chilean production costs and affect its competitiveness in food exports, again making productivity increases essential.

Conclusions

The Chilean export boom of the mid-80s to the mid-90s has been quite unlike that of the Asian "tigers." As Moguillansky's (1999) in-depth study of Chilean investment clearly demonstrates, government export policy has promoted investment in existing areas of international competitiveness. This has resulted in an export profile that evidences little upgrading out of resource-based activities. Although Chile has enjoyed a comparative advantage in natural resource based products due to its climate, soil, mineral accessibility, and relatively cheap labor, rising real wages and appreciating currency have threatened the profitability and continued international competitiveness of Chile's principal exports.

Under these circumstances, continued competitiveness in the long run depends on increases in productivity, either through productivity increases in existing product lines, or by upgrading into products with higher-value added production processes. As we have seen, Chilean firms have had limited success with respect to the development of new bases for continued export competitiveness. The move from cost-based to "investment-driven" competitiveness requires a conceptual shift on the part of firms that few in Chile have sought to achieve. While there is a growing recognition of the need for this paradigm shift, government policy in Chile has been slow to support its development. Peres (1997) argues that in Chile, as in the region as a whole, "policies have tended to strengthen the existing pattern of comparative advantages, more than the creation of new competitive advantages," despite the consensus around the need to "move into a second export stage (that is to say, one more intensive in manufactures of high value added)" commonly accepted as a policy objective in Chile in the early 1990s.

On the positive side, Chile indeed enjoyed expanded capital endowments during its export boom, with increased direct foreign investment, increased overall investment rates, and increased fixed capital formation. Chile's savings rate has been high, and interest rates have been relatively low. However, investments have gone chiefly into capacity expansion in mining and other extractive industries, rather than into product and process innovation. There has been limited development of the skill and technological resources that are also necessary for the development of dynamic competitive advantage. While a few export activities have achieved the first stage of technological capacity by adopting state-of-the-art imported technology, there is little evidence of the higher-level adaptive or innovative stages of technological capacity in the country. Indeed, Chile's machine-tool industry was one of the chief casualties of the 1970s shock treatment policies. Most exporters continue to base their competitive position on low costs of raw materials and low wages.

Chile does have a number of factors working in favor of long-term success: a highly literate labor force, a nucleus of dynamic entrepreneurs, good fiscal management, and growing recognition by state and private organizations of the need to support firms' technological development. The transition to democratic rule has put the standard of living of the Chilean labor force back on the policy agenda, amid clear recognition that this necessitates a change in the competitiveness strategy of Chilean exporters. Whether this can be accomplished in time to sustain Chile's export-led growth remains to be seen.

References

Shahid, A.M. (1989) *Governments and Markets in Economic Development Strategies*, NY, Praeger.

Alcorta, L., and W. Peres (1995) "Investment in Innovation and Technological Adaptability in Latin America and the Caribbean," paper presented at the Annual Meeting of the Latin American Studies Association.

Amsden, A. (1989) *Asia's Next Giant: South Korea and Late Industrialization*, NY, Oxford University Press.

Ariff, Mohamed, and Hal Hill, (1985) *Export-Oriented Industrialisation: The ASEAN Experience*, London, Allen and Unwin.

Arze, E.C., and B.W. Svensson (1997) "Development of international competitiveness in industries and individual firms in developing countries: the case of the Chilean forest-based industry," *International Journal of Production Economics* 52, 185-202.

Asia Pulse (1998a) "World Pulp Prices Sink in First Two Months, 1998," *Asia Pulse*, May 12.

Asia Pulse (1998b) "Australian Wine Export Prices Forecast to Drop in 1998," *Asia Pulse*, May 25.

Banco Central de Chile, various years. *Indicadores de Comercio Exterior* (Santiago, Chile).

Barham, B., M. Clark, E. Katz, and R. Schurman (1992) "Non-traditional Agricultural Exports in Latin America," *Latin American Research Review*, 27, 43-82.

Biggs, T.S., and B.D. Levy, (1991) "Strategic Interventions and the Political Economy of Industrial Policy in Developing Countries." In D.H. Perkins and M. Roemer (eds.) *Reforming Economic Systems in Developing Countries*, Cambridge, MA, HIID.

Bradford, C. (ed.) (1994) *The New Paradigm of Systemic Competitiveness: Toward More Integrated Policies in Latin America*, Paris, OECD.

Bruton, H. (1998) "A Reconsideration of Import Substitution," *Journal of Economic Literature*, 36, 903-36.

Buitelaar, R. and P. van Dijck (eds.) (1996) *Latin America's New Insertion in the World Economy: Towards Systemic Competitiveness in Small Economies*, New York, Macmillan.

Casaburi, G. (1999) *Dynamic Agroindustrial Clusters: The Political Economy of Competitive Sectors in Argentina and Chile*, New York, St. Martin's Press.

CEPAL (1986) *El desarrollo fruticola y forestal en Chile y sus derivaciones sociales*, Estudios y Informes de la CEPAL no. 57, Santiago, Chile, ECLAC.

CEPAL (1990) *El comercio de manufacturas de America Latina, Evolucion y Estructura 1962-1989*, Santiago, Chile, ECLAC.

CEPAL. (1995) *El Sector de Celulosa y Paper en Chile: Un caso exitoso de reestructuracion hacia los commodities industrials*, Santiago, Chile, ECLAC.

Chowdury, A., and I. Islam (1993) *The Newly Industrializing Economies of East Asia*, London and NY, Routledge.

Cooper, C. (1994) "Relevance of Innovation Studies to Developing Countries." In C. Cooper (ed.) *Technology and Innovation in the International Economy*, United Nations University Press.

Fajnzylber, F. (1990) "Industrialization in Latin America: From the Black Box to the Empty Box," *Cuadernos de la CEPAL*, No. 60.

Fajnzylber, F. (1991) "International insertion and institutional renewal," CEPAL *Review*, 44, 137-166.

Ffrench-Davis, R., (2002) *Economic Reforms in Chile*, Ann Arbor, University of Michigan Press.

Ffrench-Davis, R. and O. Munoz G (1992) "Economic and Political Instability in Chile." In S. Teitel (ed.) *Towards a New Development Strategy for Latin America,* Washington, D.C, Johns Hopkins University Press, pp. 281-321.

Foxley, A. (1983) *Latin American Experiments in Neo-conservative Economics*, Berkeley: University of California Press.

Friedland, J. (1996) "Chile's Growth May Be Peaking Too Soon," *Wall Street Journal*, Dec. 4.

Friedland, J. (1997) "Chilean Salmon Farmers Test Free Trade," *Wall Street Journal,* Oct. 13.

Gatica Barros, J. (1989) *Deindustrialization in Chile,* Boulder, CO, Westview Press.

Gomez, S. and J. Echenique (1988) *La Agricultura Chilena: Las Dos Caras de Modernizacion*, Santiago, Chile, FLACSO.

Gwynne, R. (1986) *Industrialization and Urbanization in Latin America*, Baltimore, MD, The Johns Hopkins University Press.

Gwynne, R. (1993) "Non-traditional Export Growth and Economic Development: the Chilean Forestry Sector since 1974," *Bulletin of Latin American Research*, 12, 147-169.

Hojman, D. (1996) "Poverty and Inequality in Chile: Are Democratic Politics and Neoliberal Economics Good for You?" *Journal of Interamerican Studies and World Affairs*, 38, 73-96.

Hughes, H. (ed.) (1988) *Achieving Industrialization in East Asia,* New York, Cambridge University Press.

Huss, T. (1991) "Transfer of Technology: the Case of the Chile Foundation," *CEPAL Review*, 43, 97-115.

IDB. (2001) *Economic and Social Progress in Latin America, Competitiveness: The Business of Growth,* Washington, D.C., John Hopkins University Press.

IMF. (1999, 2000) *International Financial Statistics Yearbook,* Washington, D.C., International Monetary Fund.

Jarvis, L.S. (1991) "Chilean Fruit Development Since 1973: Manipulating the Cornucopia to What End?," Paper presented at the Latin American Studies Association, Crystal City, Virginia, April 4-6.

Lall, S. (1992) "The Role of Technology in Economic Development." In S. Teitel (ed.) *Towards a New Development Strategy for Latin America*, Washington, D.C., The Johns Hopkins University Press, pp. 169-218.

Lucchetti, A., (1997) "Woes From Asia Hit Farm Commodities," *Wall Street Journal*, December 22.

Meller, P., R. O'Ryan, and A. Solimano (1996) "Growth, Equity and the Environment in Chile: Issues and Evidence," *World Development* 24, 255-272.

Messner, D. (1993) "Shaping Industrial Competitiveness in Chile: The Case of the Chilean Wood-processing Industry." In K. Esser (ed.) *International Competitiveness in Latin America and East Asia*, London, Frank Cass.

Moguillansky, G. (1999) *La inversion en Chile: El fin de un ciclo en expansion?* Santiago, Chile: CEPAL.

Morley, S., R. Machado, and S. Pettinato (1999) "Indexes of Structural Reform in Latin America," *Serie Reformas Economicas 12,* Santiago, Chile, ECLAC.

Nazmi, N. (1996) *Economic Policy and Stabilization in Latin America*, Armonk, NY, M.E. Sharpe.

Nelson, R. (1993) *National Innovation Systems: A Comparative Analysis*, New York: Oxford University Press.

Palma Arancibia, C. (1995) "Structural Adjustment and Agricultural Performance: The Chilean Case." In J. Weeks (ed.) *Structural Adjustment and the Agricultural Sector in Latin America and the Caribbean,* London, St. Martin's Press.

Paus, E. (1994) "Economic Growth through Neoliberal Restructuring? Insights from the Chilean Experience," *The Journal of Developing Areas*, 28, 31-55.

Pearson, C. (1994) "The Asian Export Ladder." In S-C. Yang (ed.) *Manufactured Exports of East Asian Industrializing Economies,* Armonk, NY, M.E. Sharpe.

Peres, W. (1997) "Industrial Competitiveness Policies in Latin America and the Caribbean in the 1990s," paper presented at the meeting of the Latin American Studies Association, Guadalajara, Mexico, April 17-19.

Pietrobelli, C. (1993) "Non-traditional Agricultural and Agro-industrial Exports and Technological Change: A Microeconomic Approach." In D. Hojman (ed.) *Change in the Chilean Countryside: From Pinochet to Aylwin and Beyond*, Basingstoke: Macmillan.

Pietrobelli, C. (1995) *Technological Capability and Export Diversification in a Developing country: the Case of Chile since 1974*, unpublished doctoral dissertation, Oxford University.

Porter, M. (1990) *The Competitive Advantage of Nations*, London, Macmillan.

Pulp and Paper Week (1997a) "Kimberly to sell free-standing pulp mills," 19, March, 3-7.

Pulp and Paper Week (1997b.) "Southeast Asians starting up more pulp capacity," 19, March, 3-7.

Reinhardt, N. (1997) "Export-led Growth in Chile, Malaysia, and Thailand: Fast Track to Success or Dead-end Siding?" Paper presented at the Fifteenth Annual Meeting of the Association of Third World Studies, Hartford, CT.

Schurman, R. (1996) "Snails, Southern Hake, and Sustainability: Neoliberalism and Natural Resource Exports in Chile," *World Development* 24, 1695-1709.

Taylor, L. (1993) "Stabilization, Adjustment, and Reform." In L. Taylor (ed.) *The Rocky Road to Reform*, Cambridge, MA, The MIT Press.

Thorpe, A. and A.A. Ibarra (2000) "The New Economic Model and Marine Fisheries Development in Latin America," *World Development* 28, 1889-1702.

Torres, C. (2000)"Chile Mining Group Vaults to Big Leagues," *Wall Street Journal,* Feb. 1.

UN (1961) *Standard International Trade Classification, Revised*, Statistical Papers, Series M, No. 34, New York, United Nations.

UNECLAC (1992) *Social Equity and Changing Production Patterns: An Integrated Approach*, Santiago, Chile: UNECLAC.

UNIDO (1986) *International Comparative Advantage in Manufacturing: Changing profiles of resources and trade*, Vienna: UNIDO.

Wade, R. (1990) *Governing the Market: Economic Theory and the Role of Government in East Asian Industrialization*, Princeton, NJ, Princeton University Press.

White, G (ed.) (1988) *Developmental States in East Asia*, London: Macmillan.

World Bank (1987, 1991 to 1998/99) *World Development Report*, New York, Oxford University Press.

World Economic Forum (2002) *Global Competitiveness Report 2001-2002,* New York, Oxford University Press.

WSJ (2001) "Commodity prices give clues on timing of recovery," *Wall Street Journal,* Nov. 27.

6 Monetary Policy in Chile: Did it Produce Changes in the Volatility Regime, 1990-2002?

Sergio Zúñiga

Introduction

A number of fundamental modifications in monetary policy were implemented in Chile beginning in the 1990s, among which included independent status for the Central Bank, establishment of an inflation targeting regime (IT),[1] an important liberation of interest rates, and more recently the establishment of the Monetary Policy Rate (MPR). Before 1990, the mission of the Chilean Central Bank was quite limited. In effect, since 1976 monetary policy was linked to government financing, control of interest rates, and bank credit; up to 1982, a nominally fixed exchange rate existed, and until 1984 the bank was limited to supporting the banking system in the financial crises which occurred in the 1980s.

One of the most relevant aspects of monetary policy is its impact on financial markets. Unfortunately, the number of empirical studies on this point is relatively limited, and the results have been apparently contradictory. On one hand, there is ample international evidence that suggests that the independence of a central bank may be associated with lower inflation rates and greater stability in financial markets, that is, that the real interest rate variance is less than in countries that have greater levels of central bank independence (Summers, 1991; Alesina and Summers, 1993; McConnell and Perez, 2000). On the other hand, Bernanke *et al.* (1999) and Bernanke and Gertler (2000) concluded that in

[1] Beginning in 1990 several countries began to adopt an explicit policy of Inflation Targeting (IT). The first country was New Zealand in March 1990, followed by Canada (Feb.1991), the U.K. (Oct.1992), Sweden (Jan.1993), Australia (1993) and the ECB (Oct.1998). Chile (May 2000) was the first country to implement IT in Latin America.

the short term context, a policy of complete stabilization of inflation should lead to major changes in interest rates, that is, to a tradeoff between inflation and volatility of interest rates.

Regarding the IT, although international experience is relatively recent, there is some evidence that suggests that in countries that have adopted it, a real product stabilization has occurred (Corbo and Schmidt-Hebbel, 2001), although with a cost in apparent increase in financial instability (Honohan, 2000). Watson (1999) argues that the greater volatility in the interest rates is due to the increase in number of movements of the USA Fed rate, which has had good success in controlling inflation and increasing credibility in the Fed's capacity to control inflation. Chadha (2001) argues that since the IT is characterized by openness and transparency on the part of monetary policymakers, this should translate into greater credibility, thus reducing interest rates. Gruen (1995) argued that monetary policy, by decreasing inflation and its variability, should decrease financial instability, as measured for example, by volatility of prices of financial instruments. It has also been suggested that once an overnight rate is implemented as a matter of policy, central banks would tend to smooth interest rates, reducing volatility (Woodford, 1999; Srour, 2001; Kim and Sheen, 2002).

The least clear relationship would probably be between policy regarding the type of exchange and the volatility of interest rates and their level. Frenkel and Rose (1995) suggested that the exchange rate volatility appears unmatched by volatility of interest rates (and other macro variables) across different exchange rate regimes. Here, it has been suggested that, in the light of the covered interest parity condition for currency portfolio equilibrium, a reduction in volatility of the type of exchange should lead to an increase in the volatility of the short term interest rate (Svenson, 1989). Conversely, Hausmann *et al.* (1999) and Hausmann and Powell (1999) argue that in the case of Latin America, exchange rate volatility brings higher interest rates and unstable policy reactions due to the inability of Latin American countries to create demand for financial instruments in their own currencies. McKinnon (1990) suggested that the volatility of the interest rates is more likely explained by the weakness in the currency (long term rates were higher and volatile in the USA when its currency was weak against that of Japan and Germany). Laopodis (2000) suggested that it could be expected that international integration implied increases in inflation risk in other countries, which would imply more rebalancing, and both short term and long term volatility. Greater credibility in the central bank would also lead economic agents to trade less, reducing the volumes transacted and volatility in interest rates (Kim and Sheen, 2002). Other factors such as monetary aggregates, requirements for bank reserves, and economic activity also produce an impact on interest rates and their volatility.

Our focus in this chapter is to empirically analyze the behavior of the volatility of interest rates in the Chilean market by analyzing the different monetary policy regimes beginning in 1990, and following the hypothesis stated before that the behavior was different under each different regime. The chapter begins by describing the principal changes of monetary policy in Chile starting with May 1990, which allows us to propose the existence of different regimes. In the following portion of the chapter, we demonstrate how we define the real rate of market interest at a weekly frequency over the study period, and we show the difficulties in its constitution. We continue by making estimations of the volatility of the interest rates using an EGARCH specification that admits the possibility of the existence of asymmetries. Finally, we analyze the behavior of the conditional volatility by examining a window of various days around each change in the Monetary Policy Rate. The conclusions of the study are summarized at the end, and an Appendix is added explaining the calculation of the MPR.

Recent Monetary Policy Regimes in Chile

Recent monetary history in Chile begins in early 1985, a year in which the Central Bank implemented a relatively active monetary policy by means of direct control of the MPR, through the real 90-day rates of the PRBC (Pagarés Reajustables del Banco Central). In 1990, Law No 18.840 provided autonomy for the Chilean Central Bank, which implied that monetary policy would be oriented toward maintaining the evolution of the aggregate demand in line with the evolution of the potential output (expenditure to output gap must not exceed 3 to 4 %), and the explicit establishment of an IT scheme. As intermediate goals, an announcement was made of an annual goal for inflation in order to channel market expectations.[2] From 1990 to May 1995, the policy tool was the real interest rate, and the principal instrument for the regulation of market liquidity was the PRBC-90, which was offered over-the-counter at a pre-established rate, and thus implied a direct setting of medium term interest rates.

It would have been ideal to the goals of our study to have had available a continuous, high frequency rate series for the period before 1990. However, the information on market quotes of indexed instruments from the Central Bank prior to 1990 is very limited. In effect, the earliest records from the Santiago Stock Exchange reported transactions of these instruments only from the beginning of 1987 (see figure 1 in Zuñiga, 1999). There was low volume until May 1990, which is the reason the present study is initiated on this date.

---

[2] The exchange rate was discarded at this time due to the high risk and costs of external competitivity, and monetary aggregates, given the unusually high variability in the rate of money circulation.

A second regime began in May 1995, at which time the Central Bank established that the MPR would be the real daily rate on interbank loans (overnight real interbank rate). In this way, direct setting of the interest rate of the PBRC was discarded (discarding over-the-counter offers and instead, the attempt was made to influence the secondary market of the PBRC by means of Open Market Operations. Among these, in addition to the three-step liquidity credit line (rediscount) that constituted a ceiling for the interbank rate, a line of liquidity deposit appeared which represented an account into which banks could make one-day deposits and obtain an interest rate that represented a floor for the interbank rate.[3] In any case, beginning in May 1995, monetary policy became more transparent, which in the light of the preceding discussion should have contributed to a reduction of market volatility, while the uncertainty of the moment and the magnitude of the changes in the MPR could provoke an inverse effect.

A third regime began in August 2001, when the Central Bank changed the format specifying the MPR in terms of a nominal rate instead of a real rate, as had in effect been doing (nominalization of the MPR). This new format was accompanied by an important change in the structure of liabilities of the Central Bank from short and medium term indexed debt to nominal peso debt. It was expected that the only effect would be a reduction in the short term (month to month) variability of nominal interest rates and an increase in short-term volatility of UF defined rates (also month to month). It was argued that an indexed scheme (of real rates) could add volatility to the exchange rate under the real rate goal, since when faced with significant (and transitory) reductions in inflation the Central Bank saw itself obligated to intervene in order to validate a level of nominal interest rates that were extremely low. This measure has been the center of an interesting recent polemic (Fuentes *et al.*, 2003; Morandé, 2002 and Fontaine, 2002).

Our main hypothesis is that each of the previous regimes could affect the behavior of market interest rate volatility in a different way, and we wished to quantify the magnitudes of these differences. It is important to comment here on the recent change in monetary policy (not separately analyzed in this study) where it was decided that the Central Bank would, in September 1999, adopt a floating exchange rate. This process ended with complete liberalization of the capital account in 2000.

Interest Rates in Chile

Certain difficulties arise when trying to choose an interest rate representative of the short term fixed income instruments in Chile, especially when one wishes to work with high frequency (weekly or daily)

---

[3] For a historical review of Chilean monetary policy see, for example, Magendzo (1997).

data. Given that the ideal rate should be taken as risk-free, this excludes private issuers (for example, average monthly interest rates paid on deposits, used by banks and financial institutions, which are published only on a monthly basis), and that basically limits us to the instruments issued by the Chilean Central Bank,[4] in particularly the PBRC and PRC (Pagarés Reajustables con Cupones) that have the advantage of being quoted indexed to inflation.

The second difficulty is that the PBRC series is basically limited to the period in which these transactions were offered in the Santiago Stock Market (since 1987, although with few transactions until 1989, plus the existence of important gaps in 1990) and the decision of the Central Bank in 2001 to substitute them for PDBC (Pagarés Descontables del Banco Central, a nominal short term bond), implying a gradual remove from the secondary market. Since July 2001, there has been a virtual halt to these transactions (see figure 6.1). Hence, beginning in the second semester of 2001, it is not possible to use this instrument, particularly if one wishes to analyze the more recent behavior of interest rates as in the present study.

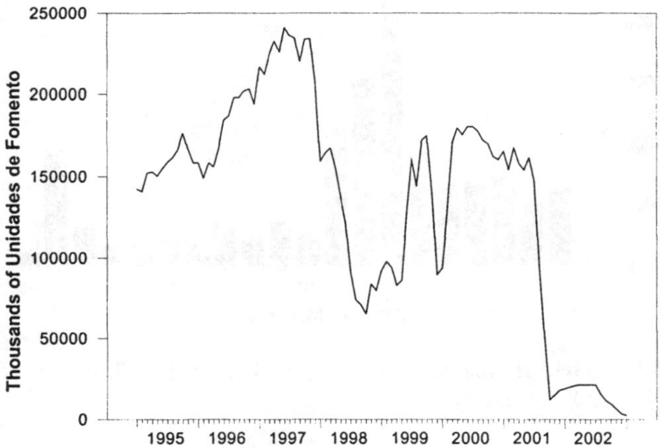

Figure 6.1 Stock of PBRC in Circulation

Alternative instruments include the PRC, which are long term, and have a relatively more stable circulation than the PBRC. Additionally, their yields are less volatile than short term instruments (in agreement with the expectations hypothesis of interest rates, long term interest rates are smoothed-out averages of short term interest rates), and should reflect a

---

4 Other issuers which have state guarantees include the Institute of Pension Normalization by means of Bonos de Reconocimiento (Zuñiga, 1999).

best-estimate for the average horizon of the average agent. Figure 6.2 shows a histogram of maturities of PRC over the period 1989:05:30 - 2002:12:30, showing that there was a high concentration of these instruments with about 7 years to maturity. On the basis of this estimation, we worked with PRC having maturities of between 8 and 10 years. This was done since in general there was a relatively low number of transactions in Chile, for which it is necessary to consider a range of days to maturity for each series, thus permitting raising the probability that there was at least one transaction per day, although with the limitation of smoothing out the yields due to the aggregation.

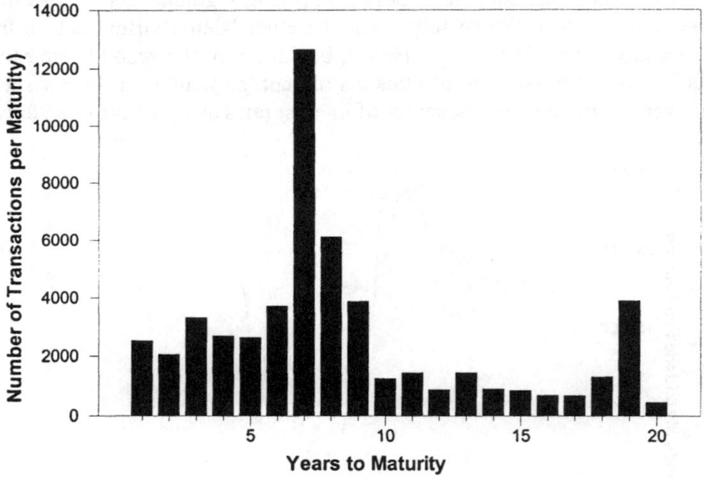

Figure 6.2 Yield Histogram for 8-10 year PRC 1989:05:30-2002:12:30

Figure 6.3 shows the evolution of this series of yields which are assumed to be stationary, together with the MPR level. First and third regimes are shaded. Note that the event of 16 September 1998 stands out, when the MPR was increased strongly by the Central Bank from 8.5% to 14.0%; it can be seen that important levels of volatility occurred around this event.

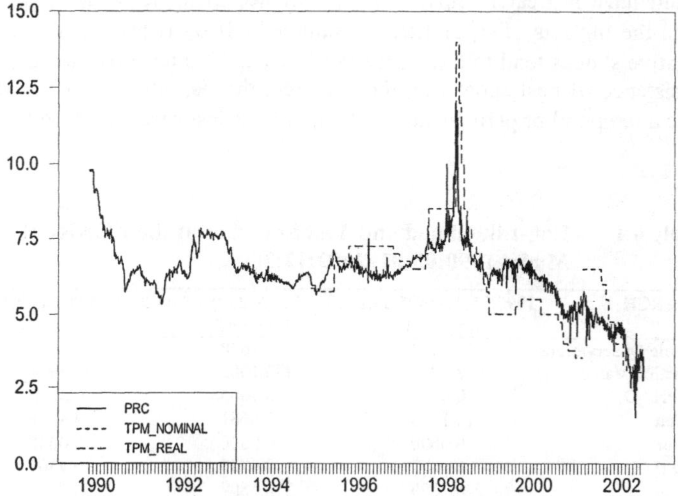

Note: In August 2001 the MPR is nominalized, going from 3.5% (real annual) to 6.50% (nominal annual)

Figure 6.3 8-10 Year PRC Yields, Real MPR, and Nominal MPR 1990:05:01-2002:12:30

Volatility of Interest Rates: EGARCH Specification

Beginning with the pioneering studies of Engle (1982) and Bollerslev (1986) that showed that it was possible to simultaneously model the mean and conditional variance, there exists a series of generalizations that allows analysis of the behavior of volatility based on interest rates (PRC). In our case, it is of interest to model volatility allowing for the possibility that this would be asymmetric around a central tendency as postulated by Nelson (1991) through an EGARCH specification. To accomplish this task, we modeled the mean as an autoregressive first-order process affecting the yield of the PRC (assumed stationary), while the conditional variance is modeled according to the following EGARCH model (1,1):

$$\log(\sigma_t^2) = \alpha_0 + \alpha_1 \left[\left| \frac{\varepsilon_{t-1}}{\sqrt{\sigma_{t-1}^2}} \right| - \sqrt{\frac{2}{\pi}} \right] + \alpha_2 \log(\sigma_{t-1}^2) + \alpha_3 \frac{\varepsilon_{t-1}}{\sqrt{\sigma_{t-1}^2}} \tag{6.1}$$

where α_1 measures the impact of the past information, which when combined with α_3 shows the sensitivity of the variance to positive and negative shocks. If α_3 is greater than zero, positive shocks on the yields would have a greater impact on the variance than the negative shocks, since the impacts of α_1 and α_3 are summed. If α_3 is less than zero, the negative shocks tend to have a greater impact. The term α_2 measures the persistence of past shocks on the variance, that is, whether or not these have a temporal or permanent effect, and in this last case α_2 would be near 1.0.

Table 6.1 Log-Likelihood and Test Statistics of the EGARCH Model 1990:05:01–2002:12:30

EGARCH	1990:05:01-1995:05:26 Regime 1	1995:05:29-2001:08:08 Regime 2	2001:08:09-2002:12:30 Regime 3
Usable Observations	1324	1618	363
Function Value	2888.3738	2470.1003	333.3974
ALPHAO	0.0782	0.1665	0.2893
T-Stat	10.1113	7.6681	4.4868
Signif	0.0000	0.0000	0.0000
ALPHA1	0.9877	0.9753	0.9307
T-Stat	910.7599	276.1804	66.7355
Signif	0.0000	0.0000	0.0000
AO	-0.0485	-0.1084	-0.1503
T-Stat	-3.2137	-5.9201	-3.6027
Signif	0.0013	0.0000	0.0003
A1	0.9888	0.9611	0.9364
T-Stat	323.3259	205.6601	56.6620
Signif	0.0000	0.0000	0.0000
A2	0.1236	0.5246	0.3355
T-Stat	8.7433	32.7530	5.9727
Signif	0.0000	0.0000	0.0000
A3	0.0141	0.0395	-0.0784
T-Stat	1.9025	2.2778	-2.1787
Signif	0.0571	0.0227	0.0294

Note: ALPHA O and ALPHA 1 represent the coefficients of the first-order autoregressive process defined for the mean.

The process of empirical estimation of the model involves maximization of the likelihood function with respect to the coefficients. For that we use the Berndt, Hall, Hall and Hausman (BHHH)[5] algorithm using the RATS® econometric program. The results of the estimation both for the entire period and for each regime are shown in table 6.1.[6]

The statistical output shows a good fit for the three regimes. The only coefficient significant at 5.7% is α_3, while the remaining coefficients are

[5] In spite of the fact that most software produces direct results, one useful reference is that of Press, Flannery, Teukolsky and Vettering (1988). 'Numerical Recipes in C'. N.Y. Cambridge Univ. Press.

[6] We carried out estimations in equation (6.1) incorporating the TPM level as an additional explicative variable without observing any impact on the results.

significant at traditional levels. Thus, the results reflect the existence of a volatility asymmetry in response to the shocks. In effect, the sign of the α_3 coefficient indicates that in the 1st and 2nd regimes the positive shocks of the previous yields have had a greater impact on the variance than the negative shocks, a situation that becomes inverted in the 3rd period. For effects of monetary policy, this asymmetric response on the part of investors may be interpreted in the sense that before August 2001 they reacted more strongly on average due to the increases in rates (fear of restrictive monetary policy), while after this date, the reaction was greater due to a fall in the previous rates. Based on the Appendix, it should be noted that the last regime only experienced declines in the MPR (although there were increases in market interest rates). Concerning the autoregressive component of the variance, the α_2 coefficient is close to 1.0 (0.98, 0.96, and 0.93 respectively) in all the regimes, although somewhat less with the beginning of nominalization, such that in the short term there exists an important transmission of volatility that persists for several following weeks.

Table 6.2 Statistics for the Adjusted Conditional Volatility 1990:05:01-2002:12:30

	1990:05:01-1995:05:26 Regime 1	1995:05:29-2001:08:08 Regime 2	2001:08:09-2002:12:30 Regime 3
Observations	1324	1618	363
Sample Mean	0.0714	0.1714	0.2615
Variance	0.0004	0.0274	0.0148
Standard Error	0.0207	0.1656	0.1216
t-Statistic	125.4544	41.6286	40.9746
Skewness	0.5588	4.3587	2.2813
Signif.	0.0000	0.0000	0.0000
Kurtosis	0.1842	28.1412	6.4871
Signif.	0.1723	0.0000	0.0000
Jarque Bera	70.7707	58512.0849	951.3499
Signif.	0.0000	0.0000	0.0000

Table 6.2 shows the statistics from the conditional volatility series constructed from the preceding estimations. As expected, the results reflect a systematic increase in volatility within each regime from 0.071 in the first to 0.171 in the second, and 0.260 in the last (3rd) case. The table shows that the dispersion of volatility was greater in the second regime, indicating that there existed periods of markedly high volatility, and others of low volatility, such as that which occurred with the event of September in 1998. However, the average volatility of this period was lower than that of the following period. As expected, the results suggested the existence of skewness and abnormality in the three regimes. Figure 6.4 shows the daily changes in the interest rate (left), and the data fitted to the model of

each regime (right), maintaining a vertical axis of the same scale to facilitate the comparison. Figure 6.5 reveals the comparative behavior of the three regimes in relation to their mean conditional volatility.

A test to verify the existence of a change in volatility with change in regime consists in running the model (6.1) incorporating two dummy variables that identify each of the preceding sub-periods (n-1 dummies are required to identify n regimes). The resulting model is as follows:

$$\log(\sigma_t^2) = \alpha_0 + \alpha_1 \left[\left| \frac{\varepsilon_{t-1}}{\sqrt{\sigma_{t-1}^2}} \right| - \sqrt{\frac{2}{\pi}} \right] + \alpha_2 \log(\sigma_{t-1}^2) + \alpha_3 \frac{\varepsilon_{t-1}}{\sqrt{\sigma_{t-1}^2}} + \alpha_4 R_1 + \alpha_5 R_2 \qquad (6.2)$$

where R_1 identifies the second regime and R_2 identifies the third regime. The results of the estimation of (6.2) for the complete period produce a good fit. The coefficient of R_1 is 0.0434 with t = 6.1803 and the coefficient of R_2 is 0.1144 with t = 9.7461, such that we conclude that significant difference exists in the conditional volatility between the three regimes.

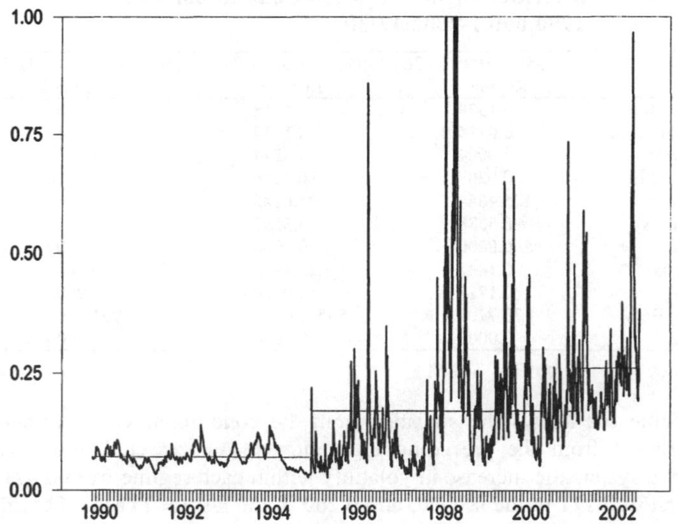

Note: Some extremely high values have been deleted to improve the visualization

Figure 6.4 Adjusted Conditional Volatility, and Mean Volatility by Regime 1990:05:01-2002:12:30

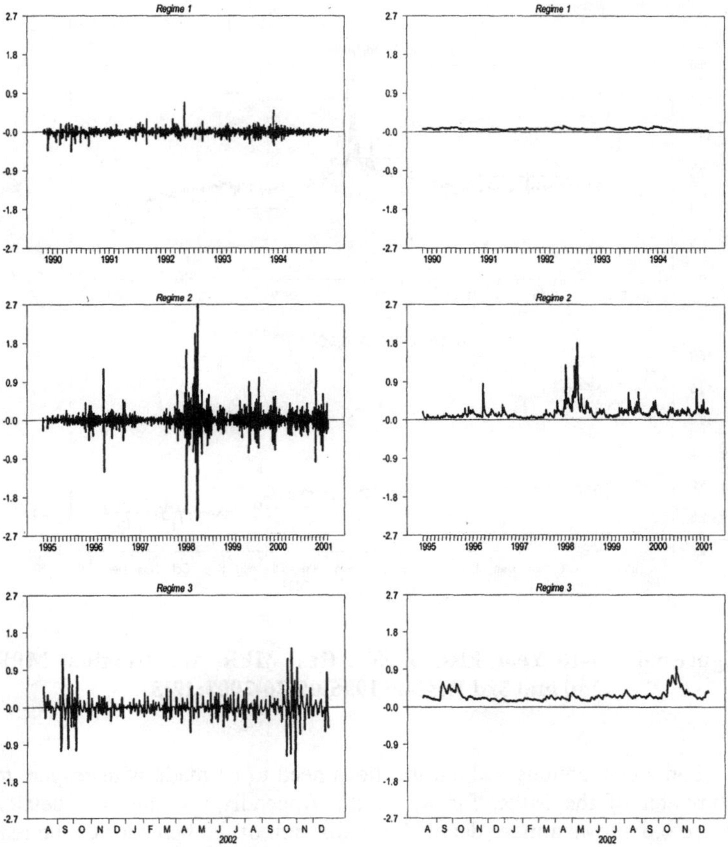

Figure 6.5 Changes in the Interest Rate and Adjusted Conditional Volatility by Regime 1990:05:01-2002:12:30

Patterns in the Conditional Volatility: a Closer Look

In this section, a more detailed analysis was undertaken of the behavior of the volatility of the interest rate. We previously suggested that the effective and potential changes in the MPR on the part of the Central Bank could generate volatility in interest rates, and there is an important group of publications that analyzes this possibility (see, for example, Thornton,

1991). Our approach analyzes the behavior of the conditional volatility in PRC yield around the days in which the Central Bank modified the MPR.

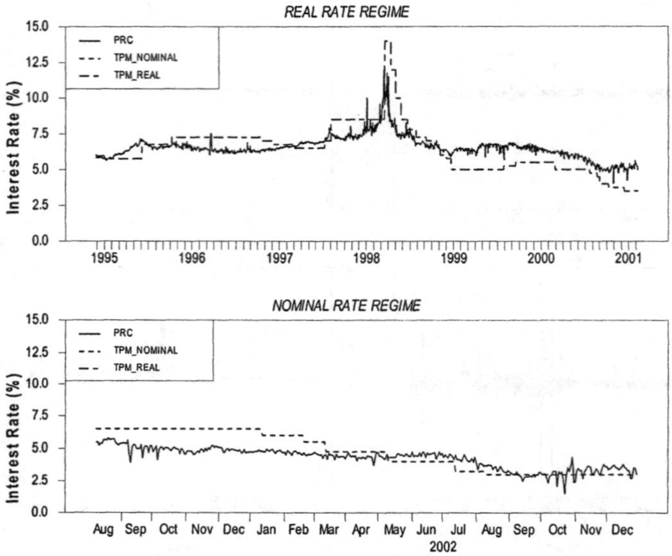

Figure 6.6 8-10 Year PRC Yields, Real MPR, and Nominal MPR 2nd and 3rd Regime 1995:05:26-2002:12:31

Some conventions and clarifications need to be made with respect to estimation of the MPR, for which the Appendix provides the details. Figure 6.6 allows a more detailed visualization of the behavior of the real MPR for each period in which it was in force (1995:05:29-2001:07:26) and the nominal MPR for the following period (2001:07:27-2002:12:30), both compared with the interest rate level.

Since the behavior of the volatility (as determined before by the EGARCH specification in 6.2) around the changes in the MPR must be affected by the size of these changes, we have standardized it by dividing it by the corresponding change in MPR. In this way, we selected information on rates using a three-day window both before and after each change in the MPR, excluding weekends and holidays. The standardized adjusted volatility is therefore:

$$adj\_\sigma_{j,t} = \frac{\sigma_t}{abs\left(\Delta TPM_j\right)} \tag{6.3}$$

where σ_t is the conditional volatility on day t (table 6.3) around the jth change in the MPR, $abs(\Delta MPR)$ is the absolute change in MPR made by the Central Bank at the end of day j, and adj_σ is the resultant series with the volatility standardized on day t around j.

The analytical model is based on linear regression with k dummy variables of the following type:

$$adj\_\sigma_{j,t} = \sum_k \beta_k \delta_{kt} + \varepsilon_t \tag{6.4}$$

where: $adj\_\sigma_{j,t}$ = conditional volatility of the interest rate set on day t around the jth change in the MPR.

δ_{kt} = dummy variable which takes on the value $\delta_k = 1$ if the volatility on day t corresponds to k days around (before or after) the change in MPR, and $\delta_k = 0$ in any other case.

β_k = is the coefficient of the dummy variable, representing the mean volatility of each event k.

ε_t = are errors which are assumed to be independent and identically distributed, $N(0,\Omega)$ with Ω not diagonal.

Since it is proposed in (6.4) that the regression has no intercept, it is characterized by the fact that the values taken by the coefficients of the dummy variables are the estimated mean of the conditional volatility. Note also that the estimates in (6.4) come from a two-step estimation.

Table 6.3 OLS and Test Statistics of the Dummy Model 2nd and 3rd Regimes, 1995:05:26-2002:12:31

	1995:05:29-2001:08:08 Regime 2	2001:08:09-2002:12:30 Regime 3
Useable observations	575	107
Degrees of Freedom	569	101
R Bar **2	-1.052	-1.551
D_ANTE_3	0.396	0.561
Test T	4.416	2.331
D_ANTE_2	0.383	0.514
Test T	4.265	2.136
D_ANTE_1	0.391	0.493
Test T	4.358	2.050
D_POST_1	0.453	0.493
Test T	4.954	2.049
D_POST_2	0.452	0.474
Test T	5.042	1.968
D_POST_3	0.434	0.479
Test T	4.835	1.993
F(5,569)=	0.126	
F(5,101)=		0.018
Significance Level	0.987	1.000

Table 6.3 shows the results from (6.4) for the two regimes in which MPR rules. The estimations appear significant at 95% for all cases, and the coefficients represent the mean standardized volatility each day around the change in the MPR. At the bottom of the table, it can be seen that the equality hypothesis for adjusted volatility over the six days that form the window cannot be rejected. Notwithstanding this finding, it is illustrative to analyze the pattern followed by the volatility (figure 6.7), where the adjusted volatility around the changes in the MPR appear greater in the last regime (3rd) than in the second regime. This coincides with our previous result, in that the 3rd regime showed greater average levels of volatility than the preceding (2nd) regime. A second observation is that the changes in the last regime apparently have been less surprising for the market, since volatility decreased systematically in the three-day window before and after. On the contrary, in the second regime the change in rate appears to provoke an increase in volatility that only tends to decrease on the third day after the change.

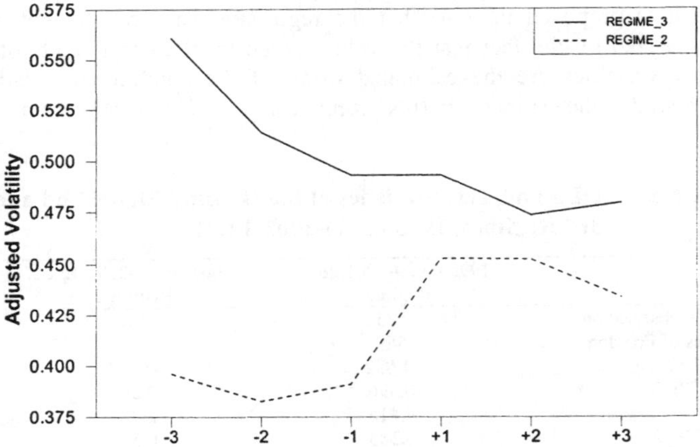

Figure 6.7 Patterns in Volatility around MPR Changes 2nd and 3rd Regimes - 1995:05:26-2002:12:31

In this way, the conclusion can be drawn that although volatility has increased towards the last regime, the responses are smoother, which suggests an increase in the anticipative capacity of the market. This appears to be associated with more degrees in the transparency of Chilean monetary policy. This result coincides with Nilsen (1977) and Lee (2002) who reported that for the United States, the size of the volatility response functions of interest rates began to weaken at the beginning of the 1980s, which they associated with response to actions of the US Federal Reserve Board which had been for the most part anticipated.

Conclusions

In this study, we have analyzed the possibility that different regimes may have different effects on the behavior of the interest rates in Chile by means of an EGARCH specification. The three regimes we analyzed are first, the initial stage towards independence of the Chilean Central Bank (1990:5-1995:5). The second represents the period in which the Central Bank used the interbank real daily rate as a tool of monetary policy (1995:05-2001:08). Finally, the third regime represented the period in which the Central Bank employed a nominal daily interest rate (2001:08-2002:12).

The present study argues that interest rates are conveniently determined by using weekly quotes on 8-10 year PRC from the Santiago Stock Market. The likelihood estimation of conditional volatility for each subperiod was satisfactory, pointing out the existence of asymmetries in the response to changes in previous interest rates, although with a clear change of sign beginning on 2001:08.

The results also demonstrated that there was a significant change in the level of conditional volatility in the three regimes. The volatility was clearly shown to be increasing through these regimes (0.07, 0.17, and 0.26, respectively). The first increase in volatility may be associated with the fact that at the beginning of 1995 the Central Bank stopped the direct fixing of the interest rate on its main policy instrument of the period (90 days PRBC), and centered on the one-day interbank rate. In this way, the market assumed a more important role in the determination of the equilibrium rates. Concerning the increase in volatility due to nominalization, this was one of the effects predicted by the Central Bank; however, it was expected that it would affect only short term real interest rates (about one month term).

Finally, a closer look at the conditional volatility around the days in which changes in the MPR were made, suggested there was decreasing reaction when comparing the third regime with the second. The evidence is derived from estimations of the average daily volatilities carried out by means of a model using dummy variables. In effect, patterns suggest that for the second regime, the increase in volatility around the MPR change may be interpreted as a lower predictive capacity of the market. In the third regime, volatility appears to decrease from three days before the MPR change to two days after the change, suggesting an important anticipation process. The preceding period coincides with that reported by some authors beginning from the middle 1980s for the United States, when the monetary policy of the US was made more transparent.

References

Alesina, A. and L. Summers (1993) "Central Bank Independence and Macroeconomic Performance: Some Comparative Evidence," *Journal of Money, Credit and Banking,* 25, 151-162.

Bernanke, B. and M. Gertler (2000) "Monetary Policy and Asset Price Volatility," *NBER Working Paper* No. 7559.

Bernanke, B.S., T. Laubach, F.S. Mishkin and A.S. Posen (1999) *Inflation Targeting*, Princeton, Princeton University Press.

Bollerslev, T. (1986) "Generalized Autoregressive Conditional Heteroscedasticity," *Journal of Econometrics*, 31, 307-327.

Corbo, V. and K. Schmidt-Hebbel (2001) "Inflation Targeting In Latin America," Central Bank of Chile *Working Papers* N° 105.

Chadha, J. and Ch. Nolan. (2001) "Inflation Targeting, Transparency and Interest Rate Volatility: Ditching 'Monetary Mystique' in the U.K," *Journal of Macroeconomics*, 23, 349-366.

Engle, R. (1982) "Autoregressive Conditional Heteroscedasticity with Estimates of the Variance of United Kingdom Inflation," *Econometrica*, 50, 391-407.

Frenkel, J. A. and A. K. Rose. (1995) "Empirical Research on Nominal Exchange Rates." In G. M. Grossman and K. Rogo (eds.), *Handbook of International Economics*, Vol. 3. Amsterdam, North Holland.

Fontaine, J. A. (2002) "Consecuencias de la Nominalización de la Política Monetaria," *Cuadernos de Economía*, Pontificia Universidad Católica de Chile, 117, 253-75.

Fuentes, R., A. Jara, K. Schmidt-Hebbel, M. Tapia and E. Arraño (2003) "Efectos de la Nominalización de la Política Monetaria en Chile," *Working Paper* N° 197, Santiago, Central Bank of Chile.

Gruen, D. (1995) "Financial Market Volatility and the World-wide Fall in Inflation," *Research Discussion Paper* 9513, Economic Research Department, Reserve Bank of Australia.

Hausmann, R., M. Gavin, C. Pages-Sierra, and E. Stein (1999) "Financial Turmoil and the Choice of Exchange Rate Regime," *Working Paper* N° 400, Inter-American Development Bank, Washington, DC.

Hausmann, R. and A. Powell (1999) "Dollarization: Issues of Implementation." Unpublished manuscript, Inter-American Development Bank, Washington, DC.

Honohan, P. (2000) "How Interest Rates Changed Under Financial Liberalization: A Cross-Country Review," *Working Paper* N° 2313, World Bank, Development Research Group.

Kim, S. and J. Sheen (2002) "International Linkages and Macroeconomic News Effects on Interest Rate Volatility - Australia and the US," *Pacific Basin Finance Journal*, 8, 85-113.

Laopodis, N. (2000) "Monetary Policy Implications of Volatility Linkages Among Long-Term Interest Rates," *Journal of Economics and Finance*, 24, 160-177.

Lee, J. (2002) "Federal Funds Rate Target and Interest Rate Volatility," *Journal of Economics and Business*, 54, 159-191.

Magendzo. I. (1997) "La Política Monetaria en Chile en la Década de los Noventa: Objetivos, Herramientas e Indicadores," *Serie Estudios Económicos* 41, Banco Central de Chile.

McConnell, M. and G. Perez Quiros. (2000) "Output Fluctuations in the United States: What Has Changed Since the Early 1980s?" In *Structural Change and Monetary Policy*. Proceedings of a conference held by the Federal Reserve Bank of San Francisco and the Stanford Institute for Economic Policy Research, 3–4 March 2000.

McKinnon, R. (1990) "Interest rate Volatility and Exchange Risk: New Rules for a Common Monetary Standard," *Contemporary Policy Issues*, 8, 1-17.

Morandé, F. (2002) "Nominalización de la Tasa de Política Monetaria: Debate y Consecuencias," *Cuadernos de Economía*, Pontificia Universidad Católica de Chile, 117, 239-52.

Nelson, D.B. (1991) "Conditional Heteroskedasticity in Asset Returns: A New Approach," *Econometrica*, 59, 347-370.

Nilsen, J. (1997) "Borrowed Reserves, FED Funds Rate Targets, and the Term Structure," EPRU Working Paper Series 97-04, Copenhagen Business School.

Srour, G. (2001) "Why Do Central Banks Smooth Interest Rates?" *Working Paper* 2001-17, Bank of Canada.

Summers, L. (1991) "Panel Discussion: Price Stability. How Should Long-Term Monetary Policy Be Determined?" *Journal of Money, Credit and Banking*, 23, 625–31.

Svenson, L. (1989) "Target Zones and Interest Rate Variability," *Centre for Economic Policy Research (CEPR) Discussion Paper* N° 372.

Thornton, D. (1996) "Does the Fed's New Policy of Immediate Disclosure Affect the Market?" *Federal Reserve Bank of St. Louis Review*, November/December, 77-88.

Watson, M.W. (1999) "Explaining the Increased Variability in Long Term Interest Rates," *Economic Quarterly*, Federal Reserve Bank of Richmond, Fall, 71-96.

Woodford, M. (1999) "Optimal Monetary Policy Inertia," *NBER Working Paper N° W 7261.*

Zúñiga, S. (1999) "Modelos de Tasas de Interés en Chile: Una Revisión," *Cuadernos de Economía*, Pontificia Universidad Católica de Chile, 36, 875-893.

Appendix: Calculation of the MPR

From the beginning of April 1996 the Central Bank of Chile only defined boundaries between which it wished the Tasa Interbancaria (TIB) to be situated, without specifying a unified objective rate. For this period, we calculated the MPR to have been an average between the rate on liquidity deposit and the rate of the 3rd interval of the credit line. Beginning on April 4, 1996, the monetary authority explicitly announced pushing the TIB to the 2nd and 3rd intervals of the liquidity line, that is, an average level of 7.25%. However, the TIB remained above this level at about 7.5%, and in the meeting of February 6, 1997 it was agreed to reduce this rate to 7.25%, making an explicit reference to a desired level for the TIB, which we interpreted as being the MPR at that time. In the following meeting (

April 11, 1997), expression was made that the TIB should be situated near 7.0%, which we took as the new MPR. Only beginning with the meeting held on February 3, 1998 did the Central Bank make specific reference to the MPR rather than the TIB (in that time MPR was termed Tasa de Instancia Monetaria).

Another operational aspect was that beginning in February 2000, the Monetary Policy meetings were convened monthly following a previously established schedule. Prior to this time the meetings had been sporadic. Table A1 shows all the changes made in the MPR by the Central Bank. In the period in which the MPR ruled (regimes 2 and 3), there were 33 total changes, including 26 decreases and 7 increases. In the second regime (real MPR), there were 20 decreases and 7 increases, while in the third regime (nominal MPR), there were six decreases and no increase.

Table A1 Changes Made in the MPR by the Central Bank

Meeting Day (new rate in effect on following working	TPM before change	TPM after the change	Date at which new rate goes into
26-05-1995	na	5.85	29-05-1995
23-06-1995	5.85	5.75	26-06-1995
05-12-1995	5.75	6.75	06-12-1995
04-04-1996	6.75	7.25	08-04-1996
11-04-1997	7.25	7.00	14-04-1997
05-06-1997	7.00	6.75	06-06-1997
02-09-1997	6.75	6.50	03-09-1997
08-01-1998	6.50	7.00	09-01-1998
03-02-1998	7.00	8.50	04-02-1998
16-09-1998	8.50	14.00	17-09-1998
13-10-1998	14.00	12.00	14-10-1998
02-11-1998	12.00	10.00	03-11-1998
24-11-1998	10.00	8.50	25-11-1998
22-12-1998	8.50	7.80	23-12-1998
26-01-1999	7.80	7.25	27-01-1999
09-03-1999	7.25	7.00	10-03-1999
06-04-1999	7.00	6.50	07-04-1999
06-05-1999	6.50	6.00	07-05-1999
01-06-1999	6.00	5.75	02-06-1999
21-06-1999	5.75	5.00	22-06-1999
27-01-2000	5.00	5.25	28-01-2000
16-03-2000	5.25	5.50	17-03-2000
28-08-2000	5.50	5.00	29-08-2000
18-01-2001	5.00	4.75	19-01-2001
20-02-2001	4.75	4.50	21-02-2001
02-03-2001	4.50	4.00	05-03-2001
10-04-2001	4.00	3.75	11-04-2001
12-06-2001	3.75	3.50	13-06-2001
08-08-2001	3.50	6.50	09-08-2001
10-01-2002	6.50	6.00	11-01-2002
19-02-2002	6.00	5.50	20-02-2002
12-03-2002	5.50	4.75	13-03-2002
09-05-2002	4.75	4.00	10-05-2002
11-07-2002	4.00	3.25	12-07-2002
08-08-2002	3.25	3.00	09-08-2002

Note: In August 2001 the MPR is nominalized, going from 3.5% (real annual) to 6.50% (nominal annual).

7 The Discrete Charm of Chilean Agriculture

Renato Aguilar and Jorge Dresdner

Introduction

Agriculture has played a central role in Chile's economic development during most of its history. After a relatively short period during the sixteenth and seventeenth centuries, when Chile was essentially a military outpost covering Peru's frontier, the country become a basically agricultural economy. The economic outcome depended heavily of a series of agricultural exporting cycles; first hides and fat, and then grains. It is not until the second half of the nineteenth and early twentieth centuries that mining became a significant economic and exporting activity. After the Second World War, together with general awareness about the problems of economic development, an attitude against agriculture became apparent. The sector was considered a major hindrance for development and its performance the main explanation for inflation, an endemic problem during the period.

On the other hand Chile's economy has shown a remarkable performance during the last few decades. From the middle of the 1980s and through most part of the 1990s, output grew at quite a high rate, with the unemployment rate falling to historically low levels. During this period, the inflation rate steadily decreased, attaining levels that could be favorably compared internationally. Finally, the foreign payments situation, a main source of concern in the previous period, was balanced. One of the most important driving forces behind this performance of Chile's economy was the exporting behavior (See, for example, Perry and Leipziger, 1999). A lot of attention was paid to mining and macroeconomic reforms during this period.

However, one of the most dynamical exporting sectors was the primary sector related to agricultural, cattle and forestry activities. We will give to this sector the general name of *agricultural sector*, even if some of these activities could formally be classified as industrial or in other sectors. One of the main achievements attained by the recent developments of Chile's economy has been to transform the agricultural sector from an initial situation of stagnation during the 1960s, characterized by a low productivity and a deficit in its small trade balance, to one of the most dynamical exporting sectors, highly diversified, aggressively engaged in international trade, and with a significant net contribution to the balance of payments. It is interesting to know how this change was made possible and especially the role played by economic policy in this process. The discussion and interpretation of this issue is the aim of this chapter.

In what follows, first we provide a short description of the historical evolution of the Chilean agriculture since World War II. Then, we sketch the development of economic policy towards the sector, suggesting the possible periods that can be identified. Thereafter, we will try to discuss and interpret the changes in the agricultural sector and their possible causes. A short section presenting a few econometric results follows. Finally, we will try to summarize the arguments and assess the role of economic policy in this change.

The Historical Evolution of Agriculture

Since World War II, agriculture has shown a secular trend to reduce its participation in total output. In 1940, the share of agriculture in total output was 10.2%, falling to 7.3% by 1960. This negative trend continued during the 1960s until 1973. However, the share of agriculture in total output recovered in the mid 1970s and although it has fluctuated since then, the ten-year average has been relative stable. This can be seen in table 7.1, where the information is presented as average figures for ten-year periods; there does not seem to be a clear tendency in any direction during the period covered by this study. In the same table it is possible to observe that during the 1960s and 1970s, agricultural output grew at a much lower rate.[1] The annual growth rate in the later decades at least doubled the growth rate in the previous decades.

Agricultural growth seems to have been affected by important structural and institutional changes. Land tenure changed drastically as a consequence of the land reforms started during the Alessandri administration (1958-1964), intensified by the Frei administration (1964-1970), and vigorously continued during the Allende administration (1970-

[1] The division of the period in decades is arbitrary from an analytical point of view. This division does not identify well the different relevant sub periods from an economic standpoint. Nonetheless, the result that is emphasized in the main text, namely that the performance of the agricultural sector improved in the later decades, is fully observable and robust to the selection of periods.

1973). To this we should add the "counter-reform" process implemented during the Dictatorship (1973-1989). During the period covered by this study farms and other productive agricultural units were capitalized, incorporated modern technology, as well as high-yield inputs. They became more efficient and export oriented. Labor productivity increased enormously and faster than in sectors in the rest of the economy. The general economic policy as well as the specific one aimed at the agricultural sector varied radically and non-monotonically. Finally, the country suffered large structural changes in the social and economic arena and important changes in the external situation that conditioned the agricultural development.[2]

Table 7.1 Share of Agricultural Product in GDP and Growth Rate in Chile 1960-1999, Period Averages (millions of 1995 pesos and percentages)

Period	GDP	Agricultural Output	Share (%)	Average Growth Rate
1960-1969	8,110,510	537,818	6.6	1.8
1970-1979	10,281,546	618,874	6.0	2.0
1980-1989	13,213,364	906,130	6.9	5.5
1990-1999	24,688,326	1,673,501	6.8	3.8

Source: Braun *et al.* (2000)

Table 7.2 Percentage of Land Tenure Structure in Chile, Selected Years

	1997		1976		1965	
Size (ha)	Units	Area	Units	Area	Units	Area
Less than 5	42.5	0.9	49.5	0.8	49.8	0.7
5-20	31.1	3.8	25.2	2.8	24.4	2.1
20-100	19.8	9.8	17.3	8.1	17.1	6.3
100-1000	5.9	18.1	7.0	21.5	7.5	18.2
1000 +	0.9	67.4	1.0	66.8	1.3	72.7

Source: Censos Agropecuarios 1965, 1976, 1997, INE.

One of the main consequences that these events had for the agricultural sector was the final eradication of the *Latifundio* system and the creation of a free land market (Jarvis, 1985). The structure of land tenure changed radically and a sector of medium and small size farms was created. As can readily be seen in table 7.2, the share of the largest units

[2] For an analysis of the changes that took place in the agricultural sector between the 1960s and the first half of the 1980s, see Jarvis (1985), Larrañaga (1991), Muñoz and Ortega (1987), Quiróz et al (1988). An analysis of the most recent period can be found in Errázuriz and Muchnik (1996).

declined between 1965 and 1997. In contrast, the medium unit's share of the total area increased in the same period.

Land use also changed; the so-called "traditional crops" (wheat, sugar beet, rice, etc.) reduced their relative share in total agricultural output. Even more, the total area used by these crops declined in absolute terms. In contrast, other uses of land, such as fruits, horticulture, wine and forestry, increased their share. It is possible to see in table 7.3 that between 1965 and 1997, the traditional crops area decreased in more than 424,000 hectares. On the other hand, in the same period, the forestry area increased by nearly 680,000 hectares. During the same period the fruit production area increased in more than 148,000 hectares, which amounts to an annual (average) growth rate of 4.6%. Moreover, the transformation process seemed to speed up as it can be seen by the comparison of the average annual growth rates of the different land uses between the periods 1965-1997 and 1976-1997.

Table 7.3 Evolution of Some Agricultural Activities in Chile, 1965-1997

Census year	Traditional crops (Hectares)	Fruit farming (Hectares)	Forestry (Hectares)
1965	1269046	85589	418800
1976	1180321	89488	627500
1997	844275	233973	1098500
Growth rate 65-97	-1.9%	4.6%	4.4%
Growth rate 76-97	-3.0%	8.7%	5.1%

Source: Census 1965, 1976, 1997, INE.

The agricultural sector's trade balance, traditionally in deficit, developed a quite significant surplus. Figure 7.1 shows the balance between exports and imports of agricultural origin between 1996 and 1988[3]. This was in equilibrium in 1978, and moreover, after 1983, it became consistently and significantly positive, reaching a surplus near 1.4 billion dollars in 1988. More recent data about the agricultural trade balance, though this information is not methodologically comparable because of inconsistent definitions, suggest that the agricultural trade surplus continues to be quite large. In 1997 the balance was about 1.218 billion dollars (Central Bank, 1999).

Summing up, Chilean agriculture underwent a deep transformation process from the 1960s onwards. This process generated a strong supply

[3] This balance includes manufactured goods based on agricultural inputs, such as paper and cellulose. Therefore, in strict terms, it does not represent the agricultural sector's trade balance. For the more recent years (1985-1998), however, it is possible to construct a proper agricultural trade balance.

response, especially in the exporting behavior of the sector. The interesting question remains: how did this come about?

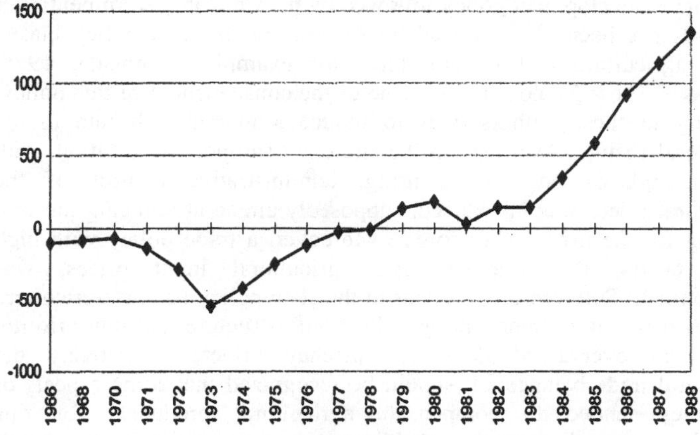

Sources: Ministry of Agriculture (1989), Central Bank and Customs Service.

Figure 7.1 Agricultural Trade Balance, Chile, 1966-1988 (million dollars)

Economic Policy and Agriculture

Before discussing economic policy and the agricultural sector in Chile during this period, it is convenient to put forward a couple of observations. First, we are using the term agricultural economic policy in this chapter in a broad sense. It does not only include the use of instruments specifically directed to the agricultural sector, but also general measures directed to the economy as a whole, but ones that do have a clear impact on agricultural development. Among these general policies we include macroeconomic policy, general trade policy and changes in the institutional setting. To make the distinction between what type of policy we are addressing we shall talk about **specific** and **general** policies, where specific policies are those particularly directed to the agricultural sector, and general are those policies not directed to any particular sector, but that do affect the development of the agricultural sector. Secondly, it is important to bear in mind that the performance of the agricultural sector does not depend only on economic policy, but also on circumstances beyond the control of the economic authorities, such as international events, and the behavior of the private sector. What economic policy can do is establish an adequate incentive framework for the private agents to take decisions consistent with the policy goals, subject to the external market restrictions.

Agriculture Before the 1960s

The general development policy followed by the Chilean government after the 1940s has been characterized by several authors as a policy biased against agriculture and exports (see, for example, Ahumada, 1958; Mamalakis, 1965; Muñoz, 1986). One of the consequences of this policy, according to these authors, was to induce a low growth rate in the agricultural sector. As a lead in the strategy of import substitution, with special emphasis on manufacturing, administrative control of the agricultural prices was introduced, supposedly aimed at reducing the cost of living for the urban labor force. Moreover, a trade policy with high import tariffs, that implied high agricultural input prices, was implemented. Furthermore, the bias in the state policy against agriculture meant also that investment in agriculture infrastructure had low priority. Finally, an overvalued domestic currency affected negatively the agricultural trade balance. It should be recognized that some aspects of the policy tended to compensate agricultural producers for this discrimination, such as credit subsidies, special tax regimes, etc. In all probability, it is also true that these aspects were insufficient to completely compensate for the higher costs or lower incomes implied by the general strategy followed by the authorities during that period.

An alternative interpretation of the stagnation of Chilean agriculture during this period argued that the prevailing land tenure system, strongly based on a Latifundium – Minifundium relationship, prevented the development of the sector. According to this approach, the prevailing ownership structure, with a class of large landlords lacking positive entrepreneurial characteristics, created imperfect factor markets and affected productivity growth and technical innovation in a negative way. These phenomena explained the very low response of agricultural supply to price incentives.[4] The corollary was, therefore, that in order to dynamize the sector it was necessary to go first through a land reform process modifying the land tenure structure and allowing for the creation or incorporation of price conscious producers.

Period 1960-1973: The Restless Agricultural Sector

Since the early 1960s, three different land reform processes were attempted in Chile.[5] A first timid land reform law was introduced during the Alessandri administration (1958-1964). This resulted in only small

---

[4] References and an analysis of this hypothesis are found in Dresdner (1990).

[5] It is not the aim of this chapter to evaluate the results of the land reform in Chile. Those interested in this subject can find two well-known evaluations in Barraclough and Fernández (1974) and Jarvis (1985). There exists also an interesting debate over the response that the agricultural output had during the Frei administration; see Quiroz *et al.* (1988), Jarvis (1990) and Barahona *et al.* (1990).

areas changing hands without significant effects for the performance of the sector, neither in the short nor in the long term. During the Frei administration (1964-1970), land reform largely increased its pace resulting in the expropriation of significant land areas. Land reform during this period included the organization of agricultural cooperatives and unions to manage the expropriated land, important resources were reallocated to agriculture through technical and financial aid to the reformed sector, and the application of government policies that improved agricultural prices. On the external side, the policies were mostly aimed to enhance trade through tariff reductions, to release and simplify the system of quantitative import controls, and an attempt to encourage exports. The macroeconomic policies prevailing during the period led to an increase in the real exchange rate (Ffrench Davis, 1974).

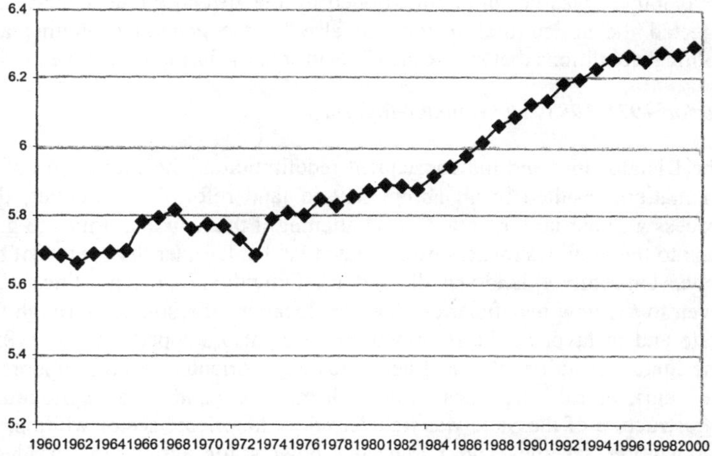

Source: Braun et al. (2000).

Figure 7.2 Logarithm of the Agricultural Output in Chile, 1960-2000

During the Allende administration (1970-1973), land reform was sustained and even accelerated. On the other hand, a return to price controls and a reversal in the process of trade opening was implemented (De Vylder, 1974). That is, macroeconomic policies were again unfavorable for the sector. It should be noted that the acceleration of the pace of land reform during this period took place mostly on the side of land expropriation while the reorganization of expropriated land lagged behind.

At the macroeconomic level, the real exchange rate increased during the 1960s, but then appreciated strongly during the first years of the 1970s. The real interest rate was low or even negative for most of the period. The relation between agricultural prices and non-agricultural prices, the internal terms of trade, remained relatively stable over the whole period.

The performance of the agricultural sector was very poor during this period (see figure 7.2). In the 1960-1970 period the output barely grew at a 1.9% annual rate. If the whole period is taken into account (1960-1973), the sector did not grow at all. The product share of total output fell from 7.5% in 1960 to 4.8% in 1973. However, due to a huge fall in employment in the sector, labor productivity grew in the whole period; for the period 1960-1970, productivity grew on average at a 3.6% per year. The share of agricultural exports in total exports fell steadily along the whole period reaching a lowest mark of 2% in 1973. Naturally, this whole development was not only conditioned by the special circumstances that affected the agricultural sector, but also by the general economic and political conditions that shook the Chilean society during these years.

Period 1973-1983: The Counter-Reform

The Dictatorship, and the consequent redefinition of the economic policy orientation, resulted in an abrupt halt in land reform. Thereafter, this process was partially reverted by an attempt of the new authorities to give back to the previous owners expropriated land still under the control of the State. Un-returned land was divided and individual ownership titles were given to the new beneficiaries. The reallocation of resources through the State and in favor of the reformed area was also stopped (Jarvis, 1985). The State institutions that had been created or oriented to give support to the agricultural activities were dismantled and the agricultural infrastructure of the State was transferred to the private sector while price stabilization schemes and purchasing powers for agricultural products were progressively eliminated.[6] The agricultural prices were left free and the subsidies to the sector were eliminated. The general policy was directed to the liberalization and free-working of the markets, and to encourage the role of the private sector in the economy. A process aimed at trade and financial opening was initiated. The use of specific policies oriented to favor specific economic sectors was ended as a general principle. Consequently, the establishment of general measures that would not discriminate among sectors, and with the active participation of private agents in a free and competitive framework, was encouraged. Thus, industrial, price and technology transfer policies became practically non-existent. Trade policy was aimed to attain general tariff reductions and

---

[6]In an exceptional way, the price target zones for wheat, sugar bet and oil plants were sustained until 1979 (Larrañaga, 1991).

equal protection for all goods. Finally, the policy of property rights stimulated the acquisition of individual land property.

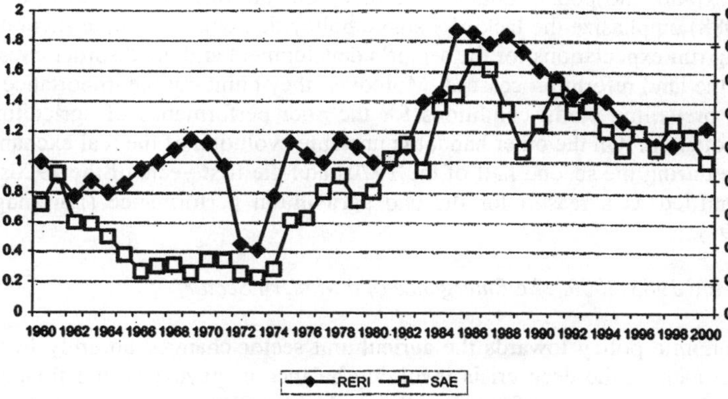

Note: The value of the RERI is read on the left hand axis and the value of the SAE on the right hand axis.
Source: Braun *et al.* (2000)

Figure 7.3 Real Exchange Rate Index (RERI) and Agricultural Share of Total Exports (SAE)

There exists a broad consensus in studies about the agricultural sector that the experiences of the 1960s and 1970s, although rich in different policies, did not imply a better performance in production (see Hurtado 1984; Jarvis 1990; Larrañaga 1991; Muñoz and Ortega 1987; Quiroz *et al.* 1988). The average annual growth rate for the period 1973-1983 was 4.3%. However, if one excludes the first year (1973), the average growth rate for the period falls to 2.2%. This can be explained considering the very special circumstances experienced by the economy in general and agriculture in particular and that meant a temporarily depressed agricultural output. On the other hand, agricultural production was almost unaffected by the recession that the economy experienced in 1975. Consequently, the share of agriculture in the GDP, increased radically during the first years of the period and fell in the second part. On the macroeconomic plane, the real exchange rate depreciated until 1978 and real interest rates became highly positive. The internal terms of trade became favorable for agricultural products. Consequently, agricultural exports grew extremely rapidly in this period at an average rate of 25.1% per year and the agricultural trade gap was closed. As can be observed in figure 7.3, displaying the real exchange rate on the left-hand axis and the share of agricultural exports on the right-hand axis, it seems that the performance of agricultural exports was highly conditioned by the real exchange rate.

Different reasons, of general as well as of specific character, are given to explain the poor production results. On the one hand, Quiroz et al. (1988) emphasize the lack of a stable policy that could generate favorable long run expectations for the sector's development and the disorder caused by the land reform processes.[7] Moreover, they point out the importance of the prevailing credit conditions for the poor performance of agricultural production. On the other hand, the unstable evolution of the real exchange rate during the second half of the 1970s and the first years of the 1980s is identified as a reason for the bad agricultural performance (Larrañaga, 1991).

Period 1983-2000. The Emergence of a Modern Sector

Economic policy towards the agricultural sector changed abruptly in the aftermath of the deep crisis involving balance of payments and financial issues with serious effects on the real side of the economy that was experienced by Chile in 1982. The agricultural sector was affected by the crisis, as were most of the other sectors of the economy, although the timing was somewhat different and the relative impact was much less severe. Agricultural product fell slightly during the period 1982-1983, while its share in GDP increased. While total production fell by 16%, agricultural production declined by only 2.8%. One of the consequences of the crisis, however, was that many agricultural firms went bankrupt and their lands were seized by the banks to be sold later to new owners, strongly reactivating the land market. In this sense, this economic crisis worked as a mechanism to reallocate land and other agricultural assets, probably eliminating less efficient agents.

The orientation of agricultural economic policy changed radically after 1983. From a non-selective and general policy, it was transformed to one with a selective policy directed to support specific activities. Many different factors lie behind this switch in the policy; the bad performance of the agricultural sector within the frame of non-selective policies might have been among the most important factors. Official documents and statements from that period recognized the specific nature of the sector, especially with regards to risk and uncertainty management. Among the measures that were taken, we can name price support schemes for various agricultural products, special tariffs for milk imports,[8] new subsidized

---

[7] This last point is discussed and challenged in Jarvis (1990).

[8] Later the government has employed special tariffs, minimum customs fees, and compensatory rights to reduce the most important fluctuations of the international prices for different agricultural products.

credit lines, technology transfer programs, and direct support to the production of sugar beet. (Larrañaga, 1991).

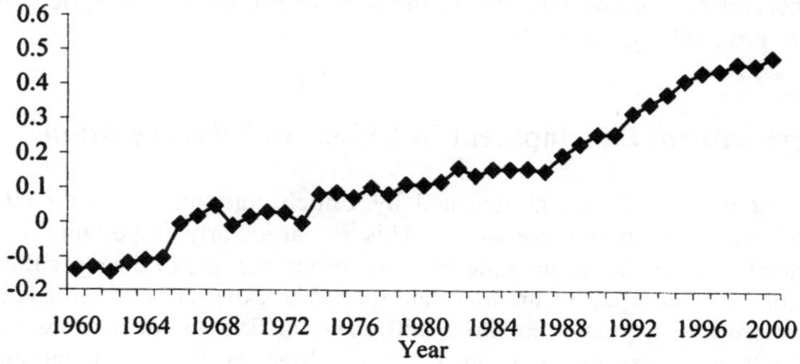

Source: Braun *et al.* (2000)

Figure 7.4 Log of Agricultural Average Labor Productivity, Chile 1960-2000

At the level of general policies, an adjustment program that was gradually implemented allowing the real exchange rate to improve, reducing the cost of credit, and increasing demand for non-tradable agricultural goods. The real exchange rate increased by 67% between 1982 and 1988. Moreover, protection against international competition was augmented by way of a general increase in tariffs. This set of measures seems to have contributed to the agricultural sector's takeoff. The process of land reallocation from traditional crops to fruit tree plantations was intensified and the forestry area was expanded considerably. Between 1983 and 1990, the sectorial output grew annually at an average rate of 8.2% but dropped to 3.9% in the following period, 1990-2000. Thus, the share of agriculture in total output increased up to 1990, and then began to fall again.[9] Actually, around 1990 the participation of agriculture in total production was similar to the share in the late 1950s. Agricultural exports grew at an annual rate of 15.3 percent between 1983 and 1990. Later, between 1990 and 2000, this growth rate was reduced to a yearly average of 5.6 percent. However, this rate is still quite high when compared to the overall performance of the economy. Thus, there was a vigorous expansion of exports of agricultural origin that,

[9] The evolution of the share of agricultural product in GDP, as well as the share of agriculture in total exports, showed this inverted U-shape during the period with the peak around 1990. This development is well synchronized with the real exchange rate, suggesting the importance of this price for agricultural development.

as noted earlier, generated a strong surplus in the agricultural trade balance. Finally, labor productivity grew very rapidly, (see figure 7.4) especially during the high growth period experienced by Chile's economy (1987-1997). During this period, the average growth rate in agricultural labor productivity was 2.9%.

Agricultural Development in Chile: An Interpretation

The notable development revealed by Chile's agricultural sector since 1983 deserves an interpretation. This is particularly important in the context of economic development theory, where the role of the agricultural sector still seems to play an important role. The experience of Chile could be interesting for many countries still trying to find an adequate role for agriculture in their development strategy. However, the interpretation of this kind of processes is complicated; a minimum conceptual framework of reference is needed. For this purpose, we distinguish between the more fundamental factors behind the change in agriculture and the more immediate factors. The fundamental factors are interwoven with the nature of societal change. Here, not only strict economic variables are analyzed, but also factors of a more sociological character. In contrast, the immediate factors of agricultural change are more amenable to a treatment using traditional econometric tools. Therefore, in this section we looked at the more basic factors, and in the next section at the more immediate ones.

The poor performance of Chile's agriculture up to the 1960s and 1970s was much debated, playing a central role in many explanations of the economic problems of that period. We use this debate as a starting point for our discussion of the development since the early 1980s. The interpretative literature about the sluggish development of the agricultural sector in Chile before the 1960s includes two main hypotheses. One of these hypotheses emphasized the lack of proper economic incentives for agricultural activities. According to this vision, the prevalence of low agricultural relative prices generated small returns and reduced the incentives to innovate. This hypothesis was termed *The Relative Price Hypothesis*. The other hypothesis stressed that an appropriate institutional setting to promote agricultural growth was missing. In this interpretation, the lack of an adequate land tenure system or the lack of a basic infrastructure did not create the necessary conditions for the development of entrepreneurial management in agriculture. This hypothesis was called *The Structuralist Hypothesis*. These hypotheses would allow us to predict rapid agricultural growth when the elements argued to be major causes of sluggish performance were eliminated. Let us try a preliminary evaluation of the predictive power of each of these hypotheses in explaining the development of Chilean agriculture from the 1980s. We will also try to complement them with other factors not taken into account in the traditional debate.

First, data on the period suggest that it is not correct to say that during the mid 1980s agricultural prices in general showed a more favorable development that in other periods. It would have been more accurate to say that relative agricultural prices were more stable in the mid 1980s than in previous periods (see table 7.4). In fact, after 1983 agricultural prices did not grow relative to general prices. On the other hand, different variability indicators show that prices were more stable than in previous periods. Thus, uncertainty as measured by relative price variability was lower after the early 1980s.

Table 7.4 Domestic Terms of Trade for Agriculture by Periods

Period	Growth rate	Coefficient of Variation	Variance
1960-1973	-0.073	0.180	0.039
1974-1982	0.049	0.208	0.031
1983-2000	0.002	0.082	0.006

Notes: Annual average continuous growth rate.
Source: Own estimations.

On the other hand, the real exchange rate did increase strongly during the 1980s, and it seems that the exporting performance of the agricultural sector is more strongly tied to this variable than is the case for other sectors. In this sense, it seems that the agricultural rate of return has a stronger dependency on relative input costs than on the internal terms of trade (see figure 7.5). This rapid development during the 1980s clearly contrasts with the development during the 1990s, where the relative agricultural prices did remain stable, but the real exchange rate tended to fall. The external performance of the agricultural sector during the 1990s, although still good, was much worse than during the 1980s. Moreover, as Quiroz et al. (1988) emphasize, agricultural prices were favorable also during the 1970s, and for that matter also during some years during the 1960s. Nonetheless, the supply response to these prices was very low.

The apparent lack of response of agricultural output during the 1970s, as compared with the strong response observed in the subsequent period, has been a matter of debate. The relevant literature includes opinions arguing that additional factors were active and neutralized the positive effect of favorable prices (see Quiroz *et al.*, 1988). These factors were, according to these authors, the slow response of the reformed sector as a consequence of lack of experience and the reduction of State technical assistance and credit; the high cost of credit during this period, and finally the absence of economic stability, that affected economic expectations and inhibited new investments in the sector. Hurtado (1984) provides a similar interpretation. He points out that the productive deterioration of the sector as a consequence of the land reform and counter-reform; the high interest rates that hindered productive adaptation and innovation; and the short period of analysis to observe the long run effects were the factors that explained the poor productive performance during the 1970s.

Source: Braun *et al.* (2000).

Figure 7.5 Domestic Terms of Trade in Chile, 1960-2000

One should remember that the effects of land reform on land reallocation at that time were already present. In effect, even if the Dictatorship attempted, at least partially, to reverse the land distribution to pre-reform situation, this attempt was not really successful. An efficient land market was created, facilitating an enormous amount of land reallocation. This generated a large change in the structure of land tenure, marking the end of the great latifundia and the upsurge of a new entrepreneurial class in the agricultural sector, with plenty of medium and small sized farms (see table 7.2). These new farms were also fundamentally "outward looking" (Muñoz and Ortega, 1987).

The discussion above leads to a simple conclusion; it seems unlikely that the Relative Price Hypothesis alone could be enough to explain the rapid development of the agriculture sector since the early 1980s. Adequate incentives might have been important, but incentives in the form of favorable relative prices are not enough to explain the observed results.

On the other hand, during the 1980s, land reform and its effects on the allocation of land had already taken place. In fact, most of land reallocation took place during the 1960s and 1970s, although the land market had a new and important spell of high activity as a consequence of the crisis in 1982. It is difficult to properly assess the role that institutional changes had in the takeoff of Chile's agricultural sector. The analysis of the causal links between changes in institutions and changes in economic variables such as output and exports lacks both a well-developed theoretical framework and a sound empirical basis. However, there is no doubt that the large changes that took place in agricultural development could have been hindered, if not stopped, by the lack of an efficient and active land market. This market was created as a consequence of previous land reform and counter-reform.

Available studies suggest that important changes in the social composition of farm managers occurred during the 1970s and 1980s. Many farm managers came from other sectors of activity, especially from manufacturing, and moved into agricultural business (see, for example, Cruz, 1988). These managers had a more entrepreneurial and innovative background and thus they had a profound impact on technology choice and the organizational aspects of economic activity in the agricultural sector. Also during this period, an important group of people with university education bought land and entered the sector. For this group, farming was mostly a secondary activity, but they confronted production from a more developed technological perspective (see Cruz, 1988). This process embracing social and economic changes in agriculture reached a high point during the crisis of 1982-1983. At this point in time, we observed an important new reallocation of land and the entrance of new farmers and farm managers.

Notwithstanding our discussion above, the explanation of growth and development in Chile's agriculture cannot be complete unless we consider other aspects, not included in the basic hypotheses. One aspect is the presence in Chile's agriculture of a group of qualified workers and farmers with a long experience in production and acquainted with modern technology. This group was the result of long term programs and policies oriented to education and technology transfer and it played a leading role in the development of agricultural exports. For example, the development of fruit plantations and even the early development of exports in this branch can be dated at least back to the 1960s. State-driven programs for technical and credit assistance succeeded in creating an important group of skilled farmers and producers with enough knowledge and experience in modern agriculture.

Secondly, already in the 1960s the government was aware that the possibilities to expand agricultural exports were limited by technological constraints, such as lack of warehouse capacity and transportation, and disease and plague control. At the end of that decade, the first packing plants and cold storage warehouses were built with help from the State; this initiative represented a critical capital stock for the producers with export expectations. These capital goods were later leased out and transferred to the new emergent entrepreneurial agricultural class after the land counter-reform and when the State infrastructure for direct intervention in agriculture was dismantled. This infrastructure was the technological base that made possible the start of massive exports of agricultural products.

Thirdly, it is evident that the new economic framework that emerged after the 1982-1983 crisis also contributed to the change in agricultural development. In particular, the opening of the external sector exposed agricultural producers to many good business possibilities in international markets. The literature accepts the idea that at least after the 1982-1983 crisis, returns to agricultural export goods was much higher than for traditional products with the result that they attracted investors and managers from other sectors of the economy, and helped to change the social composition of agricultural managers and farmers. Moreover, trade liberalization led to administrative simplifications, cheaper imported inputs, and lower costs for technology incorporation, helping and accelerating the technological development of this sector.

Finally, the working of the land market tended to eliminate the less efficient producers. The price of land, especially in those zones where exports goods were produced, increased substantially, generating an enormous opportunity cost for idle or inefficiently cultivated land. In other words, the Latifundia tended to disappear, not only because of the direct effects of the land reforms and counter-reform, but also because of the more efficient workings of the land market.

Our main conclusion is that neither of the two basic hypotheses on the sluggish development in Chile's agriculture discussed above is capable, by itself, of providing a reasonable explanation of the fundamental aspects of the agricultural take off that took place in the early 1980s. An eclectic view, to which we subscribe, is that favorable prices are important for good agricultural performance, but not enough. Additionally, an adequate incentive structure is required that generates favorable conditions for agricultural production, with a manageable degree of uncertainty to promote investment. In this incentive scheme, the existence of an efficient land reallocation mechanism is of primary importance to generate productive dynamism. Another element that emerges clearly in this account is the necessity of a balanced and growth promoting macroeconomic policy. Further, the State's active support in such matters as subsidies to promote activities (forestry activities, for example), provision of public investment in infrastructure (roads and irrigation) and technical assistance, has proven to be crucial. Finally, the presence of an innovative and entrepreneurial class, and the existence of a group of professional farmers and managers with high technical skills, seems to be an indispensable ingredient.

Testing a Few Hypotheses

Our analysis of Chile's agriculture, focused on the last half century, allows us to raise several hypotheses about the main immediate factors explaining its development. Here we try to test four of them. First, we must mention that up to the early 1970s, the discussion was dominated by the view that the problems of the agriculture were mostly a consequence of structural problems, expressed in a rather skewed structure of land tenure. These problems were solved by strong shocks during the Frei government, mostly during the Allende regime, but also at the beginning of the dictatorship. Thus, the nature of the different land reforms and contra-reforms should be reflected in clearly differentiated periods in the recent economic history of Chile's agriculture. Secondly, particularly in the late 1980s and 1990s, agricultural development seems to be strongly dependent on the general macroeconomic environment and domestic policies, including policies directly oriented to favor this sector. Thirdly, the linkage with the external sector must have played an important but varying role in the development of Chile's agriculture. We could assume that this relationship became stronger with the increasing opening of the economy. Finally, one can wonder if the agricultural sector did contribute positively to the remarkable economic development observed in the country during the last few decades. Alternatively, one can speculate whether agriculture was a hindrance or deadweight on the country's general economic growth. From a formal point of view we are interested in the main direction of causality.

It is difficult to construct empirical tests of these hypotheses. The first difficulty is the paucity of the databases of macroeconomic data related to agriculture. The nature of the productive cycle of agriculture suggests that we should collect time series of annual data. Shorter periods, such as quarterly or monthly data, would imply too arbitrary definitions in most cases. Thus, our database contains only 41 annual observations of a number of macroeconomic variables, covering the period 1960-2000. It is possible to compile longer series, but they will include periods where agriculture, the economy, and the external environment are too different. On the other hand, we need to use statistical methods and tests where only the large-sample properties are known. Thus, our statistical results must be considered from this point of view. They are mostly large-sample results obtained with the help of inherently small samples.

Our second difficulty is that our main hypotheses refer to variables that are difficult to quantify and capture in a database. Thus, our models contain proxies of the variables that we really want to discuss, generating a significant error of measurement in the variables of the model, and possibly leading to an underestimation of the standard errors of the estimates. The consequences for our inferences are obvious.

Finally, our macroeconomic variables, both the national and the sectorial ones, can be rather ill behaved. In fact, our variables are non-stationary. However, we found significant evidence suggesting that the first differences could be stationary. That is, we can assume that our variables are integrated of order one. Results of an Augmented Dickey-Fuller test are presented in the Appendix. This suggests that a non-spurious regression could be estimated for the first differences of these variables. However, we ruled out this possibility because such a model fails to capture long-term relationships and effects, which are our main aim. It was, then, only natural to turn our attention to the Error Correction Model. This specification has the important advantage of allowing us to capture both short- and long-run effects. Unfortunately, many of these variables were ill-behaved in terms of cointegration. The data suggested that only a few long-run relationships could be identified. Thus, we finally estimated the following Error Correction Model:

$$\Delta GDG_t = \delta_1 \Delta GDT_t + \delta_2 \Delta RXR_t - \lambda\left(GDG_{t-1} - \beta_0 - \beta_1 GDT_{t-1} - \beta_2 RXR_{t-1}\right) + \varepsilon_t. \qquad (7.1)$$

In this specification variable *GDG* stands for the GDP of agriculture, which we assume to be a measure of the overall performance of the sector. Variable *GDT,* the national GDP, would capture the general macroeconomic and policy environment, as well as some kind of a pull from the domestic market. Finally, we try to capture the effect of the external environment including the real exchange rate *RXR*. Equation (7.1) is much suited to our purposes as the delta-parameters capture the short-run effects and the beta-parameters capture the long-run effects. However, we cannot estimate this equation directly; instead we estimated:

$$\Delta GDG_t = \alpha_0 + \delta_1 \Delta GDT_t + \delta_2 \Delta RXR_t + \alpha_1 GDG_{t-1} + \alpha_2 GDT_{t-1} + \alpha_3 RXR_{t-1} + \varepsilon_t. \qquad (7.2)$$

Then, we used the estimates of the alpha-parameters to recover the lambda- and beta-parameters. Table 7.5 shows the results of the estimation of equation (7.2). Notice that our estimations include a first-order autoregressive structure for the stochastic disturbance, because of the inclusion of lagged dependent variables among the regressors. The matrix of variances and covariances of the estimates was calculated using the White estimator. This model was estimated for the logarithms of the variables, in order to capture possible non-linearities and to be able to read the coefficients directly as elasticities.

Table 7.5 Estimation of Equation (7.2) for the Whole Sample

Variables	Coefficient	Standard Error	t	$P>\|t\|$
GDP national, 1st diff.	0.637892	0.197632	3.228	0.0030
Real exchange rate, 1st diff.	0.238800	0.050744	4.706	0.0000
GDP agriculture, 1 lag	-0.263736	0.109117	-2.417	0.0210
GDP national, 1 lag	0.250561	0.105000	2.386	0.0230
Real exchange rate, 1 lag	0.093465	0.034066	2.744	0.0100
Constant	-1.117536	0.396015	-2.822	0.0080
rho	-0.089044			
Observations	40			
F-statistic			12.79	0.0000
R^2	0.5104			

All the coefficients were estimated with a level of significance better than three percent. Table 7.5 gives us directly the short-run elasticities as 0.637892 and 0.238800. Both coefficients have the expected sign and were estimated with a level of statistical significance better than one percent. These results basically indicate that both internal and external forces are important for explaining the development of agricultural output. Notice that the elasticity of agricultural output with respect to national output seems to be larger than the elasticity with respect to the real exchange rate. This hypothesis was tested and the empirical evidence supports it with a significance level better than two percent.

We cannot read the long-run parameters beta from this table. Thus, table 7.6 recovers these parameters. Note that because the relationship between these long-run parameters and the parameters actually estimated is non-linear we use a Wald test statistic, *F*-distributed with 1 and 34 degrees of freedom.

Table 7.6 Long-Run Parameters: The Whole Sample

	Parameter	F(1, 34)	Prob > F
Constant	-4.237324	55.5200	0.0000
GDP national	0.950043	244.5000	0.0000
Real exchange rate	0.354388	7.2900	0.0107
Different parameters[1]	0.595655	13.7700	0.0007

[1] This is a test where the null hypothesis is the equality of the last two parameters.

All the parameters were estimated at a level of significance about 1% or better. Notice that once again, the long-run elasticity of agricultural output with respect to national output is larger than the corresponding elasticity with respect to the real exchange rate. It is important to note that the long-run elasticities are larger than the corresponding short-run elasticities.

Previously, we have introduced the idea that changes of structure, mainly associated to changes in the land tenure system, could be an important factor explaining the performance of the agricultural sector. Consequently, we divided our sample in two periods; one of them for 1960-1975 and the other one for 1976-2000. The breaking point was chosen considering the start of the Dictatorship, the end of the land reforms and counter-reform. We can assume that the main issue differencing between both periods is the existence of two different land markets, with the second one becoming institutionalized after 1975. Table 7.7 shows the estimates for both the short-run and the long-run elasticities.

Not surprisingly, both sub-samples estimate the short-run elasticities with a lower level of significance than the corresponding exercise with the whole sample. It is important to notice that the sample for the first period did not allow us to estimate the short-run elasticity with respect to the national output with a reasonable level of significance. On the other hand, the short-run elasticity with respect to the exchange rate is still significant at a level better than one percent. These two short-run elasticities cannot be considered different at any reasonable level of significance. For the period 1976-200 the situation is the opposite. We could estimate the parameter corresponding to national output as significant at a level better than 2%, while the parameter corresponding to exchange rate is quite small and not different from zero at any reasonable level of significance. Not surprisingly, these parameters appear as different with a rather acceptable level of significance.

Table 7.7 Short- and Long-Run Elasticities, Two Periods

Variables	Parameters	test	Prob.
Period 1960-1975			
GDP national, short-run	0.452840	1.19	0.2640
Real exchange rate, short-run	0.268899	3.86	0.0040
Different parameters[1]	0.183941	0.48	0.3199
Constant, long-run	-2.816120	25.96	0.0006
GDP national, long-run	0.601513	16.04	0.0031
Real exchange rate, long-run	0.205369	4.57	0.0612
Different parameters[1]	0.396143	5.36	0.0458
Period 1976-2000			
GDP national, short-run	0.284338	2.60	0.0170
Real exchange rate, short-run	-0.004450	-0.07	0.9450
Different parameters[1]	0.288786	3.53	0.0011
Constant, long-run	-6.761960	42.89	0.0000
GDP national, long-run	0.878728	65.42	0.0000
Real exchange rate, long-run	0.939149	11.90	0.0027
Different parameters[1]	-0.060420	0.03	0.8672
Structural change[2]		151.72	0.0000

[1] This is a test where the null hypothesis is the equality of the last two parameters.
[2] Likelihood ratio test.

We estimated the long-run elasticities with satisfactory levels of statistical significance in both periods. It is important to see how the pattern of long-term elasticities changes drastically between both periods. During the first period (1960-1975), the domestic effect is larger than the external effect, and this difference is significant at a level better than 5 percent. However, in the second period, the coefficient affecting the exchange rate is larger than the coefficient affecting domestic output. These parameters seem to be different with significance level of about 4.5 percent. The data do not provide evidence of a significant difference between these two parameters in the second period. Much in accordance with these results, a likelihood ratio test of structural change turns out to be highly significant.

Alternatively, we broke down our sample into three sub-samples. The first one covers the period 1960-1973, the second one covers the period 1973-1985, and the last one covers the period 1986-2000. The first breaking point coincides with the beginning of the dictatorship and the second one with the deep change in the orientation of economic policy that occurred after the crisis in 1982. Table 7.8 shows the results of our estimation for these periods.

Table 7.8 Short- and Long-run Elasticities, Three Periods

Variables	Parameters	test	Prob.
Period 1960-1973			
GDP national, short-run	1.171191	1.55	0.166
Real exchange rate, short-run	0.153382	2.27	0.057
Different parameters[1]	1.017809	1.31	0.115
Constant, long-run	-2.404190	9.86	0.0164
GDP national, long-run	0.596813	5.56	0.0505
Real exchange rate, long-run	0.100790	0.41	0.5403
Different parameters[1]	0.496023	2.27	0.1757
Period 1974-1985			
GDP national, short-run	0.314449	3.04	0.0230
Real exchange rate, short-run	0.230313	3.83	0.0090
Different parameters[1]	0.084136	0.82	0.2224
Constant, long-run	0.503532	54.25	0.0003
GDP national, long-run	0.283816	115.39	0.0000
Real exchange rate, long-run	0.219716	9.29	0.0226
Different parameters[1]	0.314449	3.04	0.0230
Period 1986-2000			
GDP national, short-run	0.598194	1.77	0.110
Real exchange rate, short-run	0.270683	1.24	0.247
Different parameters[1]	0.327511	1.00	0.172
Constant, long-run	-14.974882	4.56	0.062
GDP national, long-run	1.687848	11.00	0.009
Real exchange rate, long-run	2.075410	3.34	0.101
Different parameters[1]	-0.387562	0.30	0.595
Structural change[2]		159.10	0.0000

[1] This is a test where the null hypothesis is the equality of the last two parameters.
[2] Likelihood ratio test.

Once again, it is difficult to estimate all the short-run parameters with satisfactory levels of statistical significance in all the periods. However, in the second period (1974-1985), both parameters were estimated with significance better than 2.5%. Note that these short-run parameters are close in size to the long-run parameters, suggesting that during these periods, a short-term horizon is important for the economic agents. The structural changes and the differentiated behavior are still clear in the results for the long-run parameters. Not surprisingly, we could test the structural change with an important level of significance. Notice that the long-run parameters are quite small during the period 1974-1985 reflecting a period with deep crises, insecurity, and a drastic reallocation of land, both in terms of ownership and use. On the other hand, in the latter period, 1986-2000, these long-run parameters become surprisingly large, reflecting a more mature but dynamic sector. This division of our sample is also successful in capturing the change in the relative importance of domestic and external factors in the long-run.

Table 7.9 Testing Granger Causality

	Test	Probability
From GDP agriculture to GDP total	5.0596	0.0021
From GDP total to GDP agriculture	1.2277	0.3301
Agriculture, exports to output	2.4888	0.0544
Agriculture, output to exports	0.8554	0.5421

Note: We considered autoregressive models with 6 lags.

Finally, we addressed the issue of the dynamic relationship between sectoral output and national output, as well as the issue of sectoral exports and sectoral output. Granger causality tests are presented in table 7.9.

These results suggest that agriculture provided, especially during the last two decades, a net positive contribution to national output. This seems to be a more important effect than the possible pull that increasing national output might have on agricultural output. On the other hand, it seems that exports are an important factor in explaining this sector's output, rather than the other way around. These results, while not strong from a statistical point of view, are coherent with our previous econometric results, and with a number of sectorial indicators such as average labor productivity and exports.

Summing up the results, we can say that there is empirical evidence supporting most of the hypothesis presented in this study. The strong empirical evidence suggesting the existence of clearly differentiated periods supports the idea that land reforms and counter-reform were a crucial element explaining the behavior of Chile's agriculture. Both the external environment as well as the domestic environment (especially in terms of policies), seem to have played an important role. However, the relative importance of these factors changed over time, with the external factors becoming more important in latter periods.

Conclusions

After these few reflections about the development and performance of Chile's agriculture, we can present some conclusions. Many of them reflect a broad consensus among the analysts that have studied this sector.

In a few cases, we were able to find some support in the empirical data, while additional research remains to be completed.

The main conclusion is that the deep structural changes that took place at the end of the 1960s and beginning of the 1970s were critical for enabling a positive sectorial behavior in later years. In this sense, the consequences of the crisis of 1982 contributed to the modernization and efficiency of the sector, mainly through a reactivation of the land market. We have found some empirical evidence supporting this hypothesis. However, the structural changes during this period were far more complex than a change in the structure of land tenure. For example, one should consider the maturation of a long-term and massive educational effort that can be dated back to the 1930s during the Aguirre Cerda administration. These investments changed the educational profile not only of the rural population, but also of Chile's population as a whole. We can also mention many efforts directed towards the introduction and improvement of technology in the rural areas, through institutions such as CORFO, SAG and INDAP. Albeit with low levels of efficiency and sometimes in an inconsistent manner, these institutions largely contributed to basically change the technological base of Chile's agriculture.

Domestic policies and the general domestic macroeconomic environment also seem to be determinant for the performance of the agriculture. We have also found some empirical support for this hypothesis. The importance of these factors seems to change with time; unfortunately, we are not able to uncover the empirical basis that would enable identification of the relative importance of general and specific policies. However, secondary evidence seems to favor the hypothesis that the general policies and general macroeconomic environment have been more important, at least in the medium and long run.

During the period following the crisis of the early 1980s, the real exchange rate seems to be an important factor to explain the performance of agriculture. We present here some empirical evidence supporting this hypothesis. In some sense, the previous period can be seen as a preliminary period, dominated by necessary structural changes. The crisis induced the last act of the structural change and the restoration of a reasonable real exchange rate, correcting the relative prices, and putting Chile's agriculture firmly towards exports and a strong engagement in trade.

Finally, supported by some empirical evidence, we were able to promote the idea that agriculture made a net contribution to the rapid development of Chile's economy. This is not surprising, when we observe that Chile's economy is quite open, strongly relying on trade, and with an agricultural sector that has performed better than the other sectors of the economy.

References

Ahumada, J. (1958) *En Vez de la Miseria,* Santiago, Editorial del Pacífico.

Banco Central de Chile (1999) "*Indicadores de Comercio Exterior,*" (March), Santiago.

Barahona, P., J. Quiroz and A. Valdés (1990) "Respuesta al Comentario del Profesor Lovell, S. Jarvis," *Cuadernos de Economía*, 27, 115-117.

Barraclough, S, and J. Fernández (1974) *Diagnóstico de la Reforma Agraria en Chile,* México D.F., Ed. Siglo XXI.

Braun, J., M. Braun, I. Briones, J. Díaz, R.Luders, and G. Wagner (2000) "Economía Chilena 1810-1995 Estadísticas Históricas,", *Documento de Trabajo* N° 187, Instituto de Economía, Pontificia Universidad Católica de Chile.

Cruz, J.M. (1988) "La Fruticultura de Exportación Una Experiencia de Desarrollo Empresarial," *Colección Estudios CIEPLAN,* 25, 79-114.

De Vylder, S (1974) *Chile 1970-73. The Political Economy of the Rise and Fall of the Unidad Popular,* Stockholm, Unga Filosofers.

Dresdner, J. (1989) "The Structuralist Theory of Inflation and Structural Inflation in Chile, 1950-1972 The Lagging Food Supply Hypothesis Revisited," *Acta Universitatis Uppsaliensis*, Studia Oeconomica Upsaliensia 19, Uppsala.

Errázuriz, F. and E. Muchnik (1996) "Visión Crítica de la Agricultura Chilena y sus Problemas,", *Estudios Públicos*, 61, 141-88.

Ffrench-Davis, R. (1973) *Políticas Económicas en Chile, 1952-1970*, Santiago, Ed. Nueva Universidad.

Hurtado, H. (1984) *"Política Agraria y Desarrollo Sectorial en Chile"* Programa Postgrado en Economía Agraria, Universidad Católica, Santiago.

Instituto Nacional de Estadísticas (INE) (1997) "*VI Censo Nacional Agropecuario. Principales Resultados Un Anticipo*", (October), Santiago.

Jarvis, L. (1985) *Chilean Agriculture under Military Rule,* Institute of International Studies, University of California Berkeley.

Jarvis, L (1990) "Reformas de las Políticas Económicas de la Agricultura Chilena y la Respuesta de la Oferta Agregada Otro Punto de Vista," *Cuadernos de Economía,* 27, 103-114.

Larrañaga, O. (1991) "*Ajuste Macroeconómico, Agricultura y Pobreza Rural Chile en los Ochenta*" Programa de Postgrado ILADES-Georgetown, Serie Investigación I-36, Santiago.

Mamalakis, Markos (1965) "Public Policy and Sectoral Development A Case Study of Chile 1940-1958." In M. Mamalakis and L. Reynolds (eds.) *Essays on the Chilean Economy*, Homewood, IL., Richard D Irwin Inc.

Muñoz, O. (1986) "*Chile y su Industrialización,*" Santiago, CIEPLAN.

Muñoz, O. and H. Ortega (1987) "*La Agricultura Chilena y la Política Económica 1974-86*" Notas Técnicas 98 (March), CIEPLAN, Santiago.

Perry, G. and D. Leipziger (1999) "Chile. Recent "Policy Lessons and Emerging Challenges", *World Bank Institute Development Studies*, The World Bank, Washington D.C.

Quiroz, J., P. Barahona and A. Valdés (1988) "Reformas Económicas en la Agricultura y Respuesta de la Producción Agregada Chile 1960-1987," *Cuadernos de Economía*, 25, 391-403.

Appendix: Unit Root Results of the Augmented Dickey-Fuller Test on Selected Variables

Table A.1 Variables in Levels, 40 Observations

	AR(1)	Constant	Constant + trend	Constant + trend + 1 lag
GDP total	6.226	3.386	0.491	-0.129
GDP agriculture	4.661	2.060	-1.031	-0.950
Real exchange	-0.207	-1.500	-1.722	-2.492
Domestic terms of trade	-0.207	-1.500	-1.722	-2.492
Total exports	3.023	1.549	-0.955	-0.934
Agricultural exports	2.855	1.242	-1.597	-1.740
1% Critical Value	-2.636	-3.648	-4.242	-4.251
5% Critical Value	-1.950	-2.958	-3.540	-3.544
10% Critical Value	-1.606	-2.612	-3.204	-3.206

Table A.2 Variables in First Differences, 39 Observations

	AR(1)	Constant	Constant + trend	Constant + trend + 1 lag
GDP total	-2.598	-3.567	-4.458	-3.579
GDP agriculture	-4.241	-5.706	-6.734	-3.620
Real exchange	-4.626	-4.575	-4.528	-4.565
Domestic terms of trade	-4.626	-4.575	-4.528	-4.565
Total exports	-4.757	-5.558	-6.199	-5.182
Agricultural exports	-4.392	-5.093	-5.531	-4.948
1% Critical Value	-2.638	-3.655	-4.251	-4.260
5% Critical Value	-1.950	-2.961	-3.544	-3.548
10% Critical Value	-1.606	-2.613	-3.206	-3.209

Table A.3 Variables in Logarithms, 40 Observations

	AR(1)	Constant	Constant + trend	Constant + trend + 1 lag
GDP total	4.585	0.797	-0.875	-1.359
GDP agriculture	-0.575	0.538	-1.940	-1.749
Real exchange	0.041	-1.902	-2.343	-3.462
Domestic terms of trade	0.041	-1.902	-2.343	-3.462
Total exports	1.701	-0.507	-3.581	-4.013
Agricultural exports	-2.121	-0.125	-1.870	-2.844
1% Critical Value	-2.636	-3.648	-4.242	-4.251
5% Critical Value	-1.950	-2.958	-3.540	-3.544
10% Critical Value	-1.606	-2.612	-3.204	-3.206

Table A.4 Variables in First Differences of Logarithms, 39 Observations

	AR(1)	Constant	Constant + trend	Constant + trend + 1 lag
GDP total	-3.507	-4.631	-4.717	-3.799
GDP agriculture	-5.237	-6.497	-6.591	-4.561
Real exchange	-4.701	-4.645	-4.586	-5.944
Domestic terms of trade	-4.701	-4.645	-4.586	-5.944
Total exports	-5.082	-6.389	-6.309	-5.767
Agricultural exports	-3.885	-4.350	-4.319	-4.148
1% Critical Value	-2.638	-3.655	-4.251	-4.260
5% Critical Value	-1.950	-2.961	-3.544	-3.548
10% Critical Value	-1.606	-2.613	-3.206	-3.209

Part III

Regional Analysis

8 Regional Growth and Convergence in Chile 1960-1998: The Role of Public and Foreign Direct Investment

Patricio Aroca, Mariano Bosch Mossi and Geoffrey J.D. Hewings

Introduction

The purpose of this chapter is to re-examine the convergence process in Chile, utilizing more recent data and focusing on the role of public (domestic) and foreign direct investment in shaping the welfare levels across regions. There have been many prior studies focusing on the problem of regional convergence in Chile. Morandé *et al.* (1996) argue that some evidence is found to support regional GDP/pc absolute convergence in Barro-style estimations for the period 1960-1992. Here, they estimated that convergence occurred at an annual rate of 1.2%. However, the same authors find that using time series analysis results raises doubts about the convergence properties derived from their equation system. Fuentes (1996) obtains similar results postulating an annual convergence rate of 1.3%; in addition, he also estimated convergence rates with income per capita data, and found this to be much higher, of the order of 7.4% per annum.

However, the vast majority of the economic literature about regional convergence has considered the regions in isolation, regardless of their geographical location and potential interregional linkages. Rey and Montouri (1999) argue that of the theoretical mechanisms that are said to drive regional convergence, such as technological diffusion, factor mobility and transfer of payments, most of these have explicit geographical components. However, the role of spatial effects in convergence analysis has been widely ignored.

There are several theoretical contributions that support the idea that space may play an important role on the process of regional development. For example, Krugman (1991), Puga (1998), Benabou (1993), Durlauf (1996) and Quah (1999) argue that under certain sets of circumstances, economic development may lead to spatial concentrations of wealth and production. For example, Krugman (1991) and Puga (1998) maintain that interregional migration may provoke the existence of center-periphery schemes where the productive industry is concentrated in a few regions. At a different spatial scale, Benabou (1993) and Durlauf (1996) model the existing relationship between neighborhood choice, education performance and productivity within a city. The spatial concentrations, in this case, are generated by the associated externalities to human capital accumulation.

Recently, some authors such as Lopez-Bazo *et al.* (1999), Rey and Montouri (1999), Fingleton (1999), Pons-Novell and Viladecans-Marsal, (1999) and Magalhães *et al.* (2005), have criticized the use of traditional methods employed in convergence analysis. From their point of view, the use of spatially referenced data, like the GDP per capita of regions or countries, should not be overlooked when estimating convergence equations. Their finding of strong spatial patterns of income and productivity for different samples seems to support this claim. Lopez-Bazo, *et al.* (1999) state that these patterns may be due to the territorial location of productive factors, their mobility across adjacent regions, interregional commerce, and, in summary, to any possible relationship between the spatial units analyzed.

Quah (1996, 1997) follows a different empirical approach to study these issues. Quah explicitly introduces the influence of space in the study of regional dynamics. In Quah (1996), he makes use of traditional Markov chain tools in the comparisons of the influence of national and spatial factors on the welfare of European regions. He concludes that the spatial factors are more important than the national ones.

Drawing on these recent methodological developments, the present paper sheds additional light on the process of economic growth in Chile. In particular, the profound transformations that occurred in the 1980s, may have had very important impacts on regional cohesion. Spatial statistics techniques reveal a high and increasing spatial dependence in regional GDP/pc throughout the period 1960-1998. A more detailed analysis confirms that two clusters of regions are present in Chile at the end of the 1990s. This indicates that Chile's economic development may be spatially segmenting the country into highly productive and dynamic regions (North) and other regions that are slowly falling behind (South).

This process has been remarkably intense during the 1990s coinciding with a long period of growth of the Chilean economy. Interpretation of the traditional β-convergence equations would result in the rejection of the hypothesis of convergence; further, strong evidence of spatial correlation in the residuals is found. In the search of possible causes triggering the clustering of the regions, we have found that that foreign direct investment would appear to have strongly contributed to this process.

The chapter continues as follows. The next section describes the data, while the succeeding section uses spatial statistical techniques to detect spatial concentration in Chile's regional GDP/pc. The following section estimates convergence equations using panel data and fixed effects and studies the existence of spatial correlation in the residuals. Thereafter, the models are implemented to control for spatial correlation and then the variables to measure the influence of public and foreign direct investment are introduced into the analysis. A final section concludes the paper with some evaluation of the results and implications for development policy.

Data

The regional GDP time series has been constructed from two different sources. The Ministerio del Interior (Subsecretaría de Desarrollo Regional y Administrativo) and CIEPLAN edited a regionalized GDP disaggregated into productive activities covering the period 1960-1992. The second source makes reference to official data from the Banco Central de Chile covering the period 1985-1998.[1] As far as possible, we have made use of the official data. Population data have been obtained from Instituto Nacional de Estadística estimates based on the 1960, 1970, 1982 and 1992 census. Regionalized public investment data have been provided by MIDEPLAN (Ministerio de Desarrollo Regional) for the period 1980 to 1998. Finally, Foreign Direct investment data have been collected from the Chilean Comité de Inversiones Extranjeras.

In Search of Spatial Concentration

This section takes up the issue of the degree to which the per capita GDP is concentrated in some particular regions. In other words, we try to answer the question of whether regions with high (low) relative GDP tend to be nearby regions with similar characteristics or, quite the opposite, regional wealth and poverty is randomly distributed. The spatial statistics literature has made available a number of methods and indicators to capture geographical interlinks (See Anselin 1988, 1995 and Griffith 1996). A first approach stems from the need to derive a measure of overall spatial dependence of a determined variable within a set of spatially located units, as in our case per capita GDP of regions within a country. The spatial dependence measure is provided by a global statistic such as Moran I,[2] which can be represented by equation 8.1.

[1] Data for 1997 and 1998 are still provisional.
[2] Geary C family statistics have been computed showing very similar results.

$$I_i = \frac{n}{S} \frac{\sum_i \sum_j w_{ij} z_i z_j}{\sum z_i^2} \qquad (8.1)$$

where n is the number of regions; w_{ij} are the elements of a binary contiguity matrix $W(nxn)$, taking the value 1 if regions i and j share a common border and 0 if they do not; S is the sum of all the elements of W; and z_i and z_j are normalized vectors of the log of per capita income of each region. Values around 1 represent strong and positive (clustering of similar values) spatial dependence, whereas values around -1 show negative spatial correlation (clustering of different values).

Figure 8.1 reports the evolution of Moran I and of the standard deviation of the income per capita of Chilean regions. Several facts are worth mentioning. First of all, the Moran I happens to be positive and significant for 37 out of 39 years in the sample, indicating that we can no longer assume a random distribution of the regional GDP in Chile. This means that the rich (poor) regions have a propensity to be close to other rich (poor) regions.

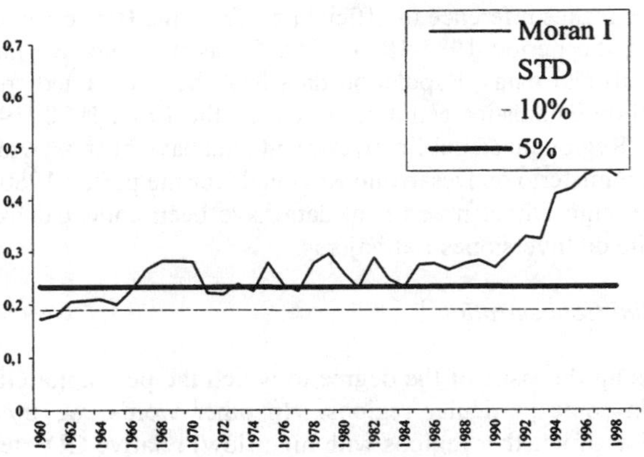

Figure 8.1 Moran I and Standard Deviation of Regional GDP Per Capita 1960-1998

Observing the evolution of the Moran statistic, we can infer several facts. There seems to be an initial period of modest growth of the statistics in the 1960s up to 1970. During the 1970s and mid 1980s there seems to be a certain stabilization in the statistic whereas from 1985 onwards there is a clear upward trend, especially from 1990. When we use a measure of dispersion such us the standard deviation (often used to study sigma convergence), there is a general trend[3] of diminishing disparities throughout the period studied, but there is evidence of a slowing of this trend during the 1990s, coinciding with a period when the Chilean economy was opened to global competition.

However, the global Moran *I* unable to capture which specific observations concentrate to generate greater spatial instability. The identification of groups of regions concentrating high (low) values of per capita GDP is the main objective of number of techniques developed by Anselin (1993, 1995). A first tool contributing to a more disaggregated picture of the spatial dependence is the Moran scatterplot. Here, the values of Wz_j on z_i, where W is the row-standardized[4] first order contiguity matrix and z_i are the standardized values of the analyzed variable are displayed. In the present context, the standardized log of per capita income of a region was presented against its spatial lag (also standardized). A region's spatial lag is a weighted average of the log of GDP/pc of its neighboring regions. The Moran scatterplot divides the space in four areas, which correspond to the four types of possible local spatial association between a region and its neighbors; quadrant I: high-income per capita regions with high-income per capita neighbors; quadrant II: low-income per capita regions surrounded by high-income per capita neighbors; quadrant III: low-income per capita regions surrounded by low-income per capita neighbors; and finally quadrant IV: regions with high-income per capita with low-income per capita neighbors (Rey and Montouri 1999). Regions located in quadrants I and III represent the association of similar values (positive spatial correlation) whereas quadrants II and IV show association of opposite values (negative spatial correlation). The concentration of regions in quadrants I and III is expected in a scenario where rich and poor regions cluster separately, generating differentiated areas of high and low income. If regions were located randomly around the origin, occupying indifferently the four quadrants, no pattern of spatial dependence would arise.

The Moran scatterplot has been calculated for the four decades of the samples and these are shown in figures 8.2 through 8.5. Some aspects may be highlighted. Coincident with the global indicator of spatial dependence, regions are mainly located in quadrants one and three; thus, there exists a dominance of positive spatial association. This is most clear for the last period of the sample (figure 8.5), where an appreciable linear relationship between the regional GDP and its spatial lag occurs. Additionally, the Moran scatterplot allows us to establish a first identification of the possible regions or groups of regions that are bound to present a higher spatial instability, although this topic will be treated more

---

[3] This global trend may be the result of the generalised approached of all the regions to region XII, that has during most of the period an extremely distorted GDP.

[4] In the row standardised matrix the rows sum to 1.

extensively elsewhere. A first group of regions will be formed by those situated in the first quadrant. Regions I and II have remained in the first quadrant throughout the analyzed period (1960-1998). Region III joins the first quadrant in the 1990s. Another group of regions (VII, VIII, IX and X) has permanently remained in the third quadrant, indicating a cluster of low production in the South of the country.

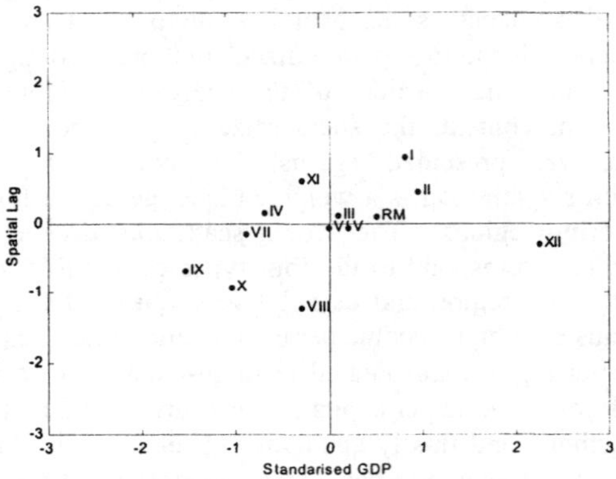

Figure 8.2 Moran Scatterplot: Regions' Per Capita GDP 1960-1969

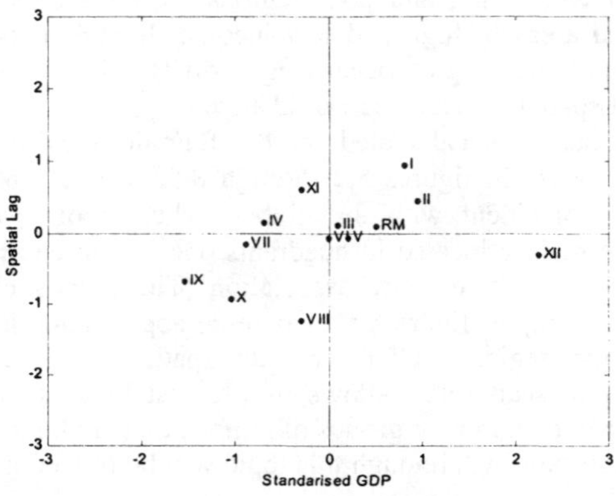

Figure 8.3 Moran Scatterplot: Regions' Per Capita GDP 1970-1979

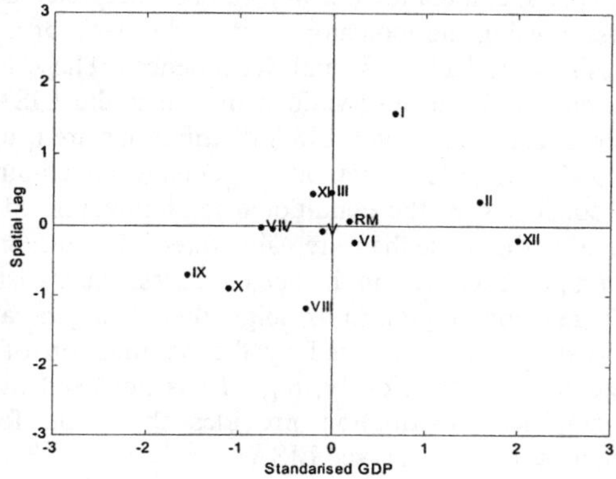

Figure 8.4 Moran Scatterplot: Regions' Per Capita GDP 1980-1989

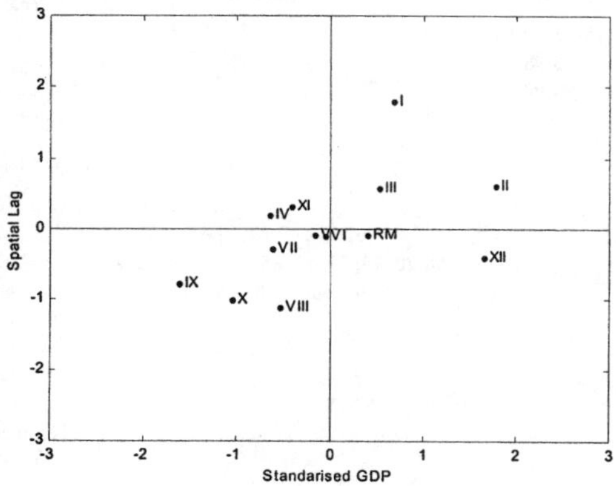

Figure 8.5 Moran Scatterplot: Regions' Per Capita GDP 1990-1998

It is possible to obtain additional evidence of cluster formation and patterns of spatial dependence. Anselin (1995) decomposed the global indicator into local indicators of spatial dependence, such as the one shown in (8.2)

$$I_i = \frac{z_i \sum_j w_{ij} z_j}{\sum z_i^2 / n} \qquad (8.2)$$

Local indicators of spatial association (LISA), can be interpreted as an indicator of spatial cluster, using the indicator itself as the basis of a test where the null hypothesis is the lack of spatial dependence. These local clusters can be identified for those observations in which the LISA is significantly different from zero. However, LISA distributions are usually unknown. Anselin (1995) suggests a method to generate an empirical distribution for LISA, consisting of the conditional randomization of the vector z_j. It is conditional in the sense that z_i remains fixed. The reasoning behind the randomization procedure lies in the need to assess the statistical significance of the linkage of one region to its neighbors. The generation of the region's LISA distribution is inferred by the permutation of the neighbors that surround region *i* (obviously, region *i* is not used in the permutation). This empirical distribution provides the basis for a statement on the extremeness of the observed LISA.

Table 8.1 Local Moran Statistics

Significant at 10%	Quadrant I	Quadrant III	Number of Years
I	78-80; 94-98		8
II	95-98		4
III	94-98		5
IV			0
V			0
VI			0
VII			0
VIII		62-70 ;75; 82; 87-98	23
IX		68-70; 75; 79; 82; 85-86; 88-89; 91-98	18
X		62; 64; 66; 85; 88-89; 91-96	12
XI			0
XII			0
RM			0
Global		62-98	38
Significant at 5%	I	III	Number of Years
I	96-98		3
II	97		1
III	96-98		3
IV			0
V			0
VI			0
VII			0
VIII		75; 82: 90-98	11
IX		94-96	3
X		95	1
XI			0
XII			0
RM			0
Global		67-70; 73 74-75; 82-83; 85-98	26

Table 8.1 shows, in first place, the interval and the specific region for which LISA is statistically different from zero and, secondly, the Moran scatterplot quadrant in which the region was located in that particular year. This will allow us a more strict identification of the clusters in their space-time dimension. Table 8.1 only shows the first and third quadrants, as these are the only ones that contain significant LISA statistics. The regions revealing greater spatial association are those previously identified as candidates to form clusters, in the North, regions I, II and III located in the first quadrant and in the South regions VIII, IX and located in the third quadrant. Therefore, a picture of the existence of two clusters emerges.

However, some disparities can be found between the two clusters. The Northern cluster only becomes apparent from the mid 1990s onwards whereas the Southern cluster presents higher temporal consistency. Consequently, it seems feasible that the high growth of the global indicator of spatial association and the behavior of LISA may be demonstrating that regional growth in Chile has been spatially biased, especially in recent years. This may have contributed to the slowing of the reduction of GDP disparities between regions.

Convergence Equations Estimation

High and growing spatial dependence has been found in the regionalization of Chile's GDP in the previous section. The next step is to evaluate, to what extent, this spatial dependence may influence the convergence estimations. In this section, we deal with the estimation of a convergence equation using panel data for the 13 regions of Chile for 39 years, and perform a number of tests with the aim of detecting the presence of spatial correlation among the residuals of the convergence equation.

De la Fuente (1996) argues that one of the main conclusions reached when estimating traditional convergence econometric models is that it happens, unconditionally, at an extremely slow pace. Additionally, the specifications used in most of the models may not be appropriate to capture the unobserved differences between the distinct regions or countries of the sample. In order to overcome these types of problems, alternative techniques have been proposed; one uses panel data with the inclusion of fixed effects, allowing for differences in the steady states of the regions of the sample.

A number of studies have used convergence models with panel data and fixed effects, such as those proposed by Raymond and Garcia (1994), Canova and Marcet (1995), de la Fuente (1996), Mancha (1999), and Morandé *et al.* (1996). The fixed effects model is based on the estimation of a standard convergence equation such as:

$$\Delta \ln y_{it} = \alpha_i + \ln y_{it-1}\beta + u_{it} \quad \forall\ i = 1,\ldots,N;\ t = 1,\ldots,T \tag{8.3}$$

where y_{it} is the relative (to the nation) per capita GDP of region i in time t, α_i corresponds to the individual fixed effects for each of the i regions. Equation (8.3) establishes that there is a relationship between the growth of a region's relative per capita GDP and its associated per capita GDP gap with the country observed in the previous time period. The appearance of significant fixed effects would denote the presence of characteristics that are specific to the regions for which the dummy variable is different from 0, and therefore particular and differentiated steady states.

Moreover, the α_i allows for the recovery of an estimate for every particular steady state. If we assume the steady state y_{it}^* may be expressed as,

$$\Delta \ln y_{it} = 0 \qquad (8.4)$$
$$y_{it}^* = \alpha_i / \beta$$

If it is assumed that all regions tend to the same steady state (unconditional β-Convergence), the fixed effects should not be significant. A natural and common way of testing unconditional convergence is estimating equation (8.3) allowing for a common intercept for all regions, $\alpha_i = 0$, since we are dealing with deviations from the mean. One of the main advantages of this sort of specification is that it relies on the lack of explicit conditioning as a dummy variable is assigned to every region, accounting for all the possible factors contributing to the differentiated steady states. This sort of conditioning, however, does not provide us with any clue of the fundamentals provoking the existence of dissimilar steady states within the regions of a country.

The constrained ($\alpha_i = 0$) and the unconstrained estimations of the model have been carried out for five different periods of time (1960-1998 and four sub-periods 1960-1970, 1970-1980, 1980-1990 and 1990-1998). Table 8.2a reports the results of the constrained model to evaluate the existence of unconditional β-Convergence taking annual periods of growth. The calculation of the unconditional convergence equation summarizes well-known results of Chilean regional growth studies (see, for example, Fuentes 1996, and Morandé *et al.* 1996). The hypothesis of unconditional β-Convergence cannot be rejected for the period as a whole. The estimate of the convergence parameter is 1.2%, which implies a very slow speed of convergence. However, in only two out of the four sub-periods in which the sample has been divided, is there any evidence of a process of convergence. The 1960s and 1980s have seen periods of convergence, especially in the latter where the convergence rate reaches the 2.3% annual. On the other hand, the 1970s, a time of great economic and political convulsions in Chile, is characterized by an absence of convergence. Nevertheless, new insights can be provided with the availability of new data. The period covering Chile's high growth period of the 1990s (around 6% per annum), happens to return a positive, but non-significant, convergence parameter.

Table 8.2a Constrained Model Estimation (Unconditional β-Convergence)

	1960-1998	1960-1970	1970-1980	1980-1990	1990-1998
Coefficient β	-0.0120	-0.0137	-0.0069	-0.0229	0.0003
t-statistic	-2.6883	-1.7816	-0.7244	-2.4254	0.0386
p-value	0.0074	0.0772	0.4702	0.0167	0.9693
$\overline{R}^2$	0.0144	0.0179	-0.0045	0.0434	-0.0125
o^2	0.0032	0.0032	0.0039	0.0035	0.0019
Durbin-Watson	2.0890	2.2614	1.9296	2.2840	1.7728
Observations	494	130	130	130	104

Table 8.3a Unconstrained Model Estimation (Conditional β-Convergence)

	1960-1998	1960-1969	1970-1979	1980-1989	1990-1998
Coefficient β	*-0.0881*	*-0.2509*	*-0.3016*	*-0.3687*	*-0.2378*
t-statistic	-4.4857	-3.6336	-4.7810	-5.3458	-3.9775
p-value	0.0000	0.0004	0.0000	0.0000	0.0001
$\overline{R^2}$	0.0391	0.0739	0.1048	0.1479	0.2346
o^2	0.0031	0.0030	0.0035	0.0031	0.0014
Durbin-Watson	2.0370	2.1094	1.8520	2.0635	2.0361
Obs	494	130	130	130	104
Fixed Effects					
I	0.0287**	0.0963**	0.1261***	0.1217***	0.0812***
II	0.0803***	0.1518***	0.2635***	0.3251***	0.2239***
III	0.0082	-0.0066	-0.0664***	0.0168	0.0868***
IV	-0.0345***	-0.1286***	-0.1280***	-0.1246***	-0.1022***
V	-0.0092	0.0055	0.0097	-0.0230	-0.0424***
VI	-0.0037	-0.0222	0.0086	0.0446**	-0.0335**
VII	-0.0384***	-0.1629***	-0.1672***	-0.1470***	-0.0790***
VIII	-0.0243**	-0.0670***	-0.0450**	-0.0604***	-0.0987***
IX	-0.0809***	-0.2785***	-0.2757***	-0.3195***	-0.2104***
X	-0.0546**	-0.1986***	-0.2154***	-0.2140***	-0.1341***
XI	-0.0115	-0.0355	-0.0306	-0.0460**	-0.0637***
XII	0.0778***	0.3264***	0.3420***	0.4026***	0.1518***
RM	0.0142	0.0727***	0.0453**	0.0378**	0.0439**

***Significant at 1%.** Significant at 5%.* Significant at 10%

However, although some of these results may reinforce the Chilean regional convergence literature, some remarks should be noted about some of the peculiarities in the sample. First of all, region XII enjoys the highest GDP/pc in 1960 and its economic performance during the period is the worst. This provides an idea of the type of convergence process taking place in Chile. Region XII, though, exhibits special characteristics. It is a sparsely populated region with a distorted per capita production due to oil extraction and refining. This situation, together with a low average economic growth throughout the period studied may have biased our analysis about the nature of regional convergence in Chile. Fuentes (1996) argues that by excluding region XII from the sample, there is a reduction in the convergence speed (from 1.3% to 1%), for a sample period from 1960-1990. In our case, the time interval is longer. When excluding region XII from the sample, the constrained model allows us to reject convergence for the whole period and only the 1980s report some sort of regional convergence.

The unconstrained model, which includes fixed effects for every region, has also been estimated and the results are shown in table 8.3a. Once the dummy variables have been introduced, the hypothesis of β-Convergence cannot be rejected for any of the periods studied. The speed of convergence increases sharply for the whole period, rising from 1.2% to 8.8%. The dummy variables result turns out to be significant for 8 out of 13 regions for the period 1960-1998. This may indicate that the majority of Chilean regions are approaching their own steady state. Some regions develop positive fixed effects (I, II and XII), whereas other regions hold negative effects (VII, VIII, IX and X). These effects could be considered as factors promoting or preventing growth, positive and negative effects respectively. Region II has its own positive effect to a prosperous copper mining extraction activity, whereas region I has seen a rapid development of it's industrial and trade sectors. In this sense, region XII behaves oddly. Although its economic performance has been mediocre for the whole period (with the lowest growth rate), a positive fixed effect has been obtained. The reason for this stems from the enormous distance in terms of GDP separating region XII from the national average. With a convergence parameter of –0.088, the growth should have been even lower so the value of the fixed effects is positive. On the other side of the scale, regions VII, VIII, IX and X report negative effects in all five periods.

However, these effects have not been constant over time. Changes have been located in regions III, V and VI. Region III overcame its negative fixed effect during the 1970s achieving a positive one in the 1990s, which would explain its transition to the first quadrant of the Moran scatterplot of high product with high product neighbors. Region V only showed a significant effect in the 1990s while Region VI presented a positive effect in the 1980s, but a negative one in the 1990s.

Nevertheless, one of the most remarkable results is the presence of significant fixed effects for all regions in the 1990s, a period of high growth, the end of the period when disparities declined and the appearance of GDP spatial clusters. Observing the disposition of Chilean regions, it is not difficult to see that positive fixed effects have been located in the North of the country (with the exception of region XII) and the negative effects have been concentrated in the South. Therefore, the fixed effects spatial distribution is consistent with the previous spatial statistics analysis, which provides addition insights about the growth patterns of the different regional clusters.

We turn now to the detection of spatial correlation in the convergence equation OLS residuals. As we are dealing with panel data with fixed effects for N individuals (regions) and T periods of time, the spatial correlation detection will require a slight transformation of the usual binary connectivity matrix, defined in the previous section. A brief description of a panel data general model will serve as a starting point to present the transformed connectivity matrix in order to allow for the time-space dimension.

Following Balestra (1992) a fixed effects model can be defined as follows,

$$\Delta \ln y_{it} = \alpha_i + \ln y_{it-1}\beta + u_{it} \tag{8.5}$$

First, the T observations for each region can be conveniently expressed as:

$$\Delta \ln y_i = l_T \alpha_i + \ln y_i \beta + u_{it} \tag{8.6}$$

where $\Delta \ln y_i$ is a Tx1 vector of y_{it}, l_T is a T dimension unity column vector, y_i is a Tx1 matrix of every time observation of the independent variable of individual i and, u_{it} is a Tx1 error vector. The complete system may be presented as follows:

$$\underset{(NT\text{x}1)}{\underset{y}{\begin{bmatrix} \Delta \ln y_1 \\ \Delta \ln y_2 \\ \cdots \\ \Delta \ln y_N \end{bmatrix}}} = \underset{(NT\text{x}N)}{\underset{D_N}{\begin{bmatrix} l_T & 0 & 0 \\ 0 & l_T & \\ & \cdots & \\ 0 & 0 & l_T \end{bmatrix}}} \underset{(N\text{x}1)}{\underset{\alpha}{\begin{bmatrix} \alpha_1 \\ \alpha_2 \\ \cdots \\ \alpha_N \end{bmatrix}}} + \underset{(NT\text{x}1)}{\underset{X}{\begin{bmatrix} \ln y_1 \\ \ln y_2 \\ \cdots \\ \ln y_N \end{bmatrix}}} \beta + \underset{(NT\text{x}1)}{\underset{\text{u}}{\begin{bmatrix} u_1 \\ u_2 \\ \cdots \\ u_N \end{bmatrix}}} \tag{8.7}$$

Once the data are organized in this way, the creation of the connectivity matrix is straightforward. The main objective is to capture the spatial correlation of the contemporaneous errors. In order to show how the construction of the transformed matrix has been completed, a standard connectivity matrix is defined in equation 8.

$$W = \begin{bmatrix} 0 & 1 & 0 & 0 & \dots & 0 \\ 1 & 0 & 1 & 0 & \dots & 0 \\ 0 & 1 & 0 & 1 & \dots & 0 \\ & & & & \dots & 1 \\ 0 & 0 & 0 & 0 & \dots & 0 \end{bmatrix} \tag{8.8}$$

$$(N\text{x}N)$$

Finally, an *NT*x*NT* matrix is defined where each unitary element of a connectivity matrix has been substituted by W and each 0 by a 0 matrix with W dimensions:

$$W_p = \begin{bmatrix} 0 & W & 0 & 0 & \dots & 0 \\ W & 0 & W & 0 & \dots & 0 \\ 0 & W & 0 & W & \dots & 0 \\ & & & & \dots & W \\ 0 & 0 & 0 & 0 & \dots & 0 \end{bmatrix} \tag{8.9}$$

$$(NT\text{x}NT)$$

Therefore, $u'W_pu$ is the weighted average of the products of the contemporaneous errors of those regions that share a common border. Several tests have been performed with the transformed connectivity matrix with the goal of detecting traces of spatial correlation in the residuals of the OLS estimates. The first test for spatial dependence in the disturbances of OLS regression model is the Moran *I*-statistic:

$$I = \frac{u'W_pu}{u'u} \tag{8.10}$$

where u are the OLS errors and W_p has been standardized. It can be shown the asymptotic distribution of the Moran I based on the OLS residuals corresponds to a normal distribution. Consequently, tests can be performed under the null hypothesis of no spatial correlation. There are, however, other asymptotic tests that can be used to establish whether spatial correlation is present or not in the OLS residuals. These tests are derived from the traditional likelihood ratio tests, Wald tests, and Lagrange Multiplier tests, all based in the estimation of the Spatial Error Model (SEM):

$$
\begin{aligned}
& y = X\beta + u \\
& u = \lambda W_p u + \xi \\
& \xi \sim N(0, \sigma^2 I)
\end{aligned}
\qquad (8.11)
$$

The likelihood ratio test (LR) is based on the difference between the log likelihood from the SEM model and log likelihood of the OLS regression. This value represents a statistic distributed as a χ^2 with one degree of freedom $\left[\chi^2(1)\right]$. A Wald test can also be used to test for spatial autocorrelation and takes the following expression:

$$
\begin{aligned}
& W_p = \lambda^2[t_2 + t_3 - (1/n)(t_1)^2] \sim \chi^2(1) \\
& t_1 = tr(W_p .* B^{-1}) \\
& t_2 = tr(W_p B^{-1})^2 \\
& t_3 = tr(W_p B^{-1})'(W_p B^{-1}) \\
& B = (I_n - \lambda W_p)
\end{aligned}
\qquad (8.12)
$$

where λ is the maximum likelihood estimation and * denotes element-by-element multiplication.

Finally, the Lagrange Multiplier test (LM) is based on the OLS residuals and calculations involving the spatial weight matrix. The LM statistic takes the form:

$$
\begin{aligned}
& LM = (1/T)[(u'W_p u)/\sigma^2]^2 \sim \chi^2(1) \\
& T = tr(W_p + W_p')*W_p
\end{aligned}
\qquad (8.13)
$$

The results are shown in tables 8.2b and 8.3b for the constrained and unconstrained models respectively. The null hypothesis of no spatial autocorrelation is not rejected for the whole period and also is not rejected for the first three sub periods. However, for the last period (1990-1998), the null is rejected and therefore the presence of spatial correlation supports the previous results obtained using Moran's I and the Moran scatter plot. The results imply that the cluster formation in this decade has been intense, making the regional GDP per capita growth highly spatial correlated. The results in table 8.3b are very similar to those obtained in the constrained model. The introduction of fixed effects to the model did not reduce the spatial correlation, implying that the spatial correlation is associated more with the growth process than to other regional characteristics that are captured by the dummies.

Table 8.2b Spatial Autocorrelation Tests (Constrained Model)

	1960-1998	1960-1970	1970-1980	1980-1990	1990-1998
Moran					
Moran I	0.0757	0.0156	0.0877	0.0358	0.2168
Marginal probability	0.1018	0.3914	0.2409	0.3645	0.0348
LR test					
LR value	2.5233	0.0273	0.8492	0.1665	4.7728
Marginal probability	0.1122	0.8687	0.3568	0.6832	0.0289
Wald test					
Wald value	2.4996	0.0130	0.5239	0.0983	7.3862
Marginal probability	0.1139	0.9091	0.4692	0.7539	0.0066
LM test					
LM value	2.6800	0.0302	0.9463	0.1579	4.6324
Marginal probability	0.1016	0.8621	0.3307	0.6911	0.0314

Table 8.3b Spatial Autocorrelation Tests (Unconstrained Model)

	1960-1998	1960-1969	1970-1979	1980-1989	1990-1998
Moran					
Moran I	0.0804	-0.0423	0.1368	0.0645	0.2501
Marginal probability	0.0906	0.3556	0.1327	0.3121	0.0242
LR test					
LR value	2.8649	0.2210	2.1742	0.5659	5.5254
Marginal probability	0.0905	0.6383	0.1403	0.4519	0.0187
Wald test					
Wald value	3.0520	0.1276	1.9731	0.4116	7.4349
Marginal probability	0.0806	0.7210	0.1601	0.5212	0.0064
LM test					
LM value	3.0290	0.2206	2.3047	0.5130	6.1611
Marginal probability	0.0818	0.6386	0.1290	0.4738	0.0131

Considering Space

The presence of spatial correlation has important consequences on the inference of parameters when estimated through OLS. The spatial econometrics literature provides several specifications to control for spatial correlation; we have adopted techniques described in Anselin (1988) and LeSage (1999). Two different models are considered to treat the effects of the possible interrelationships between regions previously detected.

Autocorrelation test have shown that the hypothesis of a non-spatially autocorrelated errors can be rejected marginally for the whole period (1960-1998) and more strongly in the last period considered (1990-1998). This reinforces the earlier results derived from the Moran *I* statistics. The problem faced is whether this autocorrelation is operating through the levels, for which we should incorporate on the right hand side of equation (8.3) the dependent variable spatially lagged, or, on the contrary, whether the spatial relationship is working through the errors. Both models are described and their economic implications discussed.

The Spatial Lag Model

This model assumes that the interdependence effect is captured by the spatial lag of the dependent variable in the convergence equation. Then, if ρ is the parameter associated with the spatial lag, we can factor the dependent variable creating the matrix (I - ρW_p). Anselin (1988) provides the framework of the maximum likelihood estimation of this model. If the Spatial Lag Model is the correct one but the estimation is undertaken without considering the spatially lagged dependent variable, the estimation of the parameters would be biased and, therefore, any inference invalid.

$$\begin{aligned} \Delta \ln y_{it} &= \alpha_i + \rho W_p \Delta \ln y_{it} + \ln y_{it-1}\beta + u_{it} \\ \Delta \ln y_{it} &= (I - \rho W_p)^{-1}(\alpha_i + \ln y_{it-1}\beta + u_{it}) \end{aligned} \tag{8.14}$$

The economic interpretation of the model may be considered by evaluating the matrix (I - ρW_p). This matrix can be understood similarly to the Leontief matrix in the input-output context. If W_p is considered as a matrix capturing the spatial chaining between regions and ρ is a weighting parameter determining the importance of the level of these chaining, then (I - ρW)$^{-1}$ takes an identical form of the inverse of Leontief's matrix. Therefore, in our regional growth framework, we could say that the relative growth rate of a region does not only depend on its initial relative position but on the initial relative level (y_{it-1}), the fixed effects (α_i) and the random realizations (u_{it} different from zero) of the neighbor regions and the neighbors' neighbors. In input-output terminology, the relative growth rate of a region is determined by its own characteristics (immediate effect), its neighbors' (direct effect) and its neighbors' neighbors (indirect effect).

Spatial Error Model

Spatial interdependence now is assumed to affect the model through the error structure:

$$\begin{aligned} u_{it} &= \lambda W_p u_{it} + \varepsilon_{it} \qquad \textit{where} \qquad \varepsilon_{it} \sim N(0, \sigma_\varepsilon^2) \\ \Delta \ln y_{it} &= \alpha_i + \ln y_{it-1}\beta + (I - \lambda W_p)^{-1}\varepsilon_{it} \end{aligned} \tag{8.15}$$

where λ is an autoregressive parameter affecting the error term. The spatial error may arise because of measurement problems in the data or because of the omission of variables (Pons-Novell and Viladecans-Marsal, 1999). This model implies, in similar fashion to the spatial lag model, that a shock produced in a region will have impacts, not only in the region but on its neighbors, and finally to all the other regions. If this were to be the true model but autocorrelation ignored the parameters, the estimations would still be unbiased, however, they would be inefficient.

Table 8.4a Spatial Lag Model Estimation

	1960-1998	1990-1998
Coefficient β	-0.0121	-0.0022
t-statistic	-2.7313	-0.2649
p-value	0.0063	0.7911
rho	0.0613	0.1907
t-statistic	1.4126	2.0842
p-value	0.1578	0.0371
$\overline{R}^2$	0.0205	0.0476
o^2	0.0032	0.0018
Log- likelihood	891.1846	216.6813
Observations	494	104

Although there are econometric similarities between the two models (failure to account for autocorrelation yields inefficient parameters), the economic interpretation is radically different (Pons-Novell and Viladecans-Marsal, 1999). Bernat (1996) provides an interpretation of the differences between the two models as follows. Whereas in the spatial lag model the relative growth of a region influences directly its neighbors, in the spatial error model, the realization of a region would only affect its neighbors if its growth does not match what may be expected from its initial situation.

Table 8.4b Spatial Error Model Estimation

	1960-1998	1990-1998
Coefficient β	*-0.0127*	*-0.0062*
t-statistic	-2.8156	-0.6826
p-value	0.0049	0.4948
Lambda	0.0673	0.2058
t-statistic	1.5816	2.3127
p-value	0.1138	0.0207
$\overline{R}^2$	0.0217	0.0538
o^2	0.0032	0.0018
Log- likelihood	891.3894	216.8572
Obs	494	104

Tables 8.4 and 8.5 summarize the result of the maximum likelihood estimation of equations (8.14) and (8.15). For the periods 1960-1998 and 1990-1998, the spatial error model seems to present a better fit. The coefficients of determination as well as the log likelihood estimates

support this finding. In similar fashion to the previous results, the estimation of λ and ρ representing the spatial interconnection are highly significant for the 1990s and only marginally significant for the whole period. The convergence parameter does not suffer great modifications. Once the spatial autocorrelation is accounted for, the unconditional convergence parameter turns to negative values but is still not significant (tables 8.4a and 8.4b).

Table 8.5a Spatial Lag Model Estimation with Fixed Effects

	1960-1998	1990-1998
Coefficient β	-0.0885	-0.2296
t-statistic	-4.5858	-4.2321
p-value	0.0000	0.0000
rho	0.0650	0.1767
t-statistic	1.5110	2.0018
p-value	0.1308	0.0453
$\overline{R}^2$	0.0458	0.2784
o^2	0.0030	0.0012
Log- likelihood	904.2061	238.267
Obs	494	104
Fixed effects		
I	0.0280 **	0.0750 ***
II	0.0805 ***	0.2132 ***
III	0.0077	0.0847 ***
IV	-0.0347 ***	-0.1009 ***
V	-0.0091	-0.0394 ***
VI	-0.0036	-0.0325 ***
VII	-0.0383 ***	-0.0720 ***
VIII	-0.0247 **	-0.0959 ***
IX	-0.0813 ***	-0.2013 ***
X	-0.0551 ***	-0.1285 ***
XI	-0.0109	-0.0580 ***
XII	0.0780 ***	0.1457 ***
RM	0.0146	0.0458 ***

***Significant at 1%** Significant at 5%* Significant at 10%

Tables 8.5a and 8.5b report the results obtained from recalculating the unconstrained model with the spatial autocorrelation correction. The convergence rate estimate remains around 23%. The spatial error model presents interesting modifications. The fixed effects seem to be more accentuated. The positive fixed effects associated with the regions forming the northern cluster are now greater and the negative fixed effects of the southern cluster are even smaller. This could be indicating that controlling the spatial autocorrelation yields a higher disparity between the steady states of the regions of Chile.

Table 8.5b Spatial Error Model Estimation with Fixed Effects

	1960-1998		1990-1998	
Coefficient β	-0.0895		-0.2408	
t-statistic	-4.6413		-4.4018	
p-value	0.0000		0.0000	
lambda	0.0718		0.2062	
t-statistic	1.6899		2.3176	
p-value	0.0910		0.0205	
$\overline{R}^2$	0.0471		0.2900	
o^2	0.0030		0.0012	
Log- likelihood	904.4243		238.8016	
Obs	494		104	
Fixed Effects				
I	0.0292	**	0.0821	***
II	0.0814	***	0.2265	***
III	0.0082		0.0874	***
IV	-0.0351	***	-0.1033	***
V	-0.0092		-0.0427	***
VI	-0.0036		-0.0337	***
VII	-0.0391	***	-0.0801	***
VIII	-0.0246	**	-0.0996	***
IX	-0.0822	***	-0.2130	***
X	-0.0556	***	-0.1358	***
XI	-0.0117		-0.0645	***
XII	0.0794	***	0.1543	***
RM	0.0144		0.0444	***

***Significant at 1%** Significant at 5%* Significant at 10%

Public and Foreign Direct Investment

How can we account for these findings? The purpose of this section is to explore some possible variables that might have caused the spatial segmentation between "wining" and "loosing" regions in the last period of growth in Chile. Analysis is focused on the impact of public and foreign direct investment (FDI) in the last two decades. A first approach to the question follows a spatial statistics point of view. Again global and local statistics, as well as the Moran scatterplot are used to study the spatial dependence of the public and foreign investment flows.

Table 8.6 and figures 8.6, 8.7 and 8.8 reveal regional public investment relative to the region's GDP. The lagging regions (XI, IX, X, IV, and VII) have received a greater investment effort from the central and regional governments for the last two years. However, no clear spatial relationships can be traced, either positive or negative. Moreover, the global statistics of spatial dependence are not significant and the local statistics only show region X as a point of public investment attraction throughout the two periods studied.

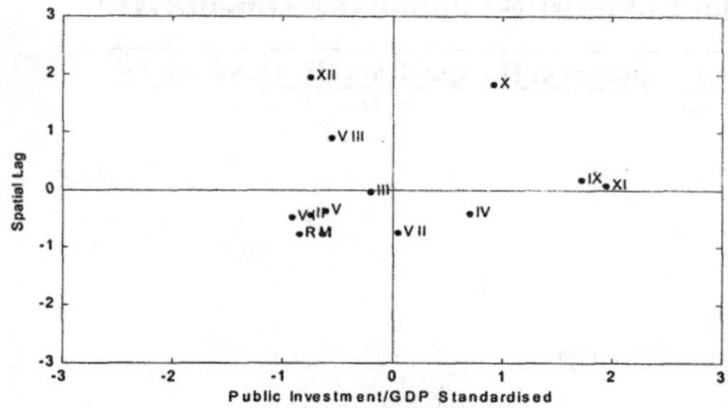

Figure 8.6 Moran Scatterplot: Regions' Public Investment/GDP 1980-1989

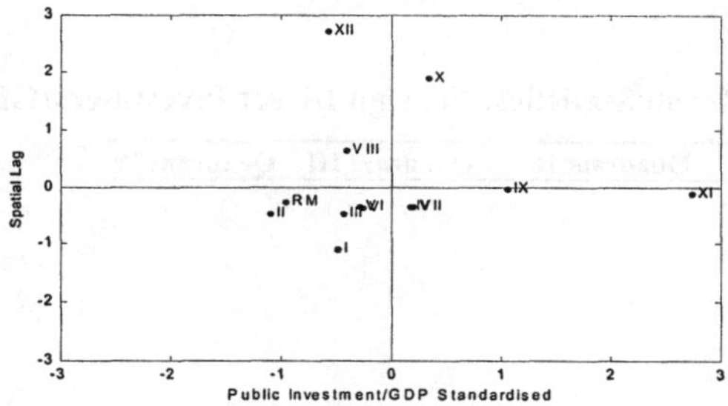

Figure 8.7 Moran Scatterplot Regions' Public Investment/GDP 1990-1998

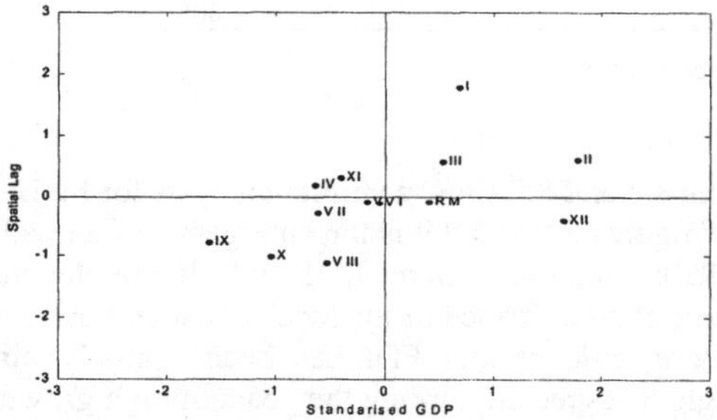

Figure 8.8 Moran Scatterplot Regions' Foreign Direct Investment/GDP 1980-1989

Table 8.6 Local Moran Statistics: Public Investment/GDP

	Quadrant I	Quadrant II	Quadrant III	Quadrant IV
I			90**	
II				
III				
IV				
V				
VI				
VII				
VIII		80*		
IX				
X	80**, 90 **			
XI				
XII				
RM				

** Significant at 5% * Significant at 10%

Table 8.7 Local Moran Statistics: Foreign Direct Investment/GDP

	Quadrant I	Quadrant II	Quadrant III	Quadrant IV
I	90**			
II	90**			
III	90**			
IV				
V				
VI				
VII		90*		
VIII				
IX				
X			80*	
XI				
XII				
RM				80**

** Significant at 5% * Significant at 10%

Table 8.7 and figures 8.8 and 8.9 show a similar analysis for FDI. The most relevant feature of figures 8.8 and 8.9 is the emergence of a quadrant I cluster during the 1990s wherein regions I, II and III are the major beneficiaries. The pattern of significance of the local statistics also reveals this fact. It is, therefore, evident that FDI has been spatially biased towards the northern regions, especially during the years of high growth.

We turn, now, to verify whether the different patterns of public and foreign direct investment have determined different steady states for the regions of Chile. In order to do so, the public investment as well as the FDI have been introduced on the right hand side of the convergence equation (3). Table 8.8a summarizes the results of including conditioning variables for the last period studied (1990-1998). Several facts are worth mentioning. First of all, both public and FDI are highly significant, especially the FDI. The public investment parameter shows a negative sign indicating that those regions that received more public investment have performed badly in terms of relative growth. This could be explained partly by the fact that public investment has been mainly aimed towards lagging regions. The FDI has the expected positive sign. The convergence parameter is now significant and fairly near to 2% per annum. Nevertheless, the most interesting result comes as a consequence of the application of the spatial autocorrelation test. Once the investment variables have been introduced in the estimation, the hypothesis of no spatial autocorrelation cannot be rejected (table 8.8b). This would indicate that some of the characteristics that are making space more important are to be found in the investment processes occurring in Chile during the 1990s.

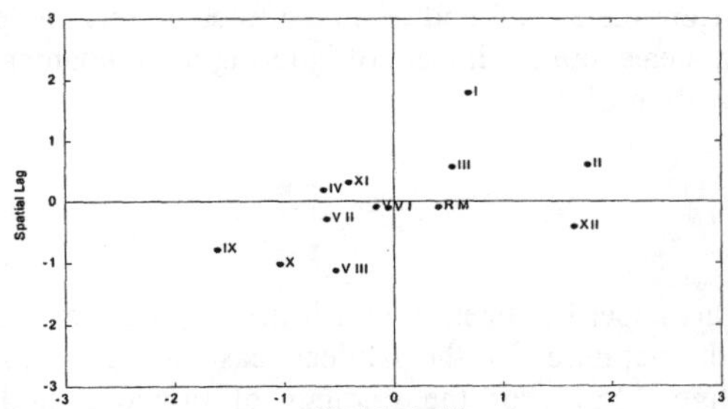

Figure 8.9 Moran Scatterplot Regions' Foreign Direct Investment/GDP 1990-1998

Table 8.8a Investment Conditioned Model (OLS Estimation)

	1990-1998	1990-1998
Coefficient β	0.0003	-0.0196
t-statistic	0.0386	-2.0080
p-value	0.9693	0.0473
Public Investment		-0.2170
t-statistic		-2.6951
p-value		0.0082
Foreign Direct Investment		0.1930
t-statistic		4.0822
p-value		0.0001
$\overline{R}^2$	-0.0125	0.1167
σ^2	0.0019	0.0017
Durbin-Watson	1.7728	2.1092
Observations	104	104

Table 8.8b Spatial Autocorrelation Tests

Tests		
Moran		
Moran I	0.2168	0.1037
Marginal probability	0.0348	0.1989
LR test		
LR value	4.7728	1.1228
Marginal probability	0.0289	0.2893
Wald test		
Wald value	7.3862	0.9448
Marginal probability	0.0066	0.3310
LM test		
LM value	4.6324	1.0595
Marginal probability	0.0314	0.3033

Finally, although the investment variables are revealed to be important in the determination of the regional steady states, the convergence rate obtained (1.9%) is far from the 23% found when the fixed effects model is used. This provides an idea about the impact of ignoring the fundamentals of uneven regional growth in Chile.

Conclusions

The main purpose of this paper has been to revisit the empirical evidence of the regional growth literature for the Chilean case using a spatial econometrics perspective. Some of the findings of previous studies, Fuentes (1996) and Morandé *et al.* (1996) have been corroborated; however, new insights have been obtained about the characteristics of the last period of prolonged growth enjoyed by Chile.

First of all, the indicators of spatial dependence show a dramatic increase of the GDP's spatial interdependence in the last 15 years. This coincides with the collapse of the reduction of disparities between the Chilean regions. It has also been shown that during this period, the formation of clusters has been remarkably intense. Actually, it is during this period that the northern cluster developed as such.

Convergence equations estimations provide additional evidence on the same grounds. The idea of unconditional convergence during this period can be strongly rejected, and only when the fixed effects are included does the convergence parameter takes its usual sign and value. The existence of highly significant fixed effects for all regions denotes the lack of a common steady state.

We have also shown that the FDI has been a major contributor to the consolidation of the Northern cluster throughout the 1990s provoking a polarization between dynamic and lagged regions. Public investment has not been able to promote lagged regions. This fact poses two main questions for the policy-maker. First, if public investment cannot promote a regional balance in development, some additional policies have to be made in order to pursue this objective. Perhaps, public investment may facilitate development but in and of itself, it would not appear to promote the needed responses from the private sector.

On the other hand, FDI appears as one of the main factors responsible for the cluster formation in the north of the country associated particularly with the mining sector. This sector has been the major attractor of FDI in the country. According to Aroca (2001) more than 50 percent of the total FDI in the last fifteen years has been directed to this zone, specifically to copper exploitation. At the same time, the creation of Mercosur and other changes occurring in Latin America, Chilean firms have invested considerable resources in Brazil, Argentina and Peru during this period. The manufacturing and services have been the main focus of these Chilean firms according to Daher (2000). It means, that location factors are attracting FDI to natural resources exploitation but at the same time the investment in manufacturing and services sector has been more attractive in the neighboring countries. Therefore, as natural resources are spatially concentrated, FDI will continue increasing the spatial dependence, while the Chilean FDI abroad will not help others regions in Chile that are poor in natural resources, reducing the likelihood that they will catch up with the northern regions. Herewith lies a tension between national policies promoting the development of a multicountry market (MERCOSUR) and those attempting to reduce internal disparities between regions. It is a problem shared by many other countries in Latin America.

References

Anselin, L. (1988) *Spatial Econometrics: Methods and Models*, Dordrecht, Kluwer.

Anselin, L. (1993) "The Moran scatterplot as an ESDA tool to assess local instability in spatial association," GISDATA Specialist Meeting on GIS and Spatial Analysis, Amsterdam.

Anselin, L. (1995) "Local Indicators of spatial association-LISA," *Geographical Analysis*, 27, 93-115.

Aroca, P. (2001) "Impacts and development in local economies based on mining: the case of the Chilean II region." *Resources Policy*, 27, 119-134.

Aroca, P. and M. Bosch (2000) "Crecimiento. Convergencia y Espacio en las Regiones Chilenas: 1960-1998," *Estudios de Economia*, 27, 199-224.

Balestra , P. (1992) "Fixed Effect Models and Fixed Coefficient Models." In L. Matyás and P. Sevestre (eds.) *The Econometrics of Panel Data: Handbook of Theory and Applications*, Dordrecht, Kluwer.

Barro, R. J. and X. Sala i Martin (1995) *Economic Growth*, New York, McGraw-Hill.

Benabou, R. (1993) "Workings of a City: Location, Education, and Production," *Quarterly Journal of Economics*, 108, 619-52.

Bernat (1996) "Does manufacturing matter? A spatial econometric view of Kaldor's laws," *Journal of Regional Science*, 36, 463-77.

Canova, F. and A. Marcet (1995) "The Poor Stay Poor: Non-Convergence across Countries and Regions," *CEPR Discussion Paper* 1265, UK.

Daher, A. (2000) "Regiones metropolitanas binacionales de en el MERCOSUR," *EURE*, 26, Santiago, Chile.

De la Fuente, A. (1997) "The empirics of growth and convergence: a selective review," *Journal of Economic Dynamics and Control* 21, 23-74.

De la Fuente, A. (1996) "On the Sources of Convergence: A Close Look at the Spanish Regions," *Discussion Paper* 1543 Centre for Economic Policy Research, London School of Economics.

Durlauf, S.N. and D.T. Quah (1998) "The New Empirics of Economic Growth," Centre for Economic Performance *Discussion Paper* 384 London School of Economics..

Durlauf, S.N. (1996) "A Theory of Persistent Income Inequality," *Journal of Economic Growth*, 1,75-93.

Fingleton, B. (1999) "Estimates of Time to Economic Convergence: An Analysis of Regions of the European Union," *International Regional Science Review*, 22, 5-34.

Fuentes, R.(1996) "¿Convergen las regiones de Chile?: Una Interpretación." En Análisis Empírico del Crecimiento en Chile. Morandé, F.G. y Vergara R. ILADES/Georgetown University, Santiago, Chile.

Getis, A. and K. Ord (1992) "The Analysis of Spatial Association by Use of Distance Statistics," *Geographical Analysis*, 24, 189-206.

Griffith, D.A. (1996) *Practical Handbook of Spatial Statistics*. CRC Press.

Krugman, P. (1991) "Increasing Returns and Economic Geography," *Journal of Political Economy*, 99, 483–499.

LeSage, J. P. (1999) "Spatial Econometrics using Matlab". University of Toledo. http://www.spatial-econometics.com

Lopez-Bazo, E., E. Vayà, A.J. Mora and J. Suriñach (1999) "Regional economic dynamics and convergence in the European Union," *Annals of Regional Science*, 33, 343-370.

Magalhães, A., G.J.D. Hewings and C.R. Azzoni, (2005) "Spatial Dependence and Regional Convergence in Brazil," *Investigaciones Regionales*, (forthcoming).

Mancha, T. (1999) "Integración Económica y Desigualdades Regionales :El Caso Español en el Contexto de la UE," Documento de Trabajo presentado en el Seminario "Integración Económicas y Convergencia Regional," Buenos Aires. Argentina.

Morandé, F.G., R. Soto and P. Pincheira (1996) "Achilles, the Tortoise, and Regional Growth in Chile." In F.G. Morandé and R. Vergara (eds.) *Análisis Empírico del Crecimiento en Chile*. Washington, D.C., ILADES, Georgetown University.

Openshaw, S., C. Brundson and M. Charlton (1991) "A Spatial Analysis Toolkit for GIS," EGIS '91 Proceedings of the Second European Conference on Geographical Information Systems, 788-96. Utrecht. EGIS Foundation.

Openshaw, S., A. Cross and M. Charlton (1990) "Building a Prototype Geographical Correlates Exploration Machine," *International Journal of Geographical Information Systems*, 4, 297-311.

Pons-Novell, J. and E. Viladencans-Marsal (1999) "Kaldor's Laws and Spatial Dependence: Evidence for the European Regions," *Regional Studies*, 33, 443-451.

Puga, D. (1999) "Rising and Fall of Regional Inequalities," *European Economic Review* 43, 303-334.

Quah, D.T. (1992) "International Patterns of Growth: I. Persistence in Cross-Country Disparities," *Working Paper*, LSE, London.

Quah, D.T. (1996) "Regional convergence clusters across Europe, *European Economic Review*, 40, 1951-1958.

Quah, D.T. (1997) "Empirics for growth and distribution: Stratification, polarization and convergence clubs," *Journal of Economic Growth*, 2, 27-59.

Quah, D.T. (1999) "Ideas determining convergence clubs," *Working Paper* (Incomplete Version), London School of Economics.

Raymond J.L. and B. Garcia (1994) "Las Disparidades del PIB per cápita de las Comunidades Autónomas y la Hipótesis de Convergencia," *Papeles de Economía Española* 59.

Rey, S.J. and B. D Montouri (1999) "US Regional Income Convergence: A Spatial Econometric Perspective," *Regional Studies*, 33, 143-156.

Rey, S.J. (2001) "Spatial Empirics for Economic Growth and Convergence," *Geographical Analysis*, 195-214.

Romer, P.M. (1986) "Increasing Returns and Long-run Growth," *Journal of Political Economy*, 94, 1002-1037.

Sachs, J. (1997) "Geography and Economic Transition,". *HIID Working Paper*, Cambridge, MA.

Sala i Martin, X. (1996) "Regional Cohesion: Evidence and Theories of Regional Growth and Convergence," *European Economic Review*, 40, 1325-1352.

Sala i Martin, X. (1997) "'I just Ran Two Million Regressions,'" *American Economic Review*, Papers and Proceedings, 87, 178-183.

9 Industrial Agglomeration in Chilean Regions, 1985-1997

Miguel Atienza Úbeda

Introduction

As development proceeds, it is generally assumed that conditions for spatial dispersion of industrial activities emerge. Diseconomies of scale in the core region render the monocentric pattern costly, while the growth and diversification of the economy allows the spread of economic infrastructure and agglomeration economies in hinterland regions. From this perspective, spatial concentration and dispersion are usually seen as moments in the process of economic development (Henderson, 1999a). In this respect, the literature shows a tendency towards quick spatial concentration and slow dispersion as countries develop.

After more than forty years (1932-1973) of import substitution industrialization, that reinforced the primacy of the Metropolitan Region (Miranda, 1997), Chile began, in 1973, a remarkable institutional and policy transformation, based on unilateral trade liberalization and radical structural reforms. From 1973 to 1997, Chile achieved an average annual rate of growth of 4.8 per cent. This growth was particularly rapid in the period 1985-1997, when the Chilean economy attained and average annual rate over 7 per cent, one of the highest among developing countries, and doubled its GDP per capita.

Despite economic growth, spatial concentration in the Metropolitan Region persists and is close to achieve the highest levels in the history of the country. In terms of primacy indices, the spatial pattern of Chile was in 1997 quite similar to 1973. At the beginning of this period, the Metropolitan Region represented 47.5 per cent of total GDP and 36.1 percent of total population, while, in 1997, concentrated 51.6 per cent of total GDP and 40 per cent of total population. In fact, several works (Henderson, 1999a, Atienza, 2000) point out that the concentration of economic activity in the Metropolitan Region can be considered excessive both in terms of the GDP per capita and the size of the country, measured through the amount of urban population.

The aim of this chapter is to analyze the factors of location that can be contributing to delay the spatial dispersion of activities in Chile. For this purpose, the study will focus on industry agglomeration factors during the period 1985-1997. The chapter has six sections. Section one presents the empirical model employed to estimate industry location factors across regions. Section two describes the data and the methodology that have been used. Section three analyses the evolution of regional industry location in Chile between 1985 and 1997. Section four explains the variables and hypotheses of the model. Section five offers empirical results and section six draws some conclusions.

Empirical model

The model aims to estimate what role are playing the main location factors – according to traditional and New Economic Geography theories – in the spread of industrial activities across Chilean regions, between 1985 and 1997. In particular, the study pays especial attention to two groups of factors.

- External scale economies arising from industrial agglomeration; and
- Regional comparative advantage based on factor endowments and, specifically, on natural resources abundance.

According to New Economic Geography models, it is plausible to think that, in the case of Chile, external scale economies are predominantly acting as a centripetal force, since the majority of industrial activity is still concentrated in the Metropolitan Region. At the same time, regional comparative advantage in natural resources would be, above all, a centrifugal force, since most non-metropolitan regions are specialized in the transformation of natural resources. This situation partly explains why the Chilean spatial pattern still remain excessively concentrated around Santiago

In order to estimate the role of external scale economies and comparative advantage in Chilean industry location, regional industrial employment is modeled as a function of historical and current regional conditions. According to Glaeser *et al.* (1992) and Henderson *et al.* (1995), it is assumed that the equilibrium level of employment for an industry *j,* in a region *i,* at time *t* is achieved when regional wages equals the industry marginal product:

$$W_{ijt} = A_{ijt} f'\left(L_{ijt}\right) P_{ijt} \qquad (9.1)$$

where W_{ijt} is the nominal wage rate for industry *j*, at time *t* for region *i*; A_{ijt} is the level of technology for industry *j*, at time *t* for region *i*; and L_{ijt} is employment in industry *j*, at time *t* for region *i*. $A_{ijt}f'(L_{ijt})$ represents the output of industry *j* and P_{ijt} is its price at time *t*. The production function of industry *j* only depends on labor. This assumption means that the model will not be able to capture the effects on productivity and innovation caused by the agglomeration of physical capital. However, it allows us to focus the analysis on the determinants of industry location that depends on employment.

P_{ijt} is a function of regional industry output, which depends on L_{ijj}; on regional characteristics (*RC*), that include factors like regional market potential, access to central markets and factor endowments; and on positive internal trade costs, which take an "iceberg" form. That is to say, only a fraction T_{ik} of every product transported from region *i* arrives to region *k*:

$$P_{ijt} = P\left(L_{ijt}, RC_{it}, T_{ikt}\right) \tag{9.2}$$

It is assumed that the level of technology, A_{ijt}, is determined by different kinds of externalities (Glaeser *et al.* 1992; Henderson, 1995). On the one hand, the so-called static externalities, mainly related to the current size of regional industry in terms of employment L_{ijt}; on the other hand, dynamic externalities which arise from historical characteristics of the region, basically, the initial concentration of labor in a given region. In this respect, it is possible to distinguish three types of dynamic externalities (Hanson, 1994):

- Within industry externalities (L_{ij0}), related to the specialization of a region in a particular industrial activity
- Related industry externalities (L_{ik0}), related to the concentration of labor from the same industrial branch *k*.[1]
- Diversity externalities (D_{ij0}), arising from the existence of a diverse industrial fabric.

$$A_{ijt} = A\left(L_{ij0}, L_{ik0}, D_{i0}\right) \tag{9.3}$$

If expressions (9.2) and (9.3) are substituted in expression (9.1), we obtain a reduced-form equation about the determinants of industry location in a region *i* based on current and historical regional characteristics:

$$L_{ijt} = L\left(W_{ijt}, RC_{it}, T_{it}, L_{ij0}, L_{ik0}, D_{i0}\right) \tag{9.4}$$

---

[1] An industrial branch is considered to include upstream and downstream activities of the same value chain.

Expression (9.4) is standardized in terms of deviations from national industry:

$$\frac{L_{ijt}}{L_{jt}} = L\left(\frac{W_{ijt}}{W_{jt}}, \frac{RC_{it}}{RC_{t}}, \frac{T_{it}}{T_{t}}, \frac{L_{ij0}}{L_{j0}}, \frac{L_{ik0}}{L_{j0}}, \frac{D_{i0}}{D_{0}}\right) \tag{9.5}$$

where L_{jt}, L_{j0}, W_{jt}, RC_t, T_t, and D_0 are the national levels of each variable and industrial activity.

Since the industrial agglomeration in a region is fundamentally a dynamic process, it is appropriate to transform expression (9.5) in terms of labor growth rates. For this purpose, it is taken the logarithm of the difference between different periods:

$$\Delta \ln\left(\frac{L_{ijt}}{L_{jt}}\right) = L\left(\begin{array}{c} \Delta \ln\left(\frac{W_{ijt}}{W_{jt}}\right), \Delta \ln\left(\frac{RC_{it}}{RC_{t}}\right), \Delta \ln\left(\frac{T_{it}}{T_{t}}\right), \\ \Delta \ln\left(\frac{L_{ij0}}{L_{j0}}\right), \Delta \ln\left(\frac{L_{ik0}}{L_{j0}}\right), \Delta \ln\left(\frac{D_{i0}}{D_{0}}\right) \end{array}\right) \tag{9.6}$$

where Δ represents the difference between each time of observation. Expression (9.6), similar to the models used by Glaeser *et al.* (1992) and Henderson *et al.* (1995), is used below as a basis for empirical estimation.

Data and Methodology

Data

The data refer to the period 1985-1997, when the Chilean economy achieved a GDP annual growth rate of over seven per cent and began a second episode of trade liberalization after 1973 (Ffrench-Davis and Sáez, 1995). Data are basically drawn from the Chilean Industrial Census (ENIA) and other data sets elaborated by the Instituto Nacional de Estadística (INE), and were collected for 1985, 1989, 1993 and 1997. According to the available data sets, three four years periods of observations were considered in order to analyze regional employment growth: 1985-1989; 1989-1993; and 1993-1997.

ENIA provides annual information on four-digit industrial activities according to ISIC revision 2, and on firms with over ten workers. This implies a sample of 13 regions and 89 industrial activities. Consequently, there was, in principle, a sample of 1157 (13 x 89) potential observations for each period of analysis. However, not all activities took place in all regions (758) and some observations were likely subject to measurement error (29). After eliminating these cases, the final sample included 370 observations for each period of analysis.

Methodology

As in other empirical studies (Hanson, 1994), the methodology used to estimate the regional location factors in Chile between 1985 and 1997 has been a panel data model. In particular, it is a balanced panel data comprising a relatively high number of cross section observations and a reduced temporal dimension. More specifically, there are 370 observations that represent the localization of one activity in one region and four time periods of observation corresponding to the years 1985, 1989, 1993 and 1997. The use of a panel data is justified due to the dynamic nature of changes in economic geography; both concentration and dispersion of activities are evolving processes.

A panel data model has generally the following structure:

$$y_{it} = \eta_{it} + \beta_{1i}x_{1it} + \beta_{2i}x_{2it} + ... + \beta_{ki}x_{kit} + v_{it}, \quad i = 1,2,...n; \; t = 1,2,...,t \qquad (9.7)$$

Normally, this general expression cannot be used directly and it is necessary to introduce some restrictions particularly related to the random error term. In this respect, there are two traditional types of panel data model: "fixed effects" and "random effects" estimations. Both expressions refer to the way non-observable transversal heterogeneity is related with the random error term. The model for k independent variables would be in both cases:

$$y_{it} = \sum_{j=1}^{k} \beta x_{jit} + \eta_i + v_{it} \qquad (9.8)$$

where η_i represents the non-observable transversal heterogeneity. In "fixed effects" estimations, this heterogeneity (related to the different regions and industrial activities that are analyzed) is assumed to be fixed, while, in "random effects" estimations, transversal heterogeneity is composed of a common fixed part and a random one that is specific for each individual. In this case, taking into account that the relationship between independent and dependent variables can be affected by the heterogeneity of Chilean regions and different industrial activities, a "fixed effect" estimation have been considered the most appropriate approach.

Regional Industry Location in Chile, 1985-1997

Primacy

In 1985, Chile began what has been called its "second episode of trade liberalization" since 1973 (Ffrench Davis and Sáez, 1995). After a deep recession in 1982-1983, nominal tariffs were progressively reduced from 35 per cent, in 1985, to a uniform nominal tariff of 11 per cent in 1992. This level of protection remained throughout the 1990s and was accompanied by several export promotion trade policies. As a result, imports and exports grew significantly from 43 per cent of PIB in 1982-1983 to more than 60 per cent in the 1990s1990s. Part of this result was due to the increase in industrial exports from 35 per cent of total exports to almost 50 per cent. At the same time, between 1985 and 1997, Chilean GDP grew at an annual rate of over seven per cent, one of the highest among developing countries. Industrial GDP achieved an annual rate of almost seven per cent and industrial employment recovered the share that it had at the beginning of the 1980s, around 16.5 per cent of total employment.

According to various studies (Henderson, 1999a; Fujita, *et al.*, 1999; Venables, 2000), these changes, trade liberalization, high rates of GDP growth and industrial recovery, should have contributed to the dispersion of industrial activities across Chilean regions. However, between 1985 and 1997, industry concentration around the Metropolitan Region persisted at a level that can be considered excessive taking into account GDP per capita and size, in terms of urban population (Atienza, 2000; Henderson, 1999a).

In order to analyze the evolution of the distribution of industrial activities across Chile between 1985 and 1997, regions have been divided in four geographical areas (see table 9.1):

1. The "north" which include regions I, II, III and IV;
2. The "center", which include regions V, VI, VII and VIII;
3. The "south" which include regions IX, X, XI and XIII; and
4. The "Metropolitan Region", considered as the core region of the country.

Table 9.1 Regional Distributions Industry, 1985-1997 (%)

Concentration indicators	Year	North	MR*	Center	South
Employment	1985	7.9	56.6	26.9	8.6
	1989	7.7	57.6	26.2	8.5
	1993	6.7	57.9	25.9	9.5
	1997	7.8	56.6	25.7	10.0
Establishments	1985	7.2	59.4	25.5	7.9
	1989	8.4	58.7	25.1	7.7
	1993	7.5	60.0	24.8	7.7
	1997	8.2	59.2	24.7	7.9
Value Added	1985	9.5	48.6	36.5	5.3
	1989	9.6	47.5	37.2	5.8
	1993	7.4	52.2	33.6	6.8
	1997	9.8	52.8	29.3	8.2

* Metropolitan region.
Source: Author using data from INE, ENIA (various years).

The primacy of the Metropolitan Region remained stable both in terms of employment (56.6 per cent) and number of establishments (59.3 per cent) while significantly grew in terms of value added (from 48.6 per cent to 52.8 per cent). Although, in general, there were no relevant shifts in industry location, it is possible to observe some trends regarding non-metropolitan regions. First, northern and particularly southern regions tended to increase their participation in national industry. The number of establishments grew in the north while employment grew in the south and both areas increased their share in the national value added. These increases were not constant in all the period and primarily took place from 1993 on, when the Metropolitan Region began to lose participation in terms of employment and number of establishments. Secondly, center regions and particularly regions V and VIII, which at the beginning of the period were the most industrialized of the country after the Metropolitan Region, progressively reduced their share in national industry.

Table 9.2 Industrial Specialization Index,[2] 1985 and 1997

Year	North	Center	South	MR*
1985	0.50	0.33	0.49	0.19
1989	0.46	0.34	0.54	0.19
1993	0.49	0.33	0.53	0.19
1997	0.46	0.32	0.52	0.18

* Metropolitan Region
Source: Derived from INE, ENIA 1985, 1989, 1993 and 1997.

Regional specialization

Economic geography in Chile is characterized not only by the concentration of activities and population in the Metropolitan Region but also by the extreme degree of specialization of most non-metropolitan regions, remarkably northern and southern ones (see table 9.2). This spatial pattern did not significantly change between 1985 and 1997. The specialization index of the Metropolitan and center regions remains almost

[2] Regional specialization is measured comparing regional and national distribution shares of employment across three digits ISIC activities:

$$Q_{jk} = 1/2 \sum_i \left| \frac{L_{ij}}{L_j} - \frac{L_{jk}}{L_k} \right|$$

Where, L_{ij}/L_j and L_{jk}/L_k are, respectively, the regional and the national shares of employment in sector *j*. Its value is close to one if a region is fully specialized in a sector, and is equal to zero if regional employment is dispersed across sectors in the same way as national employment.

constant and the most specialized areas of the country followed different paths; the northern regions tended to diversify (except region II) while the south of Chile increased its specialization (table 9.2).

The specialization or the diversification of a region, as has been calculated in table 9.2, is different from the relative specialization of a region in a particular activity, although they are usually related. A simple way of measuring regional relative specialization in one activity is the location quotient, calculated as the share of that activity in regional industry (labor, output) relative to the same share at a national level. If the location quotient of an activity is higher than one, then, the region is relatively specialized in this activity; if it is below one, there is no specialization. Location quotients for regions in Chile confirm the high degree of specialization in the north and the south of the country. The regions from these areas generally have an industrial composition that is highly concentrated around a smaller number of activities that belongs to the same industrial branch.

The most relevant changes in relative industrial specialization between 1985 and 1997 took place in northern regions where the majority of location quotients diminished. The most significant increase in the relative specialization in the north is related with its comparative advantage in natural resources, particularly mineral resources. Basic metals and non-metallic mineral industries became the main relative specialization of the area in 1997 together with industrial chemicals, and metal products that also increased their location quotients. Although the north of Chile seems to evolve towards a more diverse industrial structure, it is still a highly specialized area.

Southern regions relative specialization is also based on natural resources endowments, especially food and wood products and between 1985 and 1997, there was relative stability in structure. Location quotients increased for food products and diminished for wood products, although region IX developed a new relative specialization in printing and paper. The lack of relative specialization in industrial activities that are not natural resource intensive is particularly relevant since this area in the only one in the country that increased its share in industrial labor.

Location quotients in the central regions of Chile tend to be lower than in the extreme areas of the country. As in the case of southern regions, relative specialization is significantly higher in natural resource intense activities than in the rest of industries, in particular, wood and food products, paper and printing and petroleum products. The only relative specialization of this area that is not natural resource intensive is transport equipment. Between 1985 and 1997, no significant transformation took place in this respect.

The Metropolitan region largely has the most diversified industrial fabric of the country. All industrial activities, except industrial chemicals and transport equipment present a location quotient slightly higher than one and tended to maintain this value between 1985 and 1997, when the region developed new specialization in machinery, paper and printing. The main relative specialization of each area are summarized in table 9.3

Table 9.3 Main Relative Specialization of Chilean Regions, 1997

North	South
Basic mineral industry (ISIC, 36, 37) Industrial chemicals (ISIC, 35) Metal products (ISIC 38)	Food products (ISIC, 31) Wood products (ISIC, 33)
Metropolitan Region	**Center**
Paper and printing (ISIC, 34) Glass products (ISIC, 362) Metal products (ISIC, 38) Other industries (ISIC, 39)	Food products (ISIC, 31). Wood products (ISIC, 33) Paper and printing (CIIU, 34) Petroleum products (ISIC, 35) Transport equipment (ISIC 384)

Industrial employment growth

Between 1985 and 1997, industrial labor grew at an average annual rate of four per cent (table 9.4). This rate of growth was particularly high up to 1993 when it began to slow down. Labor growth widely differed across industrial activities: furniture, industrial chemicals, plastic products and professional goods grew at average annual rates over seven per cent; paper, non-metallic mineral, non-ferrous metals, metals products and transport equipment, over five per cent. All these activities, except professional goods and paper and printing, grew at a lower average annual rate in the Metropolitan Region than in the rest of the country. However, only in the southern regions of the country, industrial employment grew over the national average, 5.3 per cent. In any case, it is not possible to observe dramatic shifts of industrial employment toward any specific geographical area in the country. Spatial changes predominantly affected particular activities (table 9.5).

Northern regions mainly increased their share of employment in industrial chemicals (more than 21 per cent), nonferrous metals (15 per cent), rubber products (seven per cent) and iron and steel (5.8 per cent). As previously observed, these changes reinforced relative specialization in activities where the area had comparative advantages, especially in the case of the basic minerals industry. In all these activities, the share of industrial labor diminished in the center and the Metropolitan region while, at the same time, the north of Chile suffered important reductions of its share of employment in machinery (15.2 per cent), electrical machinery (7.6 per cent) and transport equipment (6.4 per cent).

Table 9.4 Industrial Employment Growth by Three Digits ISIC, 1985-1997 (%)

3 digit ISIC	North	Center	South	MR*	Chile
Food products	0.9	4.4	6.7	3.7	4.2
Beverages	5.6	2.6	2.2	5.0	4.2
Textiles	-10.0	0.6	-12.0	0.2	0.0
Wearing	9.4	3.2	1.4	2.9	3.2
Leather products		-1.1	-1.4	2.0	1.0
Footwear	15.4	2.0	-2.1	2.1	2.1
Timber products	-0.6	3.6	2.0	4.8	3.3
Furniture and fixtures	4.1	11.1	5.8	7.5	7.4
Paper and products	5,4	2.5	13.2	6.6	5.2
Printing and publishing	5.2	0.4	4.7	4.8	4.2
Industrial chemicals	13.7	2.9	8.5	5.7	7.6
Other chemicals	8.0	4.7	8.8	4.9	5.0
Petroleum refineries		0.4			0.4
Petroleum products	2,6	-1.1		3.2	2.3
Rubber products	6.4	-4.1	-0.8	0.7	1.1
Plastic products	7.0	9.1	17.6	7.0	7.4
Pottery and china		-3.8	0.8	7.5	1.4
Glass products	-0.3	0.2	4.9	5.4	4.6
Non metallic minerals	7.9	6.5	7.6	4.8	5.7
Iron and steel	3.0	-2.2		-4.3	-2.5
Nonferrous metals	7,6	3.1		5.9	6.8
Metal products	8.4	7.2	4.8	4.6	5.3
Machinery	-0.3	2.3	-0.3	9.0	4.9
Electrical machinery	-14.8	2.4	-10.0	4.0	2.8
Transport equipment	3.3	13.0	5.0	4.4	6.6
Professional goods		3.6		7.8	7.5
Other industries	4.5	1.6	5,2	4.6	4.5
TOTAL	3.9	3.6	5.3	4.0	4.0

* Metropolitan region.
Source: Calculated by Author using data from INE, ENIA (various years).

The attraction of industrial labor towards southern regions of Chile was based on employment growth in food products that, in 1997, represented more than 60 per cent of industrial labor in this area and almost 27 per cent of national industrial labor. Note that the higher increase in labor share of the country between 1985 and 1997 is almost exclusively due to food products where southern regions increased their share by 5.6 per cent. The majority of activities, except paper and printing and industrial chemicals, either diminished or maintained their labor share in the south.

The major increases in labor share in the center regions of Chile took place in transport equipment (19.5 per cent) and furniture (4.3 per cent). However, this area stands out due to the loss of participation in most industrial activities. These losses were particularly relevant in pottery and china (31.6 per cent), industrial chemicals (16.1 per cent), paper and products (12 per cent), petroleum products (9.5 per cent), glass products (7.4 per cent) and machinery (6.3 per cent). Significantly, these loses of participation in industrial labor coincided with important increases in the share of the Metropolitan Region in all those activities, except industrial chemicals that tended to locate in the north. It seems that a centripetal force is attracting industrial labor from the center of Chile towards the Metropolitan Region where firms can enjoy a more diverse industrial fabric. It is even possible to observe that the Metropolitan Region attracts some natural resource intensive activities – pottery and china, leather and timber products where – where it does not have a comparative advantage relative to the center of the country.

Table 9.5 Regional Changes in the Share of Industrial Employment by Three Digits ISIC, 1985-1997 (%)

3 digit ISIC	North	Center	South	MR*
Food products	-4.1	0.0	5.6	-1.5
Beverages	2.7	-5.9	-1.2	4.4
Textiles	-0.5	1.1	-2.1	1.5
Wearing	3.4	-0.1	-0.1	-3.2
Leather products		-6.4	-1.4	7.8
Footwear	1.2	-0.1	-1	-0.1
Timber products	-0.5	2.1	-4.1	2.5
Furniture and fixtures	-2	4.3	-3.4	1.1
Paper and products	0.4	-12	2.4	9.2
Printing and publishing	0.7	-5.7	0.3	4.7
Industrial chemicals	21.2	-16.1	2.3	-7.4
Other chemicals	1.1	-0.4	0.2	-0.9
Petroleum refineries		0.0		
Petroleum products	1.2	-9.5		8.3
Rubber products	7	-3.2	-0.1	-3.7
Plastic products	-0.1	1.9	1.8	-3.6
Pottery and china		-31.6	-0.1	31.7
Glass products	-0.9	-7.4	0.4	7.9
Non metallic minerals	2.7	2	1.1	-5.8
Iron and steel	5.8	2.4		-8.2
Nonferrous metals	15	-7.9		-7.1
Metal products	2.8	3.3	-0.1	-6
Machinery	-15.2	-6.3	-1.4	22.9
Electrical machinery	-7.6	-0.7	-3.3	11.6
Transport equipment	-6.4	19.5	-1.9	-11.2
Professional goods		-3.3		3.3
Other industries	0.0	-2.5	1.8	0.7
TOTAL	-0.1	-1.4	1.5	-0.1

* Metropolitan region.
Source: Author using data from INE. ENIA (various years).

This situation is revealed in figure 9.1 using two digit ISIC data. The most important increases in the Metropolitan Region industrial labor share -timber and furniture, paper and printing and non-metallic minerals- are related, except in the case of industrial chemicals, with significant reductions in the share of center regions. At the same time the most relevant increases in the share of northern regions -industrial chemicals, non-metallic minerals and basic minerals- also coincide with an important decline in the participation of the center.

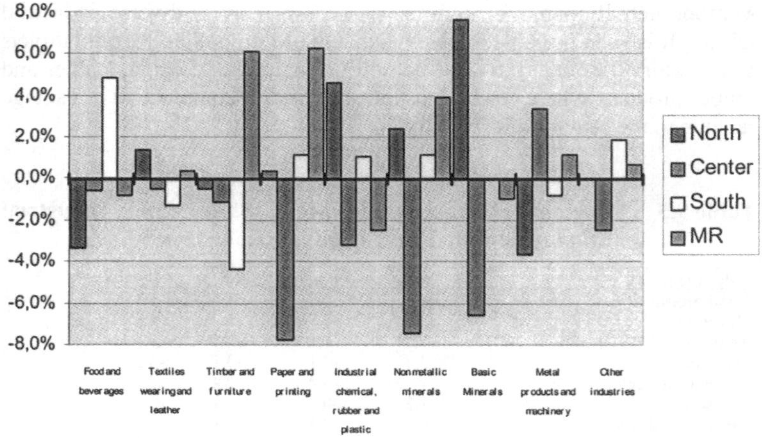

Figure 9.1 Regional Changes in the Share of Industrial Employment by Two Digit ISIC, 1985-1997 (%)

Taking into account both the evolution of location quotients and the changes in the regional share of industrial labor between 1985 and 1997, it is plausible to suggest that Chile has a spatial pattern characterized by two conflicting forces. First, agglomeration economies arising from diversity would act as a centripetal force attracting firms to the Metropolitan Region, especially from the center of the country. Secondly, comparative advantage in raw materials would act as a centrifugal force that tends to keep the relative specialization of non-metropolitan regions in natural resources intense products, normally export oriented -basic mineral industries in the north and food products in the south. It is important to explore to what extent this pattern of industry location is contributing to the slow regional dispersion of industry across Chilean regions, to what extent it is affecting the growth of regional industrial labor.

Model Estimation

This section presents the variables that have been used to estimate the model and the main hypothesis to be tested. According to expression (9.6), regional growth of industrial employment is a function of current and historical regional conditions, external scale economies, fixed factor endowments, wages and internal trade costs stand out among these conditions. Due to the lack of complete data for the whole period of analysis, it is assumed that wages are homogeneous in all regions and this variable is introduced in the model using as a proxy the productivity of labor. Basic descriptive statistics and the description of the variables used in the estimation are presented in table 9.6 and table A1 in appendix A, respectively.

Table 9.6 Descriptive Statistics, 1985-1997

Variables.	1985-1989		1989-1993		1993-1997	
	Mean	Std.	Mean	Std. Dev.	Mean	Std. Dev.
Industrial employment	-0.075	0.461	0.000	0.444	-	0.424
Productivity.	-0.365	0.807	-	0.726	-	0.728
Plant size.	-0.249	0.706	-	0.756	-	0.761
Raw materials intensity.	-0.040	0.679	-	0.770	-	0.775
Specialization in one	0.026	1.191	-	1.245	0.012	1.197
Specialization in a branch.	-0.137	1.122	-	1.149	-	1.112
Diversity.	0.965	0.652	0.985	0.663	0.982	0.674
Paved road.	0.231	1.094	0.231	1.094	0.241	0.692

Source: Author.

The dependent variable in the model is the natural logarithm of the relative variation of regional employment in industrial activities between the initial and the final observation of each time period. The model assumes that this variation is a function of the conditions that exist in regional industry relative to those of national industry at the initial point of each period, according to the following expression (9.9):

$$\Delta \ln\left(\frac{L_{ijt}}{Ljt}\right) = \beta_0 + \beta_1 \ln\left(\frac{pav_{it}/road_{it}}{pav_t/road_t}\right) + \beta_2 \ln\left(\frac{L_{ijt}/L_{it}}{L_{jt}/L_t}\right) + \beta_3 \ln\left(\frac{L_{ikt}/L_{ijt}}{L_{kt}/L_{jt}}\right) +$$

$$+\beta_4 \ln\left(\frac{\sum_{h\neq j}(L_{iht}/L_{it})^2}{\sum_{h\neq j}(L_{ht}/L_t)^2}\right) + \beta_5 \ln\left(\frac{L_{ijt}/est_{ijt}}{L_{jt}/est_{jt}}\right) + \beta_6 \ln\left(\frac{mp_{ijt}/va_{ijt}}{\sum_j \omega\left(mp_{jt}/va_{jt}\right)}\right) \quad (9.9)$$

$$+\beta_7 \ln\left(\frac{va_{ijt}/L_{ijt}}{va_{jt}/L_{jt}}\right) + \sum_j \beta_{10j} D_j + \sum_i \beta_{11i} D_i + \varepsilon_{ijt} - \overline{\varepsilon_{jt}}$$

where *i* indicates the region, *j* the four digit ISIC industrial activities, *k* the two digits ISIC industrial activities and *t* the initial period.

Variables and hypothesis.

Internal trade costs is the first independent variable of the equation. It is a proxy calculated as the percentage of paved roads in region *i* (pav_i) over total regional roads (*roads*$_i$), relative to the same ratio at a national level and at the beginning of each period of analysis. It is assumed that the smaller the percentage of regional paved roads relative to the country, the higher the regional internal trade costs. High trade costs are normally considered as a factor that reduces the incentives for industry location. Therefore, although Chilean paved roads experienced almost no change during the first two periods of analysis, it is expected that regional paved road endowment would be positively related with industrial employment growth.

The next three independent variables aim to capture the effect of external scale economies, at the beginning of each period, on regional industrial employment growth. As noted above, three types of agglomeration external economies are considered: within industry, related industry and diversity externalities. The first one arises from regional specialization in one industrial activity and implies the existence of localization externalities. The second and the third ones would be more related with the existence of urbanization externalities, arising from the interaction of various activities in a region.

Regional relative specialization in one industrial activity is measured by means of location quotients. These quotients allow us to estimate to what extent localization externalities stemming from the relative agglomeration of regional industry around just one activity affect industrial employment growth. In principle, it would be possible to think that high relative regional specialization is related to higher growth rates of industrial employment. However, empirical work, mainly based on the location of industrial activities in the United States, challenges this assumption. On the one side, Glaeser *et al.* (1992) do not find that relative specialization positively affects industrial labor growth; on the other side, Henderson *et al.* (1995) and Henderson (1999b) confirm the existence of localization externalities but only in the case of traditional and mature activities. Since the most specialized regions in Chile did not experienced significant increases between 1985 and 1997, it is plausible to think that there are few localization externalities arising from relative specialization in the country. Consequently, it might be expected that regional specialization would be insignificant as a location factor or even to be negatively related with regional industrial labor growth.

Regional relative agglomeration of activities that belong to the same industrial branch[3] is the second source of possible external economies of scale that could explain regional labor growth. Related industry agglomeration in a branch *k* is calculated as the ratio of two digit regional employment over four digit regional employment (L_{ikt}/L_{ijt}), relative to the

---

[3] Following the criteria used by Hanson (1994), an industrial branch is composed by those ISIC four digits activities that belong to the same two digits activity.

same ratio at a national level (L_{kt}/L_{jt}). Industrial branches include upstream and downstream activities of the same value chain, implying a certain level of regional diversification. Therefore, the analysis of the effect of industrial branch concentration on the growth of industrial employment partially captures the impact of some kind of urbanization economies on industry location. In principle, commercial and productive linkages between clients and suppliers of the same industrial branch are a source of positive externalities by means of the creation of more powerful linkages, labor force turnover and the diffusion of common knowledge and adapted technologies. From this perspective, industrial employment growth ought to be faster in the regions with higher related industry agglomeration.

Relative diversity of the regional industrial fabric is the third possible source of external scale economies included in the model. Diversity is estimated using a Hirschman-Herfindahl type index, which is calculated as the sum of squared regional employment shares of all activities different from *j* relative to the sum of squared national employment shares of these activities. Generally, industrial diversity is related to the existence of urbanization economies in the region, that is to say, external scale economies that arise from the co-existence and the proximity of a critical mass of diverse industrial activities in the same territory. In principle, it is generally assumed that diversity is positively related to industrial employment growth (Henderson *et al.*, 1995). Since the index of industrial diversity that has been calculated is smaller while the regional diversity is larger, it is expected that it will be negatively related to industrial employment growth. According to this hypothesis, industrial labor should grow faster in the most diverse regions in Chile, particularly, in the Metropolitan Region, where there is a larger agglomeration of different activities than in the rest of the country.

Relative plant size aims to capture the impact that the use of different technologies and the existence of internal scale economies have on industry location. Relative plant size is calculated as the establishment average size of an activity *j* in a region *i*, relative to its average size at a national level. Generally, small and medium firms are considered to be particularly effective in creating jobs, either through the formation of new business or through the expansion of existing ones (Armstrong and Taylor. 2000). At the same time, relatively large plants tend to achieve internal economies through the use of more efficient technologies. According to these ideas, it is expected that regions with a higher proportion of smaller size of plants would generate more industrial employment growth than regions where relatively large firms predominate.

Relative intensity in the use of raw material in the production is the next variable included in the model as a proxy of comparative advantage based on regional natural resources endowment. This variable is measured as the costs of raw materials divided by the value added of activity *j* in region *i* relative to the weighted-average of the same ratio at the national industry level. According to Kim (1995), activities that are natural resources intensive tend to be more localized than the rest, due to the fixed nature of these resources. From this perspective, it is expected that regions where industry is more raw material intensive would have a comparative advantage in factor endowments that favors industrial labor growth.

Relative productivity of labor is the last independent variable of the model. It is calculated as the value added per worker of activity *j* in region *i*, relative to the value added per worker of activity *j* at a national level. It is generally assumed that productivity is closely related to regional wage level. Therefore, it is expected regions with a relatively high productivity would grow faster than the rest in terms of industrial labor.

Finally, the model introduces a set of dummy variables (0, 1) whose aim is to capture the fixed effects related to the heterogeneity of industrial activities (D_j)[4] and regions (D_i) that are not explained by the independent variables of the model.

Estimation Results

Country results

Table 9.7 shows the estimation results on regional industrial employment growth in Chile between 1985 and 1997. Regressions in "a" columns are estimations of the model without the regional and industrial activity dummies variables, while in "b" columns dummies are included. Relative labor productivity, establishment size and relative intensity in the use of raw material are the variables of the model with higher explicative power, while internal trade costs and the three types of external scale economies analyzed seem to have less importance in the regional agglomeration of Chilean industrial activities.

Regressions 1a and 1b include all the variables that are not connected to the effects of external scale economies. As expected, relative labor productivity – a proxy of regional relative wages – is positively related with regional industrial labor growth and is significant at the 95 per cent level in all regressions. Those regions with a relatively higher productivity attracted more industrial labor between 1985 and 1997. The impact of this variable is the most important one in quantitative terms: a one standard deviation in relative labor productivity increases average labor growth by

---

[4] Dummy variables representing industrial activities consider three digits ISIC (27 activities), since using four digits ISIC (88 activities) would have imply the loss of excessive degrees of freedom.

17 per cent per period of analysis[5]. This variable presents relevant disparities among regions and industrial activities, which probably explains why its quantitative impact on labor growth increases to 20 per cent when the fix effects of dummy variables are considered.

Table 9.7 Regression Results on Relative Industrial Labor Growth in Chilean Regions, 1985-1997

VARIABLES	1a	1b	2a	2b	3a	3b	4a	4b	5a	5b
C	-0.018* (0.015)	-0.282* (0.124)	0.245** (0.023)	0.020 (0.170)	-0.029 (0.023)	-0.341** (0.162)	-0.016 (0.015)	-0.150 (0.120)	-0.012 (0.0157)	-0.129 (0.120)
Relative productivity	0.115** (0.019)	0.135** (0.020)	0.111** (0.019)	0.142** (0.020)	0.109** (0.019)	0.127** (0.020)	0.106** (0.019)	0.128** (0.020)	0.109** (0.018)	0.131** (0.020)
Relative plant size	-0.129** (0.019)	-0.150** (0.019)	-0.080** (0.024)	-0.091** (0.027)	-0.131** (0.019)	-0.145** (0.020)	-0.107** (0.021)	-0.119** (0.023)	-0.084** (0.023)	-0.086** (0.027)
Raw material intensity	0.079** (0.021)	0.086** (0.022)	0.066** (0.021)	0.085** (0.022)	0.075** (0.021)	0.056** (0.021)	0.071** (0.020)	0.058** (0.021)	0.065** (0.021)	0.053** (0.021)
Paved roads	-0.026* (0.014)	-0.056 (0.049)								
Within industry agglomeration			-0.042** (0.019)	-0.047** (0.024)					-0.047** (0.013)	-0.058** (0.018)
Related industry agglomeration			0.008 (0.018)	0.010 (0.021)			0.034** (0.013)	0.037** (0.016)		
Diversity			0.015 (0.021)	0.027 (0.057)	-0.002 (0.021)	0.066 (0.055)				
Dummy variables	NO	YES	NO	YES	NO	YES	NO	YES	NO	YES
R^2	0.059	0.110	0.067	0.116	0.056	0.102	0.062	0.105	0.071	0.120
N	1110	1110	1110	1110	1110	1110	1110	1110	1110	1110

* Significant at 0.1 level ** Significance at 0.05 level. Standard deviation in parentheses.
Source: Author.

Relative plant size also has the expected sign – regions where activities have relatively smaller establishments created more industrial labor – and is significant at the 95 per cent level in all regressions. This result is

[5] This and the following quantitative impacts are obtained using standardized coefficients of regressions in columns 5a and 5b.

consistent with the idea that small firms are effective in creating jobs. The quantitative impact of this variable is smaller than in the case of relative productivity; a one standard deviation in relative labor productivity increases average labor growth by 10 per cent per period of analysis (regression 5b).

The relative intensity in the use of raw materials is positively related to the growth of industrial labor, and is significant at the 95 per cent level in all regressions. As expected, raw material intensity acts as an industry location factor; industrial employment growth is higher in the regions where industrial activities are relatively more intense in the use of raw materials. Quantitatively, a one standard deviation in relative raw material intensity increases average labor growth by 7 per cent per period of analysis. Taking into account that, in Chile, these kinds of activities are predominantly located in non-metropolitan regions, which have a clear comparative advantage in natural resources, it is plausible to say that between 1985 and 1997, access to raw materials was a centrifugal force that favored the regional dispersion of industrial activities.

Regressions 1a and 1b include all the variables that are not connected to the effects of external scale economies. As expected, relative labor productivity – a proxy of regional relative wages – is positively related with regional industrial labor growth and is significant at the 95 per cent level in all regressions. Those regions with a relatively higher productivity attracted more industrial labor between 1985 and 1997. The impact of this variable is the most important one in quantitative terms: a one standard deviation in relative labor productivity increases average labor growth by 17 per cent per period of analysis[6]. This variable presents relevant disparities among regions and industrial activities, which probably explains why its quantitative impact on labor growth increases to 20 per cent when the fix effects of dummy variables are considered.

Relative plant size also has the expected sign – regions where activities have relatively smaller establishments created more industrial labor – and is significant at the 95 per cent level in all regressions. This result is consistent with the idea that small firms are effective in creating jobs. The quantitative impact of this variable is smaller than in the case of relative productivity; a one standard deviation in relative labor productivity increases average labor growth by 10 per cent per period of analysis (regression 5b).

The relative intensity in the use of raw materials is positively related to the growth of industrial labor, and is significant at the 95 per cent level in all regressions. As expected, raw material intensity acts as an industry location factor; industrial employment growth is higher in the regions

---

6 This and the following quantitative impacts are obtained using standardized coefficients of regressions in columns 5a and 5b.

where industrial activities are relatively more intense in the use of raw materials. Quantitatively, a one standard deviation in relative raw material intensity increases average labor growth by 7 per cent per period of analysis. Taking into account that, in Chile, these kinds of activities are predominantly located in non-metropolitan regions, which have a clear comparative advantage in natural resources, it is plausible to say that between 1985 and 1997, access to raw materials was a centrifugal force that favored the regional dispersion of industrial activities.

Regional relative paved road endowment, as a proxy of internal trade costs, does not seem to be a factor of location of industrial activities in Chile between 1985 and 1997. The coefficient of this variable is significant at the 90 per cent level, only in regression 1a, and, unexpectedly, it has a negative sign. That is to say, it appears that industrial labor grew faster in the regions with a relatively poorer paved road endowment. Nevertheless, this result becomes insignificant when the fixed effects of region and industrial activity are considered in column 1b and in the rest of regressions.

Regressions 2a to 5b include the variables related to the externalities that steam from the agglomeration of activities. Relative regional specialization in an industrial activity, that, in principle, could give rise to within industry externalities, is negatively related with industrial labor growth. The coefficient of this variable is significant at the 95 per cent level in regressions 2 and 5 and increases when fixed factors are considered. This result is consistent with the hypothesis that the most specialized regions of Chile, the non-metropolitan regions, were not able to attract industrial labor between 1985 and 1997. In fact, relative regional specialization implied a relative lower growth of industrial labor. Quantitatively, a one standard deviation in relative specialization in one activity reduced average labor growth by 18 per cent per period of analysis (regression 5b). Despite the high specialization of some regions, there is no evidence of localization economies in Chile. On the contrary, specialization appears to be related with the existence of diseconomies of agglomeration that delay regional industrial development.

As expected, relative regional agglomeration of activities from the same industrial branch are positively related with relative labor growth at the 95 per cent level of significance when labor growth is considered aside from other possible sources of agglomeration scale economies (regressions 4a and 4b). This result indicates that some urbanization economies could exist in the Chilean industry. However, this variable has a smaller impact on labor growth than within industry agglomeration and becomes insignificant when both sources of externalities are considered together (regressions 2a and 2b).

The relative industrial diversity is unrelated with relative regional labor growth. This variable is insignificant in all regressions. This result implies that the agglomeration of several industrial activities was not a source of relevant urbanization economies in the Metropolitan Region, whose industrial fabric is clearly the most diverse of the country.

Regressions 5a and 5b include the variables of the model that are significant at a level higher than 90 per cent. The results for relative regional employment growth between 1985 and 1997 suggest that, in Chile, external scale economies arising from relative agglomeration are not a significant factor of location. Even, within industry agglomeration could have been an obstacle for industry location in non-metropolitan regions, particularly in the north and the south of the country where relative specialization at the beginning of the period was higher. According to the model results, the factors that favored industry location were a relatively smaller size of establishments, higher labor productivity, as a proxy of wages, and intensity in the use of raw materials, as a proxy of regional comparative advantage in natural resources endowment. Taking into account previous observations, it is to be expected that relative labor productivity would be a centripetal force that attracted industrial activities to the Metropolitan Region. At the same time, it is expected that the intensity in the use of raw materials would act as a centrifugal force, that contributed to the dispersion of activities towards other regions with comparative advantage in natural resources. In order to check these hypotheses and the robustness of previous results, the model is re-estimated with some restrictions in the sample.

Regional Results

The factors that affect industry location can act differently according to the regions that are considered. The model is re-estimated, first, for the Metropolitan Region and, afterwards, for the northern and southern regions of Chile, in order to test the robustness of previous estimations. The Northern and Southern regions are the geographical areas of the country that experienced the largest increases in the share of industrial employment between 1985 and 1997, but, at the same time, both areas present relevant differences. The analysis will allow us to assess to what extent industry location factors differ between core and peripheral regions of Chile. In this respect, it is plausible to consider, in the light of the prior discussion, that labor productivity has been a factor of concentration of industrial activity in the Metropolitan Region, while fixed resource endowment, mainly natural resources, has acted as a centrifugal force. Regarding external scale economies, it is also plausible to think that industry agglomeration have played a different role in both groups of regions, since the Metropolitan Region has the most diverse industrial fabric of the country and the northern and southern regions have the highest specialization quotients.

Table 9.8 Regression Results on Relative Industrial Labor Growth in the Metropolitan Region, 1985-1997

VARIABLES	1a	1b	2[a]	2b	3a	3b
C	-0.366 (0.354)	0.362 (0.370)	-0.048 (0.064)	-0.029 (0.236)	0.013 (0.015)	0.016 (0.065)
Relative productivity	0.184** (0.031)	0.226** (0.044)	0.183** (0.031)	0.231** (0.044)	0.181** (0.031)	0.231** (0.044)
Relative plant size	-0.193** (0.046)	-0.235** (0.057)	-0.143** (0.058)	-0.143* (0.080)	-0.140** (0.058)	-0.135* (0.078)
Raw material intensity	-0.054 (0.046)	-0.027 (0.052)				
Paved roads	0.318 (0.296)	0.320 (0.304)				
Within industry agglomeration			0.035 (0.046)	-0.045 (0.479)		
Related industry agglomeration			0.072 (0.052)	0.013 (0.477)	0.043* (0.028)	0.066* (0.036)
Diversity			0.339 (0.339)	0.372 (0.400)		
Dummy variables	NO	YES	NO	YES	NO	YES
R^2	0.176	0.228	0.181	0.239	0.176	0.236
N	234	234	234	234	234	234

* Significant at 0.1 level ** Significance at 0.05 level. Standard deviation in parentheses.
Source: Author.

Tables 9.8 and 9.9, show, respectively, the results of the estimations of the model for the Metropolitan Region and northern and southern regions of Chile together. In both areas, relative productivity of labor stands out as the most important determinant of industrial employment growth of the country and is significant at the 95 per cent level in all regressions. Recalling the hypothesis previously stated, the coefficient of this variable in the Metropolitan Region almost doubles the coefficient of the north and the south of the country. As expected, industrial labor productivity predominantly acted as a centripetal force that contributed to increase the concentration of industrial activities in the core region of Chile.

The result significantly changes when the role of relative intensity in the use of raw material is estimated. This variable is positively related with relative labor growth in northern and southern Chilean regions, where it is significant at the 95 per cent level in all regressions and presents a quantitative impact similar to labor productivity. In contrast, the relative intensity in the use of raw material has no significant relationship with industrial labor growth in the Metropolitan Region. This result is consistent with the idea that natural resources endowment has acted as a centrifugal force, attracting raw materials intensive activities towards the north and the south of the country.

Table 9.9 Regression Results on Relative Industrial Labor Growth in Northern and Southern Regions, 1985-1997

VARIABLES	1a	1b	2a	2b	3a	3b
C	-0.077** (0.033)	-0.154 (0.313)	-0.130 (0.103)	-0.081 (0.351)	0.255 (0.205)	-0.077 (0.308)
Relative productivity	0.088** (0.031)	0.177** (0.040)	0.072** (0.031)	0.174** (0.040)	0.067** (0.031)	0.174** (0.040)
Relative plant size	-0.152** (0.035)	-0.199** (0.041)	-0.113** (0.046)	-0.131* (0.059)	-0.110** (0.046)	-0.128** (0.058)
Raw material intensity	0.105** (0.036)	0.158** (0.041)	0.080** (0.033)	0.150** (0.042)	0.074** (0.033)	0.149** (0.042)
Paved roads	-0.052* (0.024)	-0.061 (0.058)				
Within industry agglom.			-0.042 (0.032)	-0.045 (0.048)	-0.045** (0.024)	-0.062* (0.034)
Related industry agglom.			0.004 (0.029)	-0.022 (0.040)		
Diversity			-0.001 (0.077)	-0.018 (0.078)		
Dummy variables	NO	YES	NO	YES	NO	YES
R^2	0.067	0.152	0.068	0.157	0.071	0.157
N	411	411	411	411	411	411

* Significant at 0.1 level ** Significance at 0.05 level. Standard deviation in parentheses.
Source: Author.

Relative plant size is negatively related to industrial labor growth in both areas and significant at the 90 per cent level when region and industry fixed effects are considered. In both cases, industries with relatively smaller plants attracted more labor. Quantitatively, the impact of relative plant size on industrial labor growth is almost the same in the Metropolitan Region and the north and south of the country.

As expected, the impact of external scale economies arising from agglomeration on industrial labor growth significantly differs between the Metropolitan Region and the north and south of the country. In the later area, it possible to observe that, as in the whole country, relative specialization in one activity is negatively related to relative labor growth, at the 95 per cent level of significance, while the other sources of externalities are statistically insignificant. This result indicates the lack of powerful localization and urbanization externalities and is particularly remarkable in the case of the north and the south of Chile since the regions from these areas present the highest levels of specialization of the country.

Theoretically (Fujita. *et al.*, 1999), the increase in openness, through a reduction in external trade costs, should have promoted stronger localization economies in relatively specialized regions. The limitations of relative specialization as a source of external scale economies in northern and southern regions of Chile can be based, among other reasons, on the predominance of raw material intensive activities in these areas. However, this is a complex point that deserves a more detailed analysis of sectoral and industrial productive linkages.

In contrast, while there is no significant relation between relative specialization in one activity and relative industrial labor growth in the Metropolitan Region, it is possible to observe a positive relationship, significant a the 90 per cent level, between relative specialization in one industrial branch and relative labor growth. The diversity of the Metropolitan industry seems to favor the emergence of urbanization economies at a branch level. This result confirms the idea of the existence of powerful linkages arising from agglomeration in the Metropolitan Region. These linkages are a source of external scale economies and act as a centripetal force that attracts industrial firms to the core region of Chile, as previously observed.

Conclusions

The analysis of industry location factors in Chile between 1985 and 1997 reveal the existence of different patterns of location among regions. These patterns particularly differ in the case of the Metropolitan Region and northern and southern regions of the country and possibly contribute to maintain a core-periphery structure that has retarded the regional dispersion of industrial activities.

Drawing on the model that has been estimated, it seems that internal trade costs are not a significant factor for industry location. It would be possible to say that some regions with relatively poor paved roads endowment have attracted more employment than the rest. This unexpected result could be related with the relevance of raw materials intensity as a dispersion force. Some firms need to be located close to the sources of raw materials even if internal trade costs are high. In any case, the analysis of the impact of internal trade costs on industry location deserves more detailed attention, especially due to the changes that Chile has recently experienced thanks to the implementation of a program of roads concessions.

The main centripetal forces in the economic geography of Chile between 1985 and 1997 were the external scale economies arising from the relative specialization of the Metropolitan Region in activities from the same industrial branch and, above all, the relative productivity of labor that, in the Metropolitan Region, had a positive effect on industrial labor growth significantly higher than in the rest of the country. The main centrifugal force was the intensity in the use of raw materials, used as a proxy of regional comparative advantage in natural resource endowment.

These results imply the existence of a location pattern that, at least, contributes to preserve the primacy of the Metropolitan Region and to delay the process of regional dispersion of activities. The location pattern may be characterized as comprising two parts. The first part is a core region, with a diversified industrial fabric and mainly oriented to the domestic market; the second part comprises various peripheral regions, predominantly export-oriented and highly specialized in the production of raw materials intensive manufactures where productive linkages tend to be weak and give rise to few external scale economies.

References

Armstrong, H. and J. Taylor, J. (2000) *Regional Economics and Policy*, Oxford, Blackwell Publishers.

Atienza, M. (2000) *Apertura internacional y dispersión regional de la industria. Aplicación al caso de Chile entre 1985 y 1997*, unpublished Ph.D Thesis. Universidad Autónoma de Madrid, Spain.

Ffrench-Davis, R. and R. Saez (1995) "Comercio y desarrollo industrial en Chile," *Colección de Estudios CIEPLAN,* 41, 67-96.

Fujita, M., P. Krugman and A. Venables (1999) *The Spatial Economy. Cities, Regions and International Trade* Cambridge, MA, MIT Press.

Glaeser, E., H. Kallall, J. Scheinkman and A. Shleifer (1992) "Growth in cities," *Journal of Political Economy,* 100, 1126-1152.

Hanson, G. (1994) "Regional adjustment to trade liberalization," *NBER Working Paper* 4713.

Hanson, G. (1998) "North American economic integration and industry location," *NBER Working Paper* 6587.

Henderson, J.V. (1999a) "The effect of urban concentration on economic growth," Brown University. Draft. http://econ.pstc.brown.edu/faculty/henderson/

Henderson, J.V. (1999b) "Marshall's scale economies," *NBER Working Paper* 7358.

Henderson, J.V., A. Kunkoro and M. Turner (1995) "Industrial development in cities," *Journal of Political Economy,* 103, 1067-1090.

INE (Instituto Nacional de Estadística) (various years) "Encuesta Nacional Industrial Anual" (ENIA), Santiago.

INE (Instituto Nacional de Estadística) (various years) "Estadísticas de Transportes y Comunicaciones (ETC)," Santiago.

INE (Instituto Nacional de Estadística) (1999a) "Población de los centros poblados en Chile 1875-1992," Santiago.

INE (Instituto Nacional de Estadística) (1999b) "Estadísticas regionales de Chile 1990-1998," Santiago.

Kim, S. (1995) "The expansion of markets and the geographic distribution of economic activities: the trends in U.S. regional manufacturing structure. 1860-1987," *The Quarterly Journal of Economics,* 110, 881-908.

MIDEPLAN (Ministerio de Desarrollo y Planificación) (1993) "Compendio de estadísticas regionales," Santiago.

MIDEPLAN (Ministerio de Desarrollo y Planificación) (1998) "Población y ambiente. Prospectiva y Población," Santiago, 64-110.

MIDEPLAN (Ministerio de Desarrollo y Planificación) (1999) "Compendio de estadísticas regionales," Santiago.

Miranda, C. (1997) "Expansión urbana intercensal del Gran Santiago 1875-1992," *Estadística y Economía,* Second semester, 77-104

MOP (Ministerio de Obras Públicas) (various years) "Presupuesto ejecutado," Santiago, Dirección de Planeamiento. Departamento de Planes Intersectoriales. Mimeo.

MOP (Ministerio de Obras Públicas) (2000) "Estudio Plan Director 2000-2010," Santiago. Mimeo.

Venables, A. (2000) "Cities and trade: external trade and internal geography in developing countries," London School of Economics. http://econ.lse.ac.uk./staff/ajv/

Appendix A Variables Definitions

Dependent variable:

Relative labor growth: $$\Delta \ln\left(\frac{L_{ijt}}{L_{jt}}\right) = \left(\ln L_{ijf} - \ln L_{ijt}\right) - \left(\ln L_{if} - \ln L_{jf}\right) \quad \text{(A1)}$$

Independent variables:

Paved roads $$\ln\left(\frac{pav_{it} / road_{it}}{pav_t / road_t}\right) \quad \text{(A2)}$$

Specialization in one activity $$\ln\left(\frac{L_{ijt} / L_{it}}{L_{jt} / L_t}\right) \quad \text{(A3)}$$

Specialization in one branch $$\ln\left(\frac{L_{ikt} / L_{ijt}}{L_{kt} / L_{jt}}\right) \quad \text{(A4)}$$

Diversity $$\ln\left(\frac{\sum_{h \neq j}\left(L_{iht} / L_{it}\right)^2}{\sum_{h \neq j}\left(L_{ht} / L_t\right)^2}\right)_t \quad \text{(A5)}$$

Relative plant Size $$\ln\left[\left(L_{ijt} / est_{ijt}\right) / \left(L_{jt} / est_{jt}\right)\right] \quad \text{(A6)}$$

Raw materials intensity $$\ln\left[\left(mp_{ijt} / va_{ijt}\right) / \sum_j \omega\left(mp_{jt} / va_{jt}\right)\right] \quad \text{(A7)}$$

Relative productivity $$\ln\left[\left(va_{ijt} / L_{ijt}\right) / \left(va_{jt} / L_{jt}\right)\right] \quad \text{(A8)}$$

$\omega = L_{jt} / L_t$

t = initial period
i = region
k = activity (2-digit)
pav = km of paved roads
est = estimated number of firms
mp = raw material costs
f = final period
j, h = activity (4-digit)
l = employment
road = km of roads
va = value added

10 Regional Wage Differentials in Chile

Fernando Vial, Marcelo L. Lufin and Geoffrey J.D. Hewings

Introduction

The design of economic policy in Chile is often criticized as insensitive to the heterogeneity that is present across its regions. It is claimed that taking the country as an single spatial unit neglects the fact that effects of national policies related to taxes, public spending, and environmental regulation, sometimes generate opposite and unexpected effects in different locations.

In order to substantiate this claim, we should be able to prove that significant differences exist between regions in terms of how regional markets react to economic policy so that they should be treated as different entities in any formal economic analysis. A second step, and a more critical one, would be to identify the explanations associated with those differences so we can predict the effect of economic policy at interregional level.

Our study will focus on exploring differences in regional wages in Chile and will attempt to establish possible explanations for these differences. The Chilean National Socioeconomic Survey (CASEN) provides labor market data and socioeconomic information at the individual level. Further, individuals can be also specified by their residence at the regional, provincial, and municipality level. Accordingly, we will model the process of wage formation using data for the year 2000 at the regional level.

In the Chilean case, it is important to note that one single set of norms regulate the labor market in the whole country. Some significant examples for this work are: the existence of a single minimum wage, the employer's prerogative to fire her/his personnel at any time without any specific cause, and the right to hire substitute workers if strikes last more than certain period of time. Pension retirement and health insurance contributions are mandatory and homogenous across the whole country. At the same time, the average unionization rate is very low across all regions. Union power is only significant in certain industries and firms.

Therefore, the Chilean labor market can be pictured as one in which market forces act relatively free of intervention, with supply-demand interaction providing the main institutional mechanism that regulates wages. For the national labor market to operate as a single spatial unit within which workers and information flow freely across the country, one should expect that wages for comparable workers would not show significant differences across regions. Higher wages for some type of occupation in some regions would provide incentives for migration towards those regions. This will increase labor supply in those regions and it will decrease supply in the other regions, bringing interregional wage equality for the same type of occupations. Flows of capital from high-wage regions to low-wage regions should reinforce this result. Nonetheless, still some compensating differences may persist because of regional factors such as the endowment of amenities each region possesses. But once this effect is accounted for, interregional wage equality for the same type of job should prevail.

Several studies have gathered evidence that wage equality is not reached for comparable occupations in Chile across gender groups and locations. It is also apparent that significant differences can be found in economic structure across regions, moving costs may be not negligible for some groups because of the length of the country, market power may be exerted in some localities by large firms, and information may be imperfectly available either for workers or firms (see Aroca *et al.*, 2001; Aroca and Hewings, 2002).

In this study, we intend to assess the influence of individual characteristics and regional factors in explaining regional wages, modeling explicitly the interactions between both levels (individual and region). Most of previous studies in regional wages either have run separate models for each region or have considered the role of regional factors using fixed effects. We address the integration of individual and regional factors by using an hierarchical linear model. The model allows us to specify separately both levels of analysis and to integrate them in a single equation.

The chapter is structured as follows. In the next section, we make a brief theoretical review of causes of interregional wage differentials and methodological aspects related to their measurement. Following this review, we explain the methodological approach adopted, specify the model, and present the results of our analysis. The chapter is completed with the conclusions and suggestions for future research.

Theoretical Framework for Interregional Wage Differentials

Definition and sources of interregional wage differentials

Interregional wage equality can be defined as a situation of equal payment to some specific individual for carrying out a determined job under determined conditions, across all the regions in a country. Dickie and Gerking (1989) labeled this situation as weak interregional equality in contrast to equality in regional wage averages, which they refer to as strong regional wage equality. The latter one can be predicted only in very special settings; indeed, strong interregional wage differentials are perfectly compatible with a competitive labor market.

In a competitive economy with homogenous space, and with no significant costs on factor and information mobility, similar workers in the same type of occupation should obtain similar wages no matter where they live. Regional wage differentials for identical workers would be cleared by movements of labor and capital that sought to take advantage of those differences.[1]

Wage differentials between dissimilar workers entail no contradiction with interregional wage equality. Human capital theory has established empirical regularities that have been shown to be very stable across time and space regarding the impact on wages of individual's investment in education and training.[2] Individual wages are positively correlated with the amount and quality of education and training. Differentials may also be based on differences in individual skills that affect productivity. Higher wages to more skilled workers, everything else maintained equal, correspond to a premium for their higher productivity.

In practice, regional wage differences for similar workers exist and persist for various reasons. One line of explanation points to non monetary aspects of the job or the environment that influence individual welfare. In this context, wage differentials may arise as a compensating mechanism for differentials in environmental amenities (Roback, 1982; Berger *et al.*, 2003), risk of injury or death (Brown, 1980; Low and McPheters, 1983; and Cousineau *et al.*, 1992), employment and earning irregularities (Hammermesch and Wolf, 1990), and advancement prospects (Chapman and Hong, 1980). Highlighted not in references

---

[1] Even when no perfect mobility of factors is present, from trade theory point of view is possible to asset that wages would equalise. Note that in any case strong wage equality does not come out as a general result.

[2] Nonetheless, it must be noted that screening theory (Spence, 1973) assigns no value to education as determinant in worker's productivity. The level of education attained for an individual is rather a signal of her inherent productivity that firms use in their selection processes.

Rosen's (1974, 1986) arguments on differentiated products in pure competition may help to clarify this issue. First, we may regard each job position as a differentiated product. Each position can be characterized by a vector of characteristics. Workers choose the combinations of wages and job characteristics that maximize their utility. Firms make their decisions about job environment and wage so that they maximize profits. If a sufficiently large number of firms and workers concur at each wage-job characteristics combination, competence should produce competitive implicit prices for each characteristic. Moreover, we should observe that higher wages would be associated with a higher level of undesirable job characteristics and vice versa.

Other differentials may be grounded in conditions related to the characteristics of the economic sector or industry. In some industries, firms pay higher or "efficiency" wages in order to stimulate productivity and reduce rotation rates (Krueger and Summers, 1988). Technology may also be influential in workers productivity. Finally, some industries may exhibit a non competitive market structure which would influence the wage rates they pay to their employees.

Thus, when wage differentials play a compensating role, they are understood as equilibrium differentials for no market force acts to clear them. However, an efficient outcome requires that both workers and employers have symmetric and perfect information, whereas in many situations it can be argued that information is costly for both (Stigler, 1962). In addition, geographical barriers may reduce spatial mobility of the labor force, and as noted by Topel (1986) this immobility may induce wage differentials.

A very different rationale for wage differentials is based on the downward "stickiness" of wages because of unions and bargaining complexities (McCann, 2001). In this context, even if interregional weak wage equality prevails at some point of time, shocks that affect regions in a differentiated manner will break this equality with no prospects of automatic restoration.

Another well documented source of wage differentials is discrimination. Many studies document racial and gender discrimination in the labor market that is reflected in wage differentials (see for instance Corcoran and Duncan, 1979). As long as discrimination is not homogenous across regions, interregional wage differentials may persist for the same racial group or gender category.

So far, we have narrowed down our conceptualization of interregional wage equality so that one can distinguish between differences that arise from individual, job, and environmental heterogeneity, and those associated with market imperfections. Knowing the source of the differentials can serve as guidance for the interpretation of those differentials in the context of regional policy making. For instance, large urban infrastructure improvement may produce in the medium-term a decrease in perceived wages in some region with respect to others, but this is not necessarily an indication of welfare deterioration.

Methodological Approaches to Interregional Wage Differentials

Hedonic pricing has been promoted as a way to distinguish between compensating and non compensating wage differentials. The use of hedonic equations in labor economics can be traced back to Welch (1969). Mincer (1974) popularized an equation that related linearly the logarithm of the wage rate to individual characteristics such as education and experience. A typical specification (see for instance Berndt, 1991) is given in (10.1), where $\ln W_i$ is the natural logarithm of the wage rate of individual *i*, $Educ_i$ represents the years of schooling of individual *i*, Exp_i represents the years of experience of individual *i*, and Z_i is a column vector representing other characteristics of the individual.

$$\ln W_i = \beta_0 + \beta_1 Educ_i + \beta_2 Exp_i + \beta_3 Exp_i^{\,2} + \beta_4 (Educ_i * Exp_i) + \beta_5^T Z_i \quad (10.1)$$

We can interpret the partial derivatives with respect to workers characteristics of (10.1) - under some assumptions - as the unit price of that characteristic. Our weak wage equality condition will require these coefficients to be equal across regions after controlling for other variables. In other words, the unit returns per year of schooling and experience should be the same no matter the location.[3]

Note the close relation of this formulation to human capital theory. Schooling can be regarded as an investment in human capital and experience can be regarded as an investment in on-the-job training. Therefore, we expect positive signs for the coefficients associated with *Educ* and *Exp*. For the squared term of experience we expect a negative sign which in combination with the positive coefficient associated to *Exp* will reflect the positive effect of experience on perceived wages up to some point and then depreciation effects associated with age predominate.

Recently, other individual characteristics have been found to be important. For instance, Thomas and Strauss (2000) found for Brazilian urban workers that health condition, measured by different type of indexes such as height and body mass, yielded positive wage returns. Based on empirical testing, Millimet (2004) has claimed that job search abilities allow individuals to receive a wage closer to their maximum potential. In particular, he postulates that the cause of the sizeable residual in studies

---

[3] In other terms, we require the wage a worker perceives for carrying out some specific job in some specific surrounding environment to be spatially invariant. As we hardly could find cases of identical workers in identical jobs and identical environments across different parts of the country, the role of control variables becomes crucial.

explaining the positive correlation between firm size and wages is that applicants for vacancies in larger employers are better skilled in job search.

In the general literature, several studies on interregional wage differentials have been carried out. Earlier ones tended to test the strong interregional wage equality, but Bellante (1979) showed that an important part of wage differentials could be explained by differences in the composition of the labor force in each region and that those differences became much smaller or did not exist when similar workers across regions were compared. Later, Dickie and Gerking (1987) conducted a cross section study to determine if the interregional wage differentials were attributable to differences in average level of market valued labor characteristics or to differences in rates of returns of those characteristics. They found evidence suggesting that interregional factor and commodity movements tend to equalize rates of pay of similar full-time workers between four broad regions into which the U.S. was partitioned. Results have been mixed for the U.S. Hanushek (1973, 1981) rejected the equality in coefficients for regional wage equations but found that about 80% of the variation in earnings can be attributed to variation in returns to labor characteristics. Gerking and Weirick (1983) and Dickie and Gerking (1987) could not reject the weak interregional wage equality hypothesis,[4] and Krumm (1984) using panel data and dummy variables for locations found significant differences for nominal wages.

Farber and Newman (1987) decomposed interregional wage differentials in the U.S. for 1979 and their changes between 1973 and 1979. They found that differences in the return to worker and job characteristics may be at least as important as differences in that characteristic in regional wage variation and that returns to characteristics between the South and Non-South regions tended to converge. The authors stressed that those factors accounting for regional wage differentials cross-sectionally may not be the same as those that cause the change in differentials over time. Moreover, they point out that in a stochastic dynamic framework, short run wage differentials are expected because of incomplete adjustments to heterogeneous recent changes in the structural demand for labor across regions.

Later, Farber and Newman (1989) examined regional wage differentials integrating two competing explanations: i) regional wage inequalities are due to heterogeneous area labor markets, which produce significant differences in wage structure of earnings functions across the markets and ii) regional wage differences represent a compensating variation to offset differences in cost of living and non-pecuniary attributes. They developed a model of earnings determination where job

---

[4] It is interesting to note that they exclude from their samples workers with high percentage of earnings coming from transfers, self-employed workers, and part-time workers in an effort to improve accuracy and avoid including less mobile workers.

characteristic prices may be subject to regionally specific stochastic shocks or industry-specific factors while human capital characteristic prices are geographically invariant.

The model conceives that the wage earned by worker *i* who lives in region *k* is the product of the amount of personal and job characteristics (X_i) and their respective location specific prices (P_k):

$$W_{ik} = P_k X_i \tag{10.2}$$

Within the vector of characteristics, we can distinguish mutable characteristics (X_{im}) such as education and work experience; and immutable characteristics (X_{in}) such as race and age; and job characteristics (X_{ij}) such as safety and employment stability.

Hence, there are two causes for strong interregional wage inequality: differences in characteristic of workers and differences in the prices paid for those characteristics. If we assume that we have spatially fixed or unique factors, absence of stochastic disturbances, perfect information and factor mobility, then in equilibrium different levels of characteristics will be observed across regions but characteristic prices will converge. Therefore, strong interregional wage equality will not hold but the weak version will.

In order to incorporate the possibility of some characteristic subject to the influence of stochastic elements the authors developed the model described in (10.3). X_{it} represents a vector of human capital, personal and job characteristics of individual i at time t; X_{it}^0 is a vector representing prices that are not expected to have dominant stochastic elements, and X_{it}^1 is a vector that contain prices that potentially reflect large stochastic elements and industry specific factors leading to wage efficiency premiums.[5]

$$W_{it} = X_{it}B + e_{it} = X_{it}^0 B^0 + X_{it}^1 B^1 + e_{it} \qquad i = 1, \ldots\ldots N \tag{10.3}$$

The results supported regional homogeneity in non stochastic dominated coefficients for the two years considered in the study, 1973 and 1979.

In Chile, wage differential studies have been focused mostly on gender wage differentials. Montenegro (2001) studied gender differentials in returns to education, in returns to experience, and also gender wage differentials. Quantile regression was used to examine separately gender wage equations. The author found consistently for four different years residuals unexplained by education and experience that may be

[5] Efficiency wage theory postulates that the net productivity of workers is positively related with the wage rate. So it is possible to generate wage distributions for workers with identical productive characteristics.

attributable to negative wage discrimination for women. Also, this discrimination may be more intense when women exhibit higher levels of education and experience. Dresdner (2002) studied gender discrimination in Chile by decomposing wage residuals and analyzing their changes between 1990 and 1998. His purpose was to study how a rapid growth and anti-discriminatory policy have influenced gender gap.

Bravo *et al.* (1999) analyzed the evolution of intergroup wage inequality for two time periods, 1990 and 1996 using the methodology proposed by Katz and Murphy (1992) that ponders relative changes in labor demand and relative changes in labor supply for different groups. Groups were characterized by sector and by specific education-experience-gender levels. It was found that university workers experience a significant within-industry and between-industry increase of their relative demand. Ibarra (2001) analyzed the hypothesis of there being an increase in wage differentials between skilled and unskilled workers founding no supportive evidence for the case of Chile in the period 1992-1998.

Aroca and Vial (1998) estimated regional hedonic wage equations for the thirteen regions in Chile for each gender. Although the previous studies had used the CASEN survey (except Ibarra, 2001), they used the 1992 Supplementary Survey of Incomes of the National Institute of Statistics of Chile. As expected, education and experience turned out to be significant in almost every region. Nonetheless, the wage equations were statistically different among regions. This suggests that the weak wage equality hypothesis does not hold.

The estimation of hedonic wage equations entails some methodological considerations. There is a high dispersion in the ability to learn among individuals; for certain group of individuals is easier to acquire more education. So it is expected that there would exist a positive correlation between years of schooling and abilities. Also, Rivlin (1975) has pointed out that the individual characteristics that explain success in acquiring education are the same ones related to job success. The high correlation between abilities and the level of attained education causes an overestimation in the estimated coefficient associated with education (Willis, 1986). However Berndt (1991) affirms that there is no convincing evidence showing that individual differences in abilities explain an important portion of income differentials between individuals with different education levels.

Another issue in the estimation of hedonic wage equations is the possible influence of sample selection bias. Wages are observed only for those individuals who participate in the labor market, i.e., their market wage is greater than their reservation wage. These omitted observations may bias the value of the estimated coefficients compared with those that would be obtained from a sample drawn from the whole population. Estimation may be carried out employing a Tobit model, but likelihood functions are not easy to derive. Heckman (1979) developed a two-step procedure whereby sample bias is treated as if it were an omitted variable problem. However, this approach –known as the Heckit model after the author- does not perform well if the errors are not normal, the sample is small, the correlation between errors of the regression equation and selection equations is small, and the degree of colinearity between the regression and the selection equation is high (Kennedy, 1998).

Biased coefficients in regional hedonic wage equations would invalidate weak wage equality hypothesis testing. As can be inferred from our previous discussion, we require that coefficients across regions to be equal in order that the implicit unit prices of workers characteristics be equal.

Recapitulating, by means of hedonic equations we can explain differences in average regional wages decomposing them into differences in regional implicit prices associated with each individual characteristic and in differences in the level of average individual characteristics. This conceptualization corresponds to the Blinder-Oaxaca decomposition (Blinder, 1973; Oaxaca, 1973). We may also explain the wage differentials that the same worker would receive across regions by differences in implicit regional prices.

Nevertheless, we may push a step further in trying to explain interregional wage differentials with the intent to model the regional implicit price formation. One possible approach is to use a Linear Hierarchical Model (HLM). HLMs have been extensively and successfully used in studies related to education where variables related with students, schools they belong to, and districts containing the schools, may all be important in explaining students' performance. HLMs consist of several nested levels; in our case a two-level HLM would consider a first level represented by the hedonic wage equation (10.1) explaining individual earnings. The second level, would comprise equations explaining the level of some or all the coefficients considered in (10.1) as a function of regional variables. Thus, the first level would explain wages in terms of implicit prices, while the second level would explain coefficients as a function of regional variables related to the valuation of individual characteristics.

As the probability model associated with the error structure in multilevel modeling may become very complex, estimation is often carried out by some form of Generalized Least Squares or Maximum Likelihood. The specific error structure when we collapse all the different level models into one will be dependent upon the models we assume at each level. Raudenbush and Bryk (2002) offer a review of different variants and present applications.

HLM methodology offers an attractive way to provide a single structure for regional wage formation, assigning differentiated roles to individual and regional factors. While separated regressions provide us with specific analysis for each region, they tell us little about the causes of coefficient differences across regions. Indeed, statistical testing can be carried out to assess whether estimated coefficients or groups of them are different between two regressed equations but then only speculative analysis is possible in order to explain those results. Furthermore, the number of comparisons that result from all possible combinations often lead to a lack of parsimony in the analysis, especially if there is not a clear pattern in the results of the tests.

Model Specification and Results

A Two-level Hierarchical Linear Model for Modeling Regional Wages

Most of statistical inference is based on replicated observations of the same type of units of analysis. Normally, the analysis of such data is based on the assumption that either the sampled units themselves or the corresponding residuals are independent and identically distributed. However, in the case of labor data, observations can be regarded as coming from particular groups defined by economic sector and region. In fact, these kinds of data could be understood as units of analysis that are hierarchically nested.

In this context, and following Goldstein's ideas (2003), multilevel analysis is the appropriate statistical method for this type of data. An hierarchical linear model (HLM) can be formulated to study our case. We assume that our data can be grouped according economic sector and region, resulting in 117 different groups if we classify economic activity into 9 sectors and consider 13 regions.

Let us start by specifying a wage model at the individual level. For each group $j \in J$, where J represents the set of groups defined above, a Mincerian-type of equation can be defined. That is, the natural logarithm of wages (Y_{ij}) for individual i that belong to group j, is explained by some sectoral-regional fixed factor, and a column vector of mean centered explanatory variables (X_{ij}). The row vector b_j represents sectoral-regional slope coefficients, and ε_{ij} is an error exhibiting a normal distribution with zero mean and constant variance:

$$Y_{ij} = a_j + b_j X_{ij} + \varepsilon_{ij} \tag{10.4}$$

At sectoral-regional level, if we consider each group just as a random sample, then intercepts a_j and regression coefficients b_j should exhibit random variation. Letting a be the population mean of the intercepts across all groups and the group specific deviations from this mean by u_{0j}, the expression for each regional-sectoral coefficient would be:

$$a_j = a + u_{0j} \tag{10.5}$$

Analogously, we can define the dispersion of slopes as:

$$b_j = b + u_{1j} \tag{10.6}$$

This simple extension, leads us to a significant difference in terms of the error structure with ordinary hedonic wage models, as can be appreciated when substituting (10.5) and (10.6) into (10.7):

$$Y_{ij} = a + bX_{ij} + u_{0j} + u_{1j}X_{ij} + \varepsilon_{ij} \tag{10.7}$$

We can identify different types of residuals in (10.7). A level-1 residual ε_{ij} that varies over the population of individuals i and across groups j. Level-2 residuals u_{0j} and u_{1j} that vary over groups j. We may interpret these residuals as follows:

Large values of u_{0j} will be associated with large wage deviations with respect to the mean, for individuals belonging to j and exhibiting individual characteristics very close to the average ($X_{ij} \approx 0$).

Large values of u_{1j} are associated with a sectoral-regional group that exhibits a high wage response to increments in individual characteristics. In particular, the marginal response will be equivalent to $b + u_{1j}$.

Individuals associated with a large absolute value for ε_{ij} exhibit wages that are very different with respect to similar workers within the same sectoral-regional group.

It is interesting to point out that (10.7) differs significantly from a nation-pooled hedonic wage equation in the nature of the resulting error structure. Though both may include the same vector of independent variables, the error term in equation (10.7), $\xi_{ij} = u_{0j} + X_{ij}u_{1j} + \varepsilon_{ij}$, is heterokedastic and exhibits autocorrelation.[6]

Model (10.1), the traditional hedonic wage formulation, can be regarded as an effort to reduce the unexplained variation of wages with respect to a model where we only consider random variations about a mean, i.e. $\ln W_i = \beta_0 + \varepsilon_{ij}$. In the same fashion, we may want to push the hierarchical structure to reduce unexplained variation that arises from specifications (10.5) and (10.6). An improvement in the predictive quality of our extended model would tell us that level-2 explanatory variables

[6] Heteroskedasticity is implicitly in the term $X_{ij}u_{1j}$ and autocorrelation is given by the fact that any pair of errors associated to units of the same group j will share the common influence of the level-2 errors u_{0j} and u_{1j}.

contribute to explain the variation of wages across individuals and groups. Following Raudenbush and Bryk (2001) and Hox (1995), we will specify a Z_j vector of sectoral-regional effects at level-2. Therefore, (10.5) and (10.6) become:

$$a_j = a + c_0 Z_j + u_{0j} \tag{10.8}$$

$$b_j = b + c_1 Z_j + u_{1j} \tag{10.9}$$

Though, a_j and b_j are not directly observable, all the information needed to estimate their parameters is contained in (10.4), (10.8), and (10.9) as can be seen when we inspect the equation that results from substituting the two latter equations into the first one:

$$Y_{ij} = a + bX_{ij} + c_0 Z_j + c_1 X_{ij} Z_j + u_{0j} + u_{1j} X_{ij} + \varepsilon_{ij} \tag{10.10}$$

Now the interpretation of the error terms varies, though the error structure is the same with respect to (10.7). Note that though the terms like $c_0 Z_j + c_1 X_{ij} Z_j$ are often considered in specifications as (10.1), i.e. control variables and interactions between control variables and individual characteristics, some significant conceptual differences persist. First, as noted earlier, the error structures will differ and will make estimation methods used for an expanded version of (10.1) inappropriate in the context of (10.10). Secondly, instead of an heuristic specification of control variables, HLM provides a rationale for their inclusion and a framework for their interpretation.

The term $c_1 X_{ij} Z_j$ is known as the "interaction effect" between the individual level variables X_{ij} and the group level variables Z_j. The regression coefficient c_1 expresses how much the sectoral-regional context variables (Z_j) modifies the effect of the individual human capital (X_{ij}) on wages (W_{ij}), and it is called the "Cross-Level Interaction Effect" (CLIE). The term, u_{1j}, represents the interaction between the random term from level 2 associated with coefficient b_j and the level 1 variable X_{ij}; and it is known as the "Random Cross-Level Interaction Effect" (RCLIE).

Estimations and Results

Separated models were specified for males and females. As verified in several studies for the labor market in Chile, there are significant differences between the wages obtained by males and females. Different models allow us to go further than fixed effects in order to model wage equations for each gender. Moreover, we will verify in our study differences in model specification for each gender that reaffirm that a single model may not be appropriate to the whole population.

The model selection strategy consisted in estimating progressively more complete models and analyzing the gains in the explanation of variance when passing from one specification to another. We start with a very simple specification known as the "One-way ANOVA" model (Raudenbusch and Bryk, 2002). Then we pass to examine a model known as "Means as Outcomes Model". Though it includes level-2 explanatory variables, level-1 parameters are still modeled as a mean plus a random deviation. Next we specify the "Random Coefficient Model" that derives its name from the fact that variation in level-2 parameters is modeled as random while at level 1 we introduce explanatory variables. Finally, we consider level-1 and level-2 variables jointly in a specification known as "Intercept and Slopes as Outcomes Model."

In each stage, except the "One-way ANOVA model", different specifications of X_{ij} and Z_j were tried. The selection of variables is carried out according to sign consistency and individual significance. Note however, that in these types of models we do not have available some summary goodness of fit measure like the R^2 of standard regression. Instead, we observe from Model 1 what proportion of the variance can be attributed to level 1 and what proportion corresponds to level 2. Next, in Model 2 we analyze the effect of the introduction of level-2 variables in terms of explaining level-2 total variance. In Model 3, we apply the previous analysis for the case of level-1 variables and variance. Model 4 is a full model where we can appreciate both effects. Note that in this last step, the effect at level 2 is not simply the aggregation of effects obtained in Model 3 and Model 4 as there are interaction effects between both levels. The general purpose is to reduce the unexplained variability.

	Total Variance (0.61395+0.14029=0.75424)		
	Level I		**Level II**
Model 1	**81.94%**		**18.06%**
Model 2	**81.94%**		**62.07% out of 18.06%**
Model 3	**28.9% out of 81.94%**		**78.87% out of 18.06%**
Model 4	**28.9% out of 81.94%**		**90.66% out of 18.06%**

Note: Shaded cells indicate explained variance

Figure 10.1 Total Variance Decomposition for Female Wage Rate

Reliability estimates are also calculated for every estimate. The reliability scores measure the relative weight of the parameter variance over the sum of the parameter variance and the error variance. As the error variance shrinks the reliability increases with limit value equal to one. Supplementary statistics are also presented related to the explanation of total variance at each level. All these factors are pondered in order to choose the best specification for our data.

Female Workers

In table 10.1, we detail the results for the four different HLM formulations described above for the case of female workers. The results shown in the table are the best models obtained of each type. The formulation can be written as follows:

$$Y_{ij} = b_{0j} + \varepsilon_{ij} \tag{10.11}$$

$$b_{0j} = \gamma_{00} + u_{0j} \tag{10.12}$$

$$Y_{ij} = \gamma_{00} + u_{0j} + \varepsilon_{ij} \tag{10.13}$$

From Model 1 results, we can appreciate that the estimate associated with the grand mean wage was highly significant and the total variance around the mean to be explained amounts to 0.61395. As shown in figure 10.1 about 81.94% of this variation can be attributed to level 1 $\left[Var(\varepsilon_{ij})\right]$ and 18.06% to level 2 $\left[Var(u_{0j})\right]$. In other words, we may say that one can aspire to explain at most 81.94% of the variability of wages using level-1 variables, as in standard hedonic wage models. Additional explanation of the total variability of wages can be captured by the introduction of level-2 variables (up to 18.06%). The reliability level for the single level-1 parameter estimate of b_0, amounts to 78.3%.

In Model 2 (Means as Outcomes), two level-2 explanatory variables were significant: the proportion of workers for each sectoral-regional group that are formally hired (Formally-hired) i.e., they have permanent contracts, and the proportion of workers hired in small firms (Small-hired). We can write the final formulation as:

$$Y_{ij} = b_{0j} + \varepsilon_{ij} \tag{10.14}$$

$$b_{0j} = \gamma_{00} + \gamma_{01}(Formally-hired)_j + \gamma_{02}(Small-hired)_j + u_{0j} \tag{10.15}$$

$$Y_{ij} = \gamma_{00} + \gamma_{01}(Formally-hired)_j + \gamma_{02}(Small-hired)_j + u_{0j} + \varepsilon_{ij} \tag{10.16}$$

As shown in table 10.1, the level-2 coefficients (γ_{01} and γ_{02}) were highly significant and presented the expected signs, i.e. an increase in the proportion of formal workers in each sectoral-regional group affects positively the average wage while an increase of the proportion of employment by small size firms decreases the average wage in each sectoral-regional group. Note how the introduction of these level-2 variables reduced the unexplained variance at level-2. As shown in figure 10.1, 62.07% of the level-2 variance in wages is captured by these two variables.

Model 3 (Random Coefficients) considers level-1 variables but none of the level-2 variables. The following variables are introduced at individual level: years of schooling (Education), age as a proxy of experience (Age), the interaction of schooling and age (EducxAge), a dummy that assigns 1 to individual perceiving themselves in good health condition (Health), a dummy that assigns the value 1 to individuals working in the public sector (Public-worker), and a dummy variable that takes the value 1 if the individual works in the informal sector (Informal-worker).

We have intentionally excluded other individual variables such as the condition of being head of the households[7] or being married. Though these variables are typically included in hedonic wage equations, but their interpretation in terms of human capital theory is more controversial. In this context we should also be able to provide a theoretical explanation about why the effect of such variables may be mediated by sectoral-regional factors. We have opted here to sacrifice capturing a higher percentage of the level-1 variance as long as no convincing explanations for these effects can be provided.

The formulation selected can be represented as follows:

$$Y_{ij} = b_{0j} + b_{1j}(Education)_{ij} + b_{2j}(Age)_{ij} + b_{3j}(Educ * Age)_{ij} + b_{4j}(Health)_{ij} + b_{5j}(Public) + b_{6j}(Informal)_{ij} + \varepsilon_{ij} \quad (10.17)$$

$$b_{0j} = \gamma_{00} + u_{0j} \quad (10.18)$$

$$b_{3j} = \gamma_{30} + u_{3j} \quad (10.19)$$

$$b_{6j} = \gamma_{60} + u_{6j} \quad (10.20)$$

$$b_{lj} = \gamma_{l0} \quad (10.21)$$

for l = 1,2,4,5

$$Y_{ij} = \gamma_{00} + \gamma_{10}(Education)_{ij} + \gamma_{20}(Age)_{ij} + \gamma_{30}(Educ * Age)_{ij} + \gamma_{40}(Health)_{ij} + \gamma_{50}(Public)_{ij} + \gamma_{60}(Informal)_{ij} + u_{0j} + u_{3j}(Educ * Age)_{ij} + u_{6j}(Informal)_{ij} + \varepsilon_{ij} \quad (10.22)$$

[7] This corresponds to a self classification.

Table 10.1 Estimation Results for Female Workers[8]

		Coeff	Model 1 One-Way ANOVA	Model 2 Means as Outcomes	Model 3 Random Coefficients	Model 4 Intercept and Slopes as Outcomes
Fixed Effect						
Constant$_l$		γ_{00}	6.478135***	6.513179***	6.450551***	6.470521***
Level 2	Formally-hired (%)	γ_{01}	-	0.869782***	-	0.499047***
	Small-hired (%)	γ_{02}	-	-1.283927***	-	-0.461269***
Level 1	Education	γ_{10}	-	-	0.076903***	0.075829***
	Age	γ_{20}	-	-	0.010573***	0.010375***
	Educ X Age	γ_{30}	-	-	0.000212***	0.000199
	Health	γ_{40}	-	-	0.089089***	0.088528***
	Public	γ_{50}	-	-	0.106425***	0.110115***
	Informal	γ_{60}	-	-	-0.259488***	-0.263274***
Random Effect (Variance Component)						
Intercept		$Var(u_{0j})$	0.14029***	0.05321***	0.02963***	0.01310***
RCLIE	Educ X Age	$Var(u_{3j})$			0.00001***	0.00001***
	Informal	$Var(u_{6j})$			0.03919***	0.03443***
		σ^2	0.61395	0.61442	0.43681	0.43715
Statistics						
Model Deviance			34045.5067 91	33979.3652 55	29213.809967	29172.91792
Model Parameters			3	5	14	16
Reliability estimates[9]		b_0	0.783	0.655	0.677	0.534
		b_3	-	-	0.540	0.537
		b_6	-	-	0.500	0.480

Notes: * Significant at 10%, ** Significant at 5%, *** Significant at 1%.

From table 10.1 we can observe that all the coefficients associated with these variables are highly significant and present the expected signs. Education, experience, and health condition impact wages positively. Being a public employee also affects positively the wage but working in the informal sector results in lower labor payments. We observe also that experience and education reinforce each other. It is also observed that Model 3 improves the results in terms of variance components as the

[8] The estimations were carried out using HLM5.0, in options of Grand Centred media for independent variables and Full ML option. The sample includes 9,119 valid cases in level 1 and 113 valid groups in second level.

[9] The indicator is calculated following Raudenbush & Bryk (2001), equation 3.42, p. 46.

explained variance at level 1 increases compared to Model 2 (see figure 10.1).

Note in table 10.1, that the Random Cross Level Interaction Effects (RCLIE) associated with the interaction of education and age and to the condition of being an informal worker, were significant. These random components, acting jointly with the random intercept effect, increase the proportion of explained variance at the group level. According to these results, Model 3 offers a better explanation of regional wages than Model 2 or Model 1 do.

Model 4 (Intercept and Slopes as Outcomes) considered simultaneously both levels. Note that although random cross level interaction effects are still significant, cross level interaction effects were not significant, i.e. no statistical evidence that interaction between level-1 and level-2 variables affects wages earned by women. In other words, sectoral-regional variables do not amplify significantly the effect of individual characteristics on wages. The model can be described as follows:

$$Y_{ij} = b_{0j} + b_{1j}(Education)_{ij} + b_{2j}(Age)_{ij} + b_{3j}(Educ*Age)_{ij} + b_{4j}(Health)_{ij} + b_{5j}(Public) + b_{6j}(Informal)_{ij} + \varepsilon_{ij} \tag{10.23}$$

$$b_{0j} = \gamma_{00} + \gamma_{01}(Formally-hired)_j + \gamma_{02}(Small-hired)_j + u_{0j} \tag{10.24}$$

$$b_{3j} = \gamma_{30} + u_{3j} \tag{10.25}$$

$$b_{6j} = \gamma_{60} + u_{6j} \tag{10.26}$$

$$b_{lj} = \gamma_{l0} \tag{10.27}$$

for $l = 1,2,4,5$

$$Y_{ij} = \gamma_{00} + \gamma_{01}(Formally-hired)_j + \gamma_{02}(Small-hired)_j + \gamma_{10}(Education)_{ij} + \gamma_{20}(Age)_{ij} + \gamma_{30}(Educ*Age)_{ij} + \gamma_{40}(Health)_{ij} + \gamma_{50}(Public)_{ij} + \gamma_{60}(Informal)_{ij} + +u_{0j} + u_{3j}(Educ*Age)_{ij} + u_{6j}(Informal)_{ij} + \varepsilon_{ij} \tag{10.28}$$

Specifically, we model the mean wage in function of the proportion of individuals working in the formal sector and in function of the proportion of workers employed in small firms (γ_{01} and γ_{02} acting on b_{0j}). The level-2 variable associated with the share of each sectoral-regional group on the Gross Domestic Sectoral Product (GDSP), models the effect on wages of being an informal worker (γ_{61} acting on b_{6j}). The selected control variables are significant and exhibit the expected signs. Note that significance and signs are maintained for γ_{01} and γ_{02} when comparing

Model 2 and Model 4. The same occurs for γ_{10}, γ_{20}, γ_{40}, γ_{50}, and γ_{60} when comparing Model 3 and Model 4. However, γ_{30} the estimated coefficient associated with the interaction variable *Educ*Age* is no longer significant.

Table 10.2 Supplementary Statistics Female Workers

Test/Model	Model 1 One-Way ANOVA	Model 2 Means as Outcomes	Model 3 Random Coefficients	Model 4 Intercept and Slopes as Outcomes
Intra Class Correlation[10]				
$\hat{\rho} = \tau_{00} / (\sigma^2 + \tau_{00})$	0.18600	0.07969	0.06352	0.02909
Marginal proportion of variance explained in level 1[11]				
$PVEI = \dfrac{\sigma^2_{model\text{-}a} - \sigma^2_{model\text{-}b}}{\sigma^a_{model\text{-}a}}$		0.00000	0.28906	0.0000
Marginal proportion of variance explained in level 2[12]				
Index by b_0	-	0.62071	0.44314	0.55788
Index by b_3	-	-	-	0.00000
Index by b_6	-	-	-	0.12145
Deviance Test[13]				
Model(2) v/s Model(1)		66.14153***	-	-
Model(3) v/s Model(1)	-	-	4831.6968***	-
Model(3) v/s Model(2)	-	-	4765.5552***	-
Model(4) v/s Model(3)	-	-	-	40.8920***

Notes: * Significant at 10%, ** Significant at 5%, and *** Significant at 1%.

From the results, we can appreciate that while the fixed effect associated with the condition of being an informal worker (γ60) is negative,

---

[10] It is calculated following Raudenbush and Bryk (2002), equation 2.10 p. 24 and it is equivalent with the proportion of variance in wages (level 1) that is associated with groups in level 2. It is similar to the interpretation that Hox (1995) gives to equation 2.8 in p.14, where $\tau_{qq} = \mu_q$. For models 2, 3, and 4 this represents only an interclass correlation measure.

[11] It is calculated following Raudenbush and Bryk (2002), equation 4.2 p. 79.

[12] It is calculated following Raudenbush and Bryk (2002), equation 4.12 in p. 74 and equation 4.24 in p.85.

$$\text{Index} = \left[\hat{\tau}_{qq}a - \hat{\tau}_{qq}b\right] / \hat{\tau}a$$

[13] It is calculating following Hox (1995) p.21, in which reduction in the level of deviance are associated with improving in the model specification. Another important feature is since that the estimation is obtaining using a FML method directly the following expression can be used: DT= |Deviance Value (model b) - Deviance Value (model a)| ~ $\chi^2_{(kb-ka)}$.

the variable part, which depends on the share in the GDSP of the worker's sectoral-regional group, is positive.

Model 4 increased the proportion of explained variance at group level. As shown in table 10.2, in particular the terms associated with b_{oj} and b_{6j} have an important rate of marginal capture of level-2 variance. Figure 10.1 shows that while the level-1 explanation improves, level-2 variance explanation goes up to 90.66%. These results confirm that model 4 can be considered a better alternative to Model 3.

Male Workers

Tables 10.3 and 10.4 exhibit the HLM results for male workers. Model 1 was specified in the same way as for the case of female workers, hence equations (10.11)-(10.13) apply here too. The results showed an intra-class correlation near 15% that is very similar to the figure obtained for female workers. Therefore, at most 85% of the total wage variance can be explained by level-1 variables (see figure 10.2). The reliability level associated with b_{0j} reached 88%, indicating that the sample of estimators (means) strongly tends to capture the true parameter variance.

In Model 2, the same two level-2 explanatory variables that resulted significant in explaining the mean term, b_{0j}, in the case of female workers were also significant and sign consistent here: the proportion of male workers hired in the formal sector for each sectoral-regional group and the proportion of labor force hired in small firms for each sectoral-regional group. Hence, the specification given in (10.14)-(10.16) applies also in this case. Both variables are linked with labor demand characteristic in each group and have a positive effect on the estimated model, increasing the explained variance in the second level. In figure 10.2 we can appreciate that both variables explain about 59% of the level-2 variance.

	Total Variance (0.56317+0.10287=0.66604)		
	Level I		**Level II**
Model 1	**84.55%**		**15.45%**
Model 2	**84.55%**		58.96% out of 15.45%
Model 3	22.63% out of 84.55%		77.07% out of 15.45%
Model 4	22.63% out of 84.55%		92.34% out of 15.45%

Note: Shaded cells indicate explained variance

Figure 10.2 Total Variance Decomposition for Male Wage Rate

Model 3 yielded results that were similar to those for female workers in the sense that the same set of coefficients was significant and exhibited the expected signs (see table 10.3). The specification given in (10.17)-(10.22) applies. This formulation increased the proportions of level-1 and level-2 explained variances to 22.63% and 77.07% respectively. In Model 3, two random slopes effects were incorporated in the Education-Age-interaction variables and in the dummy variable for informal employment. Both fixed part estimators (γ30 and γ60) showed the expected signs. For the case of their random parts, the coefficients associated with the Random Cross Level Interaction Effect (u_{3j} and u_{6j}) were significant but with a very small marginal impact on the average wage.

Finally, in Model 4 there are some changes with respect to the model that was chosen for female workers (see equations 10.30, 10.31, 10.32 and 10.34). The slope associated with the level-1 interaction variable is dependent upon the proportion of formally hired workers in that sectoral-regional group and on the proportion of workers hired in small size firms (see equation 10.30). For the case of the slope associated to the level-1 interaction variable *Educ*Age*, two sectoral-regional factors appear as influential: the proportion of formally hired workers in that group and the share of that group in the national foreign direct investment during the period 1974-2000 (Share-FDI) (see equation 10.31).

$$\begin{aligned} Y_{ij} &= b_{0j} + b_{1j}(Education)_{ij} + b_{2j}(Age)_{ij} + b_{3j}(Educ * Age)_{ij} + \\ &b_{4j}(Health)_{ij} + b_{5j}(Public) + b_{6j}(Informal)_{ij} + \varepsilon_{ij} \end{aligned} \tag{10.29}$$

$$b_{0j} = \gamma_{00} + \gamma_{01}(Formally - hired)_j + \gamma_{02}(Small - hired)_j + u_{0j} \tag{10.30}$$

$$b_{3j} = \gamma_{30} + \gamma_{31}(Formally - hired)_j + \gamma_{32}(Share - FDI)_j + u_{3j} \tag{10.31}$$

$$b_{6j} = \gamma_{60} + u_{6j} \tag{10.32}$$

$$b_{lj} = \gamma_{l0} \tag{10.33}$$

for l = 1,2,4,5

$$\begin{aligned} Y_{ij} &= \gamma_{00} + \gamma_{01}(Formally - hired)_j + \gamma_{02}(Small - hired)_j + \\ &\gamma_{10}(Education)_{ij} + \gamma_{20}(Age)_{ij} + \gamma_{30}(Educ * Age)_{ij} + \gamma_{40}(Health)_{ij} + \\ &\gamma_{50}(Public)_{ij} + +\gamma_{60}(Informal)_{ij} + \\ &\gamma_{31}\{(Educ * Age)_{ij} * (Formally - hired)_j\} + \\ &\gamma_{32}\{(Educ * Age)_{ij} * (Share - FDI)_j\} + u_{0j} + \\ &u_{3j}(Educ * Age)_{ij} + +u_{6j}(Informal)_{ij} + \varepsilon_{ij} \end{aligned} \tag{10.34}$$

Table 10.3 Estimation Results for Male Workers†

Associated Variables \ Model		Coeff	Model 1 One-Way ANOVA	Model 2 Means as Outcomes	Model 3 Random Coefficients	Model 4 Intercept and Slopes as Outcomes
Fixed Effect						
Constant_I		γ_{00}	6.673156***	6.700157***	6.61101***	6.622281***
	Formally-hired	γ_{01}	-	0.976640***	-	0.429724***
Level 2	Small-hired	γ_{02}	-	-0.768165***	-	-0.452047***
	Education_I	γ_{10}	-	-	0.06190***	0.062468***
	Age_I	γ_{20}	-	-	0.00533***	0.005425***
	Educ X Age_I	γ_{30}	-	-	0.00056***	0.000565***
	Health	γ_{40}	-	-	0.09416***	0.093980***
Level 1	Public	γ_{50}	-	-	0.11862***	0.120935***
	Informal	γ_{60}	-	-	-0.1798***	-0.174938***
	Formally-hired	γ_{31}	-	-	-	0.001817***
CLIE	Share-GDSP	γ_{32}	-	-	-	-0.000410**
Random Effect (Variance Component)						
Intercept		$Var(u_{0j})$	0.1028***	0.0422***	0.0236***	0.0079***
RCLIE	Educ X Age	$Var(u_{0j})$	-	-	0.00001***	0.00001***
	Informal	$Var(u_{0j})$	-	-	0.03951***	0.04089***
		σ^2	0.56317	0.56332	0.43571	0.43584
Statistics						
Model Deviance			48560.800290	48479.262049	43196.458069	43113.644469
Model Parameters			3	5	14	18
Reliability estimates††		b_0	0.878	0.788	0.725	0.534
		b_3	-	-	0.582	0.492
		b_6	-	-	0.584	0.589

Notes: * Significant at 10%, ** Significant at 5%, and *** Significant at 1%.
†The estimations were done using software HLM5.0, in options of Grand Centered media for independent variables and Full ML option. The sample includes 18,944 valid cases in level 1 and 117 valid groups in second level.
††Raudenbush and Bryk (2001), p. 46.

This particular set of level-2 control variables, turned out to be significant and exhibited the expected signs. For the mean controls (γ_{01} and γ_{02}), we obtained similar results with respect to Model 3 for male workers, and for Models 3 and 4 in the case of female workers.

Finally, we can appreciate that Model 4's specification increases the proportion of explained variance at sectoral-regional level (see figure 10.2). Results presented in table 10.4 show that in particular the terms associated with b_{0j} and b_{6j} have an important rate of marginal capture of level-2 variance. These results confirm that Model 4 may be considered a better alternative than Model 3.

Table 10.4 Supplementary Statistics Male Workers

Test \ Model	Model 1 One-Way Anova	Model 2 Means as Outcomes	Model 3 Random Coefficients	Model 4 Intercept and Slopes as Outcomes
Intra Class Correlation[†]				
$\hat{\rho} = \tau_{00} / (\sigma^2 + \tau_{00})$	0.154450	0.069707	0.051366	0.017758
Marginal proportion of variance explained in level 1[††]				
$PVEI = \frac{\sigma^2_{model-a} - \sigma^2_{model-b}}{\sigma^a_{model-a}}$		0.00002	0.226325	0.00002
Marginal proportion of variance explained in level 2[†††]				
Index by b_0	-	0.589676	0.441127	0.665960
Index by b_3	-	-	-	0.000000
Index by b_6	-	-	-	(0.03492)
Deviance Test[14]				
Model(2) v/s Model(1)	-	81.538241***	-	-
Model(3) v/s Model(1)	-	-	5364.3422***	-
Model(3) v/s Model(2)	-	-	5282.8039***	-
Model(4) v/s Model(3)	-	-	-	82.8136***

Notes: * Significant at 10%, ** Significant at 5%, and *** Significant at 1%.
[†]Raudenbush and Bryk (2002), p. 24. For models 2, 3, and 4 this represents only an interclass correlation measure.
[††]Raudenbush and Bryk (2002), p. 79.
[†††]Raudenbush and Bryk (2002), p. 74.

Table 10.5 Cross Level Interactions Female and Male Workers

			Individual Characteristics						
			Mean Wage	Educ	Age	Ed*Age	Health	Public	Informal
Group Characteristics	Female	Formally-hired	γ_{01}						
		Small-hired	γ_{02}						
	Male	Formally-hired	γ_{01}			γ_{31}			
		Small-Hired	γ_{02}						
		Share-FDI				γ_{32}			

Analysis of Results from the Point of View of Interregional Wage Differentials

We have found evidence in the previous section that sectoral-regional variables influence the effect of individual characteristics on wages for individuals –males and females-working in those groups. In the case of

[14] Hox (1995) p. 21.

female workers, the proportion of women formally hired and the proportion of women working for small size firms turned out to be highly significant. For the case of males, the group's share of the total foreign direct investment for the 1974-2000 period was relevant together with the variables aforementioned. The way in which those variables affect wage equations differ as can be seen from an examination of (10.28) and (10.34). Table 10.5 summaries the previous findings.

Table 10.6 Sectoral-Regional Effects on Individual Hourly Wage Female Workers

	R1	R2	R3	R4	R5	R6	R7	R8	R9	R10	R11	R12	R13
Agriculture	1.000	1.049	1.262	1.259	1.336	1.366	1.222	1.218	1.155	1.341	1.267	1.367	1.417
Mining	1.818	2.031	1.817	1.735	1.921	1.765	1.513	1.690	1.391	2.077	1.899	1.968	1.822
Manufacture	1.389	1.521	1.533	1.566	1.575	1.548	1.461	1.576	1.359	1.559	1.391	1.591	1.746
Energy	1.196	1.376	1.402	1.396	1.273	1.300	1.262	1.364	1.311	1.313	1.313	1.371	1.448
Construction	2.154	1.835	1.651	1.830	1.694	1.700	1.592	1.788	1.509	1.838	1.797	2.277	1.890
Retail Servs	1.238	1.516	1.494	1.423	1.486	1.496	1.449	1.459	1.309	1.386	1.309	1.354	1.638
Transp&Tel	1.258	1.379	1.412	1.408	1.384	1.334	1.272	1.343	1.261	1.327	1.295	1.433	1.493
Financial Ss	1.567	1.751	1.444	1.590	1.581	1.655	1.600	1.651	1.510	1.583	1.605	1.766	1.777
Other	1.406	1.565	1.501	1.510	1.442	1.445	1.446	1.426	1.397	1.460	1.582	1.599	1.519

In order to analyze the effect of sectoral-regional variables we will examine the variation of wages that a specific worker would experiment of choosing different sectoral-regional groups. Table 10.6 show this effect for the case of female workers, relative to the wage that a woman would receive in Agriculture in Region 1. In other words, the following expression applies to each cell:

$$\frac{w_{ij}}{w_{i1}} = \exp\{\gamma_{01}[(Formally-hired)_j - (Formally-hired)_1] + \\ + \gamma_{02}[(Small-hired)_j - (Small-hired)_1]\}$$

Note that because no cross level interaction terms are present, the effect of personal characteristics is cancelled out in this ratio. Therefore, Table 10.6 reflects the pure effect of sectoral-regional variables on the constant term.

As can be appreciated in table 10.6, sectoral-regional variables can produce a wide dispersion of wages at intraregional level and at intrasectoral level. For instance, the same person may double her wage by moving form the base sector Agriculture-Region 1 to Mining-Region 2. This wide difference may be attributed to the greater formality of Region 2's Mining sector with respect Region 1's Agriculture Sector, and by the major importance of small firms as a hiring source in Region 1's Agriculture sector.

We can also compare wages across regions for a given sector and across sectors given regions in order to analyze what alternatives would be more convenient for a hypothetical individual. Tables 10.7 and 10.8 exhibit descending wage rankings for the figures presented in table 10.6.

Table 10.7 Sectoral Wage Ranking by Region for the Same Female Individual

Ranking/ Region	1st	2nd	3rd	4th	5th	6th	7th	8th	9th
R1	Constr	Mining	FinSer	Other	Manuf	T&T	Retail	Energy	Agric
R2	Mining	Const	FinSer	Other	Manufr	Retail	T&T	Energy	Ag
R3	Mining	Const	Manufr	Other	Retail	FinSer	T&T	Energy	Ag
R4	Constr	Mining	FinSer	Manufr	Other	Retail	T&T	Energy	Ag
R5	Mining	Const	FinSer	Manufr	Retail	Other	T&T	Ag	Energy
R6	Mining	Const	FinSer	Manufr	Retail	Other	Ag	T&T	Energy
R7	FinSer	Const	Mining	Manufr	Retail	Other	T&T	Energy	Ag
R8	Const	Mining	FinSer	Manufr	Retail	Other	Energy	T&T	Ag
R9	FinSer	Const	Other	Mining	Manufr	Energy	Retail	T&T	Ag
R10	Mining	Const	FinSer	Manufr	Other	Retail	Ag	T&T	Energy
R11	Mining	Const	FinSer	Other	Manufr	Energy	Retail	T&T	Ag
R12	Const	Mining	FinSer	Other	Manufr	T&T	Energy	Ag	Retail
R13	Const	Mining	FinSer	Manufr	Retail	Other	T&T	Energy	Ag

Key: Const (Construction); Ag (Agriculture); Manufr (Manufacturing); T&T (Transport and Telecommunications) FinSer (Financial Services)

From table 10.7, we can see that Mining and Construction appear to be in the category of highest or second highest wage category for the majority of regions; while Agriculture always is ranked as the lowest paid, second lowest paid , or third lowest paid. Financial Services are most of the time ranked as the third best paid sector, while at the other extreme, the estimated wage in Transport and Telecommunications is the second or third worst paid.

In table 10.8, we can observe that the Metropolitan Region (Region 13) exhibits wages ranked in one of the first three places for 7 out of 9 sectors. The same applies to Region 12. In the other extreme Region 9 and Region 1 wages are ranked in the three last categories in 8 out of 9 sectors and 7 out of 9 sectors respectively.

Table 10.9 shows a comparison of sectoral-regional wages taking Agriculture-Region 1 as a normalization for the case of male workers. Nonetheless, in this case personal characteristics are not cancelled out in the expression of the wage ratios, because the presence of interaction terms. Therefore, we arbitrarily have defined a male worker characterized by complete primary education (8 years), 35 years old, in good health condition, and working in the private sector as a formal worker.

Table 10.8 Regional Wage Ranking by Sector for the Same Female Individual

Ranking	Agric	Mining	Manufr	Energy	Const	Retail	T&T	Fin Ser	Other
1	R13	R10	R13	R13	R12	R13	R13	R13	R12
2	R12	R2	R12	R3	R1	R2	R12	R12	R11
3	R6	R12	R8	R4	R13	R6	R3	R2	R2
4	R10	R5	R5	R2	R10	R3	R4	R6	R13
5	R5	R11	R4	R12	R2	R5	R5	R8	R4
6	R11	R13	R10	R8	R4	R8	R2	R11	R3
7	R3	R1	R6	R10	R11	R7	R8	R7	R10
8	R4	R3	R3	R11	R8	R4	R6	R4	R7
9	R7	R6	R2	R9	R6	R10	R10	R10	R6
10	R8	R4	R7	R6	R5	R12	R11	R5	R5
11	R9	R8	R11	R5	R3	R9	R7	R1	R8
12	R2	R7	R1	R7	R7	R11	R9	R9	R1
13	R1	R9	R9	R1	R9	R1	R1	R3	R9

Key: Const (Construction); Ag (Agriculture); Manufr (Manufacturing);
T&T (Transport and Telecommunications) FinSer (Financial Services)

Table 10.9 Sectoral-Regional Effects on Individual Hourly Wage Male Worker

	R1	R2	R3	R4	R5	R6	R7	R8	R9	R10	R11	R12	R13
Agriculture	1.000	1.045	1.250	1.247	1.317	1.347	1.213	1.204	1.144	1.304	1.240	1.326	1.388
Mining	1.754	1.930	1.741	1.673	1.834	1.701	1.477	1.639	1.352	1.955	1.831	1.875	1.748
Manufacture	1.353	1.474	1.482	1.510	1.522	1.503	1.425	1.528	1.326	1.510	1.363	1.532	1.673
Energy	1.199	1.360	1.389	1.385	1.261	1.286	1.254	1.349	1.300	1.297	1.301	1.352	1.418
Const	2.041	1.766	1.617	1.767	1.639	1.629	1.540	1.720	1.469	1.751	1.714	2.140	1.805
Retail	1.218	1.474	1.449	1.390	1.444	1.449	1.408	1.422	1.282	1.348	1.278	1.325	1.578
Transp&Tel	1.232	1.336	1.377	1.373	1.344	1.304	1.245	1.307	1.234	1.290	1.261	1.387	1.441
Financial S	1.515	1.685	1.415	1.537	1.525	1.590	1.538	1.590	1.457	1.522	1.544	1.687	1.700
Other	1.380	1.525	1.463	1.470	1.404	1.404	1.408	1.393	1.363	1.418	1.533	1.549	1.470

Again significant wage differentials can be obtained by relocating the individual in different sectoral-regional groups. This time, these differentials are derived from differences in the formal level and relative importance of small firms as employers in each sectoral-regional group and by the interaction of the level of formality of each group and its share in the GDSP with Education by Age. The first cross level interaction coefficient is positive, telling us that the positive effect on wages of education and experience is amplified when a greater level of formality is present. The second term is negative. In principle, we may argue that FDI may privilege investment projects that take advantage of lower labor costs. Another explanation may be related to outsourcing practices and market power that large projects gain in determined sectors and regions. Though wages paid by a large firm may be above average, the number of direct labor that is hired may be relatively small in size because the firm may externalize a large proportion of its operations. On the other hand, this firm may have some market power in the local market that is translated into low payments to subcontractors and low wages to the individuals indirectly related to subcontractor production. However, the aggregated effect on wages of cross level interaction terms as the second one is small in absolute terms with respect to the first one.

Table 10.10 Sectoral Wage Ranking by Region for the Same Female Individual

Ranking	1	2	3	4	5	6	7	8	9
R1	Const	Mining	FinSer	Other	Manufr	T&T	Retail	Energy	Agric
R2	Mining	Const	FinSer	Other	Manufr	Retail	Energy	T&T	Agric
R3	Mining	Const	Manufr	Other	Retail	FinSer	Energy	T&T	Agric
R4	Const	Mining	FinSer	Manufr	Other	Retail	Energy	T&T	Agric
R5	Mining	Const	FinSer	Manufr	Retail	Other	T&T	Agric	Energy
R6	Mining	Const	FinSer	Manufr	Retail	Other	Agric	T&T	Energy
R7	Const	FinSer	Mining	Manufr	Retail	Other	Energy	T&T	Agric
R8	Const	Mining	FinSer	Manufr	Retail	Other	Energy	T&T	Agric
R9	Const	FinSer	Other	Mining	Manufr	Energy	Retail	T&T	Agric
R10	Mining	Const	FinSer	Manufr	Other	Retail	Agric	Energy	T&T
R11	Mining	Const	FinSer	Other	Manufr	Energy	Retail	T&T	Agric
R12	Const	Mining	FinSer	Other	Manufr	T&T	Energy	Agric	Retail
R13	Const	Mining	FinSer	Manufr	Retail	Other	T&T	Energy	Agric

Key: Const (Construction); Agric (Agriculture); Manufr (Manufacturing); T&T (Transport and Telecommunications) FinSer (Financial Services)

Table 10.11 Regional Wage Ranking by Sector for the Same Female Individual

Ranking	Agric	Mining	Manufr	Energy	Const	Retail	T&T	FinSer	Other
1	R13	R2	R13	R13	R12	R13	R13	R13	R12
2	R6	R10	R8	R3	R1	R2	R12	R2	R2
3	R5	R12	R12	R4	R13	R3	R3	R12	R11
4	R12	R11	R5	R2	R4	R5	R4	R8	R13
5	R10	R5	R10	R8	R2	R6	R5	R6	R4
6	R3	R1	R6	R12	R10	R8	R2	R4	R3
7	R4	R13	R4	R11	R8	R7	R6	R11	R10
8	R11	R3	R3	R9	R11	R4	R8	R7	R7
9	R7	R6	R2	R10	R5	R10	R10	R5	R5
10	R8	R4	R7	R6	R3	R12	R11	R1	R6
11	R9	R8	R11	R5	R6	R9	R7	R10	R8
12	R2	R7	R1	R7	R7	R11	R1	R9	R1
13	R1	R9	R9	R1	R9	R1	R9	R3	R9

Tables 10.10 and 10.11 show the same rankings developed for the case of female workers. The hypothetical individual considered here is the same as the one considered in the previous case. The results may be regarded as indications about the best choices in terms of sector and location if this individual could freely choose where to work and in which

activity. Const and Mining again appear to be as the best paying sectors in terms of hourly wages, for most of the regions, followed by Financial Services. Agriculture and Transport and telecommunications resulted once more among the less paying sectors.

In table 10.11, we can appreciate that Region 13, the metropolitan area, is ranked in 8 out of nine sectors among the first three paying locations, followed by Region 12 with 6 matches. In the other extreme Region 9 and Region 1 resulted in 8 and 6 out of 9 sectors within the last three places of this ranking respectively.

Table 10.12 Weight of the Cross Level Interaction Term for 9 years of Additional Education: Male Workers

	R1	R2	R3	R4	R5	R6	R7	R8	R9	R10	R11	R12	R13
Agriculture	0.38	0.42	0.47	0.46	0.52	0.49	0.41	0.50	0.50	0.71	0.65	0.74	0.59
Mining	0.74	0.80	0.80	0.75	0.82	0.74	0.65	0.71	0.72	0.90	0.74	0.83	0.79
Manufacture	0.69	0.73	0.76	0.78	0.75	0.71	0.66	0.69	0.67	0.73	0.63	0.78	0.75
Energy	0.21	0.47	0.42	0.41	0.45	0.48	0.41	0.45	0.44	0.50	0.45	0.53	0.54
Const	0.86	0.74	0.57	0.73	0.72	0.81	0.72	0.76	0.68	0.85	0.84	0.90	0.80
Retail	0.59	0.69	0.72	0.65	0.68	0.74	0.72	0.66	0.64	0.71	0.68	0.65	0.71
Transp&Tel	0.64	0.75	0.68	0.68	0.72	0.66	0.65	0.71	0.66	0.72	0.72	0.76	0.68
Financial S	0.75	0.77	0.61	0.75	0.77	0.80	0.80	0.77	0.78	0.80	0.80	0.83	0.73
Other	0.58	0.66	0.67	0.68	0.68	0.72	0.69	0.65	0.67	0.71	0.73	0.72	0.67

Now we turn to examine the importance of cross level interaction in our results. Several types of exercises can be carried out. We chose here to analyze how much of the impact of an increase in the education level of an individual is related to the interaction effect. For this exercise, we compare the wage rates of our hypothetical male worker in different groups with the wage rate he would obtain if he had college education (17 years) and the wage rates he would obtain with college education but assuming that the cross level interaction term is zero for the additional years completing high school and college (9 years). Table 10.12 presents the figures associated with:

$$\{1-\frac{\hat{w}_{ij}^{Education=17}-w_{ij}^{Education=8}}{w_{ij}^{Education=17}-w_{ij}^{Education=8}}\},$$

where $\hat{w}_{ij}^{Education=17}$ represents the wage rate that the individual would obtain with college education but without considering cross level interaction for the 9 years corresponding to high school and college.

Depending on the level-2 characterization of each group, the weight of cross level interaction in explaining the wage differential due to 9 years of schooling varies but in every case it explains a significant part of the total variation. On the one hand, table 10.12 results illustrate how important it is to account for interaction between individual and regional variables, and, on the other hand, how sensitive the results may be to variation in the level-2 context. As observed, the importance of cross level interaction ranges from 21% to 90%.

Conclusions

We have implemented a two level hierarchical linear model to model the interaction between individual variables and regional variables. For the case of female and male workers, we found that total wage rate variability comprised about 15% to 19% of level-2 variability. In both cases, versions accounting for full interaction between two levels resulted in the best models. In both cases, the sectoral-regional proportion of workers hired under permanent contracts and proportion of workers hired by small firms resulted in significant influences on the wage as a fixed effect.

Random cross interaction was significant in both cases but cross level interaction was significant only for the case of male workers, i.e. no systematic effect on the slopes associated with female individual characteristics was statistically relevant. In other words, women receive only a fixed premium because of choosing a different sectoral-regional group while male workers receive an additional incentive based on the amplification that sectoral-regional characteristics have on some personal characteristics such as education and experience.

Large differentials can be appreciated for the wage the same worker would obtain in different sectors and different regions. Nonetheless, these differentials should be taken cautiously as differences in regional price levels have not been considered here, because of the absence of reliable regional index prices. However, we can observe still important differences are present across sectors in a given region.

The level-1 explained variation is relatively low, and this is in part explained by our choice of keeping out of the analysis variables that are commonly used in wage equations, such as household condition, family size, and marital status, but which have no clear interpretation in terms of human capital theory. If wages are based mainly on productivity, we may wonder why a firm is going to pay more to male employees with large families as opposed to a similar worker with no children. Some explanations have been proposed, and it is possible to include additional variables relaxing these criteria. Nonetheless, it remains the problem of elaborating a reasonable explanation in case that interaction of these variables with level-2 variables results significant.

Hierarchical linear models may be seen also as a useful tool to identify regional variables affecting wages. Traditional hedonic wage models estimated on a regional or sectoral-regional basis, besides neglecting cross level interaction, allow us to test if coefficients or sets of coefficients between two regional wage equations differ or not, but do not provide clues for possible explanations. Once similarities and differences are determined, we only can speculate and develop some ad-hoc explanations. On the other hand, every regional equation must be compared with the others and unless the comparison results in some strong pattern it becomes difficult to derive some explanations for the results.

Our estimation has omitted the problem of sample selection bias commonly addressed in wage studies. In principle, this effect could be controlled by properly specifying level-2 variables or adding an additional level in the model. The other alternative is including in level-1 the inverse of the Mill's ratio as in any application of the Heckit model. We opted not to include such a term as we did not find any reliable methodology supporting this procedure and no reasonable explanation for the random or systematic cross level interaction of this ratio. To develop such methodology an explanation is an issue that may be addressed in future developments.

References

Aroca, P. and G.J.D. Hewings (2002) "Labor market adjustment and regional growth in Chile, 1982-1992," *Annals of Regional Science* 36, 197-218.

Aroca, P., G.J.D. Hewings and J.P. Godoy (2001) "Migracion interregional y el Mercado laboral en Chile: 1977-82 y 1987-1992," *Cuadernos de Economía*, 38, 321-345.

Aroca, P. and Vial, J.F. (1998) "Diferencias Interregionales: Chile 1992," Working Paper, IDEAR, Universidad Catolica del Norte.

Bellante, D. (1979) "The north-south differential and the migration of heterogeneous labor," *American Economic Review*, 69, 166-172.

Berndt, E.R. (1991) "The Practice of Econometrics: Classic and Contemporary". Addison-Wesley Publishing Company.

Blinder, A.S. (1973) "Wage Discrimination: Reduced Form and Structural Estimates," *Journal of Human Resources*, 18, 436-455.

Bravo, D., D. Contreras, and Rau, T. (1999) "Wage Inequality and Labor Market in Chile: A Non-parametric Approach," *Working Paper*, Department of Economics, Universidad de Chile.

Brown, C. (1980) "Equalizing Differences in the Labor Market," *Quarterly Journal of Economics*, 94, 113-134.

Chapman, B.J. and Hong, H.W. (1980) "Specific Training and Interindustry Wage Differentials in U.S. Manufacturing," *Review of Economic and Statistics*, 62, 371-378.

Corcoran, M. and Duncan, G.J. (1979) "Work History, Labor-Force Attachment, and Earning Differences between the Races and Sexes," *Journal of Human Resources*, 14, 3-20.

Cousineau, J-M, R. Lacroix, and Girard, A-M. (1992) "Occupational Hazard and Wage Compensating Differentials," *Review of Economic and Statistics*, 74, 166-169.

Dickie, M. and Gerking, S. (1987) "Interregional Wage Differentials: An Equilibrium Perspective," *Journal of Regional Science*, 27, 571-585.

Dickie, M. and Gerking, S. (1989) "Interregional Wage Differentials in the United States: A Survey". In Jouke Van Dijk, Hendrik Folmer, Henry Herzog and Alan M. Schlottmann (eds.) Migration *and Labor Market Adjustment*. Kluwer Academic Press.

Dresdner, J. (2002) "General and Specific Components in the Gender Wage Gap in Chile", Programa Seminarios de Investigacion, MERNYMA, Universidad de Concepcion.

Farber, S.C. and Newman, R.J. (1987) "Accounting for South/Non-South Real Wage Differentials and for Changes in Those Differentials over Time," *Review of Economic and Statistics*, 69, 215-223.

Farber, S.C. and Newman, R.J. (1989) "Regional Wage Differentials and the Spatial Convergence of Worker Characteristic Prices," *Review of Economic and Statistics*, 71, 224-231.

Gerking, S.D. and Weirick, W.N. (1983) "Compensating Differences and Interregional Wage Differentials," *Review of Economic and Statistics*, 65, 483-487.

Goldstein, H. (2003) *Multilevel statistical models*. London: Hodder and Arnold.

Hamermesh, D.S. and Wolfe, J.R (1990) "Compensating Wage Differentials and the Duration of Wage Loss," *Journal of Labor Economics*, 8, S175-S197.

Hanushek, E. (1981) "Alternative Models of Earnings Determination and Labor Market Structures," *Journal of Human Resources*, 16, 238-259.

Hanushek, E. (1973). "Regional Differences in the Structure of Earnings," *Review of Economic and Statistics*, 55, 204-213.

Heckman, J.J. (1979) "Sample Selection Bias as a Specification Error," *Econometrica*, 47, 153-161.

Hox, J.J. (1995) *Applied Multilevel Analysis*. Pi publicities, Amsterdam, Holland.

Ibarra, M. (2001) *Wage Inequality in Chile*. Unpublished Master's Thesis, University of San Diego.

Katz, L.F. and Murphy, K.M. (1992) "Changes in Relative Wages, 1963-1987: Supply and Demand Factors," *Quarterly Journal of Economics*, 107, 35-78.

Kennedy, P. (1998) *A Guide to Econometrics*. MIT Press (4th ed.).

Krueger, A.B. and Summers, L.H. (1988) "Efficiency Wages and Inter-Industry Wage Structure," *Econometrica*, 56, 259-293.

Krumm, R.J. (1984) "Regional Wage Differentials, Labor Supply Responses, and Race," *Journal of Regional Science*, 24, 431-442.

Low, S.A. and McPheters, L.R. (1983) "Wage Differentials and the Risk of Death: An Empirical Analysis," *Economic Inquiry*, 21, 271-280.

McCann, P. (2001) *Urban and Regional Economics*. Oxford University Press.

Millimet, D.L. (2004) "Job Search Skills, Employer Size, and Wages", Unpublished paper submitted for publication. Text available at: http://faculty.smu.edu/millimet/pdf/size.pdf.

Mincer, J. (1974) *Schooling, Experience, and Earnings*. Columbia University Press for the National Bureau of Economic Research.

Montenegro, C. (2001) "Wage Distribution in Chile: Does Gender Matter. A Quantile Regression Approach." Policy Research Report on Gender and Development, *Working Paper Series*, No. 20, World Bank.

Raudenbush, S. W., and Bryk, A. S. (2001) *Hierarchical linear models: Applications and data analysis methods*. (2nd ed.). Thousand Oaks, CA: Sage.

Rivlin, A.M. (1975). "Income Distribution—Can Economists Help?" *American Economic Review*, 65, 1-15

Roback, J. (1982) "Wages, Rents, and the Quality of Life," *Journal of Political Economy*, 90,1257-1258.

Rosen, S. (1974) "Hedonic Prices and Implicit Markets: Product Differentiation in Pure Competition," *Journal of Political Economy*, 82, 34-55.

Rosen, S. (1986) "The Theory of Equalizing Differences." In O. Ashenfelter and R. Layard (eds.), *Handbook of Labor Economics*, Vol. 1, Amsterdam, North-Holland, pp. 641-692.

Spence, M.A. (1973) "Job Market Signaling," *Quarterly Journal of Economics*, 87, 355-374.

Stigler, G.L. (1962) "Information in the Labor Market," *Journal of Political Economy*, 70, 94-105.

Thomas, D. and Strauss, J. (2000) "Health and Wages: Evidence on Men and Women in Urban Brazil." In Pranab Bradhan and Christopher Udry (eds.) *Readings in Development Economics*. Cambridge, MA., The MIT Press.

Topel, R.H. (1986) "Local Labor Markets," *Journal of Political Economy*, 94, S111-S143.

Welch, F. (1969) "Linear Synthesis of Skill Distribution," *Journal of Human Resources*, 4, 311-327.

Willis, R.J. (1986) "Wage Determinants: A Survey and Reinterpretation of Human Capital Earnings Functions." In O. Ashenfelter and R. Layard (editors), *Handbook of Labor Economics*, Vol. 1, Amsterdam, North-Holland, pp. 525-602.

11 The Determinants of the Regional Foreign Direct Investment in Chile

Johanna D. Robles and Geoffrey J.D. Hewings

Introduction

Over the last 30 years, Foreign Direct Investment (FDI) has played an important role in the Chilean economy. In the early 1970s, when the government exercised total control of capital movements, in addition to control of credit and the interest rate, capital inflows were close to zero and even negative. However, in September of 1973, there was an attenuation of the restrictions affecting the amount of profits and dividends of external firms that could be repatriated, in order to encourage and increase foreign investment. This was under a mechanism called Decree Law 600. In the late 1970s and early 1980s, Chile was facing a financial debt crisis, which was mostly solved through stabilization programs and the program of debt-equity swaps using foreign investors. Although there were many privatizations, by 1990, these companies were not foreign-owned. During the first years of the 1990s decade, FDI mostly concentrated in the mining sector, but it followed an evolutionary process towards investment in the services sector.

There have been many studies made concerning the impact of FDI, either as a determinant or as a dependant variable, but very few studies have considered the determinants of FDI at a regional level. The case of Chile is interesting, because the patterns for FDI tend to be clearer as the years go by; the regions have tended to specialize in their activities and in the ways in which they attract FDI. Hence, this chapter will investigate the determinants for FDI across regions and explore whether there are certain regions that are able to attract more FDI than others.

This chapter is organized as follows; in the first section, a theoretical framework is presented, followed by the introduction of the hypothesis regarding FDI and Chile. The third section presents the data and the methodology used specifically in this analysis, with the clear specification of the model used. Section five presents the main results, which are further interpreted in section six. Finally, some concluding remarks complete the analysis.

Theoretical Framework

There are many studies concerning the determinants of FDI; the traditional theory of FDI relates the profit maximization behavior of multinational enterprises, as indicated by Chen (2000) where the firm will decide whether it will enter the market of a host country or not, a decision based on the profit maximization process. Smekal and Sausgruber (2000) and Kreinin (1995) on the other hand, explain FDI based on international trade theory where capital is considered a factor with an influence in comparative costs. Moreover, when firms are asked about their motivation to invest abroad, they may not even mention increased profits, but there are two categories that they consider: cost considerations and market considerations (the second in order to increase revenues). In terms of cost considerations, one that might be relevant is the need to obtain raw materials from abroad, in fact "vast American investment in the extractive industries are motivated by the fact that the capital must follow the resources" (Kreinin, 1995). This decision is also influenced by transportation cost of the primary product; if it is very high, the first stage of processing may have to take place at or near the extraction site. Another type of cost reducing investment is related to labor, but in this case, it is important to consider whether the activity is labor or capital intensive in order to exhibit a cost-advantage. In the case of market considerations, international trade leads to firms increasing their foreign investment; in other words, the opportunities to market products abroad also encourages investment abroad in order to more easily penetrate these new markets.

In their book, Armstrong and Taylor (2000), the study for potential determinants in FDI follows an hierarchical process, beginning with the decision to locate abroad, where the question of which region of the world could be determined by trade barriers, market size, market growth and potential for import penetration. Once this question is solved, the next question probes for the choice of one or more countries. Once the country choice has been made, the final question is directed to a specific location *within* the country. There are a large set of the determinants that authors have proposed, but there are related mostly with the access to markets, labor-market conditions, promotional activities of the state, state (or regional) taxes, access to land and the industrial structure at the new location.

Empirical studies usually link FDI with economic growth, either the GDP per capita or the growth of the GDP. For example, Zhang (2001) explores the link between FDI and economic growth. The main issue in his study is the bi-directional causality that could exist between these two variables, either FDI promotes growth or growth attracts FDI. His study considered 11 economies, in different parts of the world including East Asia and Latin America, although Chile was not considered in the group of Latin American countries. Other variables usually considered are the levels of exports level and the role of international trade, as it was the case of Ruane and Görg (1996) and Lahiri and Ono (2003). In some cases, FDI may be seen to be directly export oriented or because of opportunities associated with the international trade direct investment towards an economy that is most welcoming. FDI at the regional level became more appealing since the sole study of location factors showed that there are differences in the spatial determinants, as shown by Scott (1998) in his study of location factors of FDI in early 1930s.

One of the significant studies made was done by Wei *et al.* (1999) where they study the determinants for pledged FDI and realized FDI for a panel data set of 27 provinces in China. The main variables utilized include international trade, wage rates, growth of GDP, infrastructure and investment incentives, and agglomeration, among others. They used four specifications for each kind of FDI, with the result that the use of random effects models with autocorrelation being the most powerful explanatory model against ordinary least squares. The use of fixed effects specification was not considered due the presence of perfect multicollinearity. Their results showed that there is a spatial distribution of FDI and that the determinants differ if the dependant variable is pledged FDI instead of realized FDI. In fact, whereas all the variables considered were significant for pledged FDI, only few variables were significant for realized FDI, specifically from the main equation:

FDI = f (International trade, wage rates, R & D manpower, rate of GDP growth, infrastructure, agglomeration, a dummy for time (1 for 1992 onwards and 0 before 1992), and a cross-sectional dummy for low information costs and high investment incentives)

Only international trade, wage rates and R&D manpower were significant for the case of realized FDI, indicating that the openness, labor costs and human capital are significant determinants, although they considered wage rates as a proxy for productivity levels. The results revealed that wages are considered part of the cost function rather than productivity and hence they obtained the opposite sign to the one expected. Both dummies were also significant, one of the possible explanations for the difference between pledged FDI and realized FDI is that the first one is strongly market oriented, whereas realized FDI is mainly influenced by comparative advantages of the regions in terms of human capital, trade and labor costs.

Another study considering the case of China, Sun *et al.* (2002), realized a panel data study of the determinants of FDI considering a sample of 30 provinces over 1987 to 1998 period and a large set of proxies for variables such as market demand and market size (using GDP), infrastructure (Railway per Km^2), degree of industrialization (domestic investment per worker), level of foreign investment (ratio of cumulative FDI over cumulative domestic investment), labor quality (ratio of number of engineers, scientist and technicians over total employees), labor cost (average wage) and country risk (risk ranking). Their regression considered a logarithm form for the estimation of three models: fixed effect model with a different intercept for each unit (province), a regression with common intercept and the third is with first differenced data (the latest considering the variables in term of growth). In all three cases, both OLS and GLS were estimated. Their results showed that "the importance of FDI determinants moves through time" (Sun *et al.*, 2002). The average wage was significant, although its sign changed from positive to negative, labor quality and infrastructure showed a positive relationship, meaning that they attract FDI. Other variables that were significant were the political stability and degree of openness, and the level of foreign investment had a negative impact on new FDI. This was explained in the sense that multinational corporations may want to consider investing in provinces that are not flooded with FDI competitors.

Kozlowski and Weekly (1990) were concerned with the uneven distribution of FDI among U.S. states. They pointed out that regional differences in FDI could be grouped into three categories, market-related conditions, cost-based factors and public sector policies. In their research, they used a cross-section data analysis for the purpose of measuring the dependence of FDI and a set of variables, for example, population and the growth of domestic employment were used as market size and growth hypotheses, wage levels, union membership, tax burdens, right-to work laws and estimates of business climate were used as cost-related factors; and dollar allocation in the state budget was used as public sector policies. Using correlation between changes in affiliate shares and factors linked to FDI, their results revealed that aggregate economic growth could be considered as a proxy for higher profit potential, the size of the state (or the region) could reflect market-related factors, and a staff commitment appears to enhance FDI environment. Input costs seemed not to be related directly to change in the share of the affiliates, and most of the rank correlations were not significantly different from zero, it is also important to notice that previous findings that taxes do not influence location decisions was also confirmed in their study.

A few studies have considered the way in which developing countries attract FDI. Asiedu (2002) explored the case of Africa, although in her study she considered variables such as the inverse of the real GDP per capita (as a proxy for return in investment), quality of infrastructure, openness of the host country (ratio of the trade to GDP), and political instability. The results that she obtained showed that a large share of the variation in FDI rate can be explained by openness to trade with a positive relationship, infrastructure and return on investment (also positive), for all of the specifications, but other variables such as a dummy for those countries located in the sub-Saharan Africa were not significant in the case of the ordinary least squares. In the case of the other models the effect was negative, since this part of the continent tends to attract non-market oriented FDI. Other variables considered, such as growth of GDP, government consumption rate of inflation, ratio of liquid liabilities to GDP, and political instability, were not significant. She also pointed out that there are two types of FDI that should be considered: the market-seeking or export-oriented investment FDI and non-market seeking FDI (e.g., natural resource based investments and other (Asiedu, 2002). This distinction was also made by Chen (2000), noted that the reasons for multinational enterprises to invest abroad depend on factors such as utilization of resources, attention to foreign markets, the internalization of intangible assets or specific locational advantages, each of them generating a specific kind of FDI.

Table 11.1 Main Targeted Sectors for FDI in Chile (1990-1999)

Region	Sector
I	Mining
II	Mining, electricity and transportation
III	Mining
IV	Mining, construction and services
V	Electricity and construction
VI	Industry, mining and agriculture
VII	Industry, construction and forestry
VIII	Industry, electricity and transportation
IX	Industry and forestry
X	Industry, forestry and construction
XI	Mining, industry and fishing
XII	Industry
Metropolitan	Services, industry and electricity

Source: National Institute of Statistics, Chile and Vice-Presidency of Foreign Investments Committee.

Propositions

In the specific case of Chile, we can notice that the regions have attracted different kinds of FDI, and thus it would seem probable that there is a relation between regional characteristics and certain types of FDI. As can be seen in table 11.1, the first sector mentioned corresponds to the targeted FDI made; we can distinguish three different kinds of FDI. The first one is the investment made mainly in the mining sector and others such as fishing and forestry (primary sector), the second is the investment made in the industry sector and the third is the FDI in the services sector, along with electricity and transportation.

It is important to notice that the total population of Chile for the period of study is approximately 15 million people, and the metropolitan region concentrates approximately 30% of this population. Hence, the omission of the distinction for the FDI in services is not trivial.

Consider the following hypotheses:

1. The differences in regional economic structure play an important role in attracting FDI, i.e. the specific conditions of each region are a key to attracting a specific kind of FDI.
2. There are set of independent variables that act as a factor in attracting FDI at a regional level, such as:
   The level of growth of each region (+);
   The level of Exports in each region (+);
   The unemployment level, i.e. the rate of the unoccupied force in each region (-);
   The public incentives in each region (+);
   The average wage rates of the occupied labor force in each region (- +);[1]
   The size of the market (+);
   Education levels, i.e. the percentage of people that have finished high school and college in each region each year (+);
   The infrastructure (+).
3. These main determinants act differently according to the targeted sector, i.e. these determinants differ if the FDI was oriented to the export sector, (non-market seeking FDI) which includes the primary sector; or if the FDI was made on the services sector (mainly electricity and telecommunications). Although the latter sector is related with market-seeking FDI, it is a little different from the traditional definition of market-seeking FDI, since the motives are more related with expansion with the rest of Latin America and lower costs for multinationals rather than the capturing large percentages of the Chilean market itself (ECLAC, 2000).

Data and Methodology

Taking into account previous research and the availability of the data, the methodology chosen considers a panel data set for the 13 regions in Chile over a 10-year period. The data provided information about two cases of

---

[1] The expected sign is not clear; according to Chen (2000), wages are part of the cost function of the investing and hence a negative effect of the wages on FDI would be anticipated, especially when the activities are labor-intensive. On the other hand, wages can also be viewed as a measure of productivity levels, as it was pointed out by Wei *et al* (2001) and Q. Sun *et al* (2002); from this point of view, a positive relationship would be expected.

FDI, Authorized level of FDI and Realized FDI, and also a detail of FDI for nine sectors in each region per year. The dependant variable in each case is the FDI and the set of independent variables are:

$$\text{Ln}FDI = f(\text{Ln}Gdp,\ \text{Ln}Exp,\ \text{Ln}Une,\ \text{Ln}Pexp,\ \text{Ln}Pinv,\ \text{Ln}Ing,\ \text{Ln}Pop,\ \text{Ln}Edu,\ \text{Ln}Inft\ )$$

where, Ln*Gdp* is the growth of regional GDP lagged one year; (Ln*Exp*) is the level of regional exports; (Ln*Une*) is the unemployment rate in each region; (Ln*Pexp*) is public regional expenditure; (Ln*Pinv*) is level of public investment in each region; (Ln*Ing*) is the average monthly income of the workers per region; (LnPop) is the population in each region each year; (Ln*Edu*) is the percentage of population that have at least finished high school in each region and (Ln*Inft*) is the approved and initiated buildings in m^2. The variables are in log form. There are many reasons for the use of the log form in this equation, as it was pointed by Wei *et al.* (1999), this is a way to obtain directly the elasticities of FDI with respect to several explanatory variables and the relationship between the explanatory variables with the dependant variable seems to be non-linear.

The rationale for the choice of variables is now briefly discussed. *The Rate of Growth (*Ln*Gdp)* is here considered to be one of the determinants of FDI, and as noted earlier, it is expected to have a positive relationship with FDI. While this relationship may hold at the aggregate (national level), it could be possible that it might not be significant for certain kinds of FDI. Chile is still a developing economy and the rate of growth of each *region* may not be powerful enough to act as an attractive factor that independently of the overall rate of growth of the whole country. The data for GDP are lagged one year, because the possibility of a bi-directional causality is not discarded for the case of Chile.

The *Level of Exports (*Ln*Exp)* has been used in a number of studies, although the causality is not clear. This variable acts also as a measure of openness to external trade and the "experience" of the region with exports, in the case of Chile. Some descriptive studies have shown that FDI has been oriented directly to export activities, especially in the northern regions of the country, and these exports are mostly aimed for developed economies in Asia and North America. Hence, a positive relationship is expected because it might reflect also the accessibility to a needed resource in larger, external markets.

The *Unemployment Rate (*Ln*Une)* is considered to operate in two ways, one as a measure of the availability of inputs, the other one as a part of the level of development in the region. According to Armstrong and Taylor (2000), the density of the manufacturing employment acts as a way to describe the industrial structure, and it has a positive relationship. Since, in the present case, we are using the unemployment rate, the expected result is the opposite; if this rate is high, it is expected that it deflects FDI to other regions. However, it is also expected that it does not have an influence on investments made in the services sector, for example, because this variable used as availability of inputs does not reflect completely the quality of the human capital and thus may not influence FDI in contrast with the same variable used in the primary and manufacturing sectors.

Although *Public Expenditure (*Ln*Pexp)* and *Public Investment (*Ln*Pinv)* are not often used in studies of FDI, either or both variables are considered as a proxy for incentives made by the central government in order to attract FDI. The variable often utilized is the expenditure for regional development alone; however, it seems reasonable to take a closer look at the public investment in order to narrow the scope of the government expenditures to something directly oriented to development. A positive relationship is expected, although the opposite is also possible. For example, since the economic policy of Chile concerning FDI is the attraction of capital inflows towards development in general, when FDI concentrates in some of the regions, the central government tends to focus on those regions that do not receive these inflows in order to balance economic growth. Hence, it might be possible that FDI and public incentives compete with each other.

The *Average Income of the workers per region (*Ln*Ing)* variable is considered in two ways, the first one is for the case of market-seeking FDI. The total population of Chile is approximately 15 million, then the level of income could be a factor in the case of multinationals looking for profits in a small market. The second alternative, since it is specifically the income of the workers (on average) is that it could be used as a proxy for wages in the case of non-market (or export-oriented) FDI, either as a cost variable or a proxy for productivity levels, as was indicated in Broadman and Sun (1997), Wei *et a*l. (1999), and Q. Sun *et al.* (2002)

*Population (*Ln*Pop)* is a common proxy used for agglomeration, such as the case in Wei *et al.* (1998); however, it is expected that this variable might be only significant for the case of a specific kind of FDI, such as the authorized FDI or the FDI in the services sector (in a certain way, considered market-seeking FDI). It is unlikely to be important for export-oriented FDI, since agglomeration and vertical integration for the case of Mining or Fishing, is not necessarily related to a large population. Since many activities are associated with significant capital inflows, and the potential for technology transfer, the quality of human capital would be more important than the size of population.

Hence, *Education (*Ln*Edu)* is used as a surrogate for the attraction of FDI that is very dependent on the quality of "human capital." Prior work (for example, Noorbakhsh *et al.* 2001) claims that the quality of education and training is important since it serves as a proxy for lower costs, and better productivity. As an attractive factor for FDI, the use of educational levels provides an idea of the future quality of the workers and the ease with which employees could be trained.

There are several studies that support the use of *Infrastructure (*Ln*Inft)* to help explain FDI, such as Broadman and Sun (1997), Wei *et al.* (1999), Asiedu (2002) and Sun *et al.* (2002). The idea is that more infrastructure provides better comparative advantage in terms of costs or market accessibility. The proxies utilized in each case were completely different; in the present analysis, the proxy utilized was the approved and initiated building construction in m^2; in the longer run, more traditional forms of infrastructure such as length of paved highways, railroads, or ports would be more appropriate measurers but there was little variation in these attributes over the 10 year frame of the analysis.

The Model

We can consider, for the specific case of Chile, two kinds of FDI: (1) Non-Market seeking FDI – Investments made primarily for Export activities, with special attention to availability of natural resources and (2) "Market Capture" FDI. The latter form is slightly different from the definition of market-seeking FDI, since these investments are mainly targeted to a market whose demand tends to be inelastic, for example water and electricity, or were the market is not limited to the country itself, but aims to capture bigger market in neighboring countries.

There are 4 dependent variables for which we will estimate the parameters: (1) authorized FDI; (2) realized FDI; (3) FDI in the export sector and (4) FDI in the services sector. Four alternative econometric models to be compared are employed to capture potentially different functional forms in the relationships of various types of FDI. Model 1 employs a fixed effects model (one-way fixed effects); Model 2 is a random effects model for the unobservable individual effects (one-way random effects); Model 3 is a two-way fixed effect model (group and time effects) and Model 4 is a random effect model for both individual and time effect. (two-way random effects).

Although all the regions of Chile are included in the model (13 regions), it is likely that the random effect model will be found to be more powerful than the fixed effects for some of the dependent variables, especially in the case when the FDI is divided into sectors such as exports and services. This arises from the fact that Chile presents a significant degree of concentration of certain activities in specific regions, for example the mining sector is greatly concentrated in the northern regions of Chile, and the services sector is concentrated in the metropolitan region. The random effects model might be better in explaining the influence of the regions themselves by assuming these as an error component rather than a fixed effect, especially when this influence is uneven among all 13 regions, in contrast to the assumption of the fixed effects specification. The random effects model takes into account that this influence is only due to selected regions of the total, and it is assumed to be random, and hence, part of the error term. The use of two-way fixed effect models was mainly in order to compare with the parsimonious one-way model and to obtain a more complete error-component model (random effect model for individual and period effects). The criteria for the decision of which model is more powerful to explain the dependant variable was based on the likelihood ratio and *F* tests for the fixed effects and the Hausman Test in the case of random effects versus fixed effects. In cases where the values were close to each other, the parsimonious principle was used to select the most appropriate model.

Table 11.2 Results for the First Dependent Variable, Fixed and Random Effects Model

Dependent Variable: Total Authorized FDI

	Model 1 One Way Fixed effects	Model 2 One Way Random effects	Model 3 Two Way Fixed effects	Model 4 Two Way Random effects
LOGGDP	8.023 (6.726)	13.951** (6.402)	5.875 (7.482)	13.654** (6.860)
LOGEXP	-3.868*** (1.502)	0.461 (0.417)	-4.646*** (1.748)	0.328 (0.427)
LOGUNE	-0.709 (1.162)	1.158 (0.910)	2.346 (1.663)	2.463*** (1.039)
LOGPEXP	11.989*** (4.881)	2.174 (2.859)	8.851 (7.737)	2.666 (3.458)
LOGPINV	-1.153 (2.157)	-0.892 (1.909)	-2.353 (2.268)	-2.317 (2.024)
LOGING	6.886* (3.880)	1.214 (2.106)	6.763 (5.037)	1.719 (2.258)
LOGPOP	-45.271 (26.950)	0.609 (2.218)	11.316 (33.858)	2.518 (2.977)
LOGEDU	4.953* (3.015)	5.777** (2.726)	6.581** (3.074)	6.419*** (2.709)
LOGINFT	-3.386** (1.777)	-0.886 (1.457)	-4.152** (1.934)	-2.449 (1.566)
Constant		-7.144 (29.494)	-166.105 (443.490)	-6.910 (30.950)
R Squared	47.45%	30.75%	53.72%	25.64%
Log - Likelihood	-314.325		-306.060	
Likelihood Ratio Test (χ^2)	31.639 (1.57%)		16.530 (5.66%)	
F Test	2.187 (1.70%)		1.492 (16.15%)	
Hausman (9)	20.02 (1.17%)		18.71 (2.77%)	

***significant at 10%, **significant at 5%, ***significant at 1%**

Table 11.3 Results for the Second Dependent Variable, Fixed and Random Effects Model

Dependent Variable: Total Realized FDI

	Model 1 One Way Fixed effects	Model 2 One Way Random effects	Model 3 Two Way Fixed effects	Model 4 Two Way Random effects
LOGGDP	3.941 (3.891)	6.219* (3.812)	2.628 (4.150)	5.260 3.915
LOGEXP	-0.932 (0.869)	0.521 (0.413)	-0.661 (0.969)	0.574 0.416
LOGUNE	-1.705*** (0.672)	-0.762 (0.593)	-3.151*** (0.923)	-1.041 0.675
LOGPEXP	9.396*** (2.824)	5.072*** (1.840)	22.894*** (4.291)	6.498*** 2.161
LOGPINV	-1.466 (1.248)	-1.818 (1.193)	-1.309 (1.258)	-2.008* 1.188
LOGING	-2.714 (2.244)	-0.846 (1.689)	-4.227 (2.794)	-0.851 1.828
LOGPOP	-16.117 (15.590)	-2.472** (1.486)	-7.049 (18.780)	-3.080* 1.822
LOGEDU	0.977 (1.744)	2.266 (1.637)	0.195 (1.705)	1.866 1.556
LOGINFT	-1.360 (1.028)	-0.306 (0.916)	-1.022 (1.073)	-0.799 0.941
Constant		18.205 (21.628)	-74.722 (245.988)	16.678 23.052
R Squared	62.1%	24.02%	69.54%	16.43%
Log - Likelihood	-243.166		-229.439	
Likelihood Ratio Test (χ^2)	59.572 (0.00%)		27.452 (0.02%)	
F Test	5.232 (0.00%)		2.586 (1.01%)	
Hausman (9)	14.85 (9.50%)		29.65 (0.50%)	

*significant at 10%, **significant at 5%, ***significant at 1%

Table 11.4 Results for the Third Dependent Variable, Fixed and Random Effects Model

Dependent Variable: FDI in the Primary Sector

	Model 1 One Way Fixed effects	Model 2 One Way Random effects	Model 3 Two Way Fixed effects	Model 4 Two Way Random effects
LOGGDP	12.164*** (5.104)	15.894*** (4.971)	12.307** (5.374)	14.055*** (5.331)
LOGEXP	-2.327** (1.140)	0.255 (0.465)	-2.507** (1.255)	-2.595** (1.237)
LOGUNE	-1.674* (0.882)	-0.891 (0.757)	-2.758** (1.195)	-3.390*** (1.129)
LOGPEXP	3.099 (3.704)	1.952 (2.354)	23.005*** (5.556)	17.906*** (4.989)
LOGPINV	-3.533** (1.637)	-2.716* (1.540)	-3.028* (1.629)	-2.965** (1.626)
LOGING	7.310*** (2.944)	4.174** (2.040)	3.227 (3.617)	3.489 (3.563)
LOGPOP	10.651 (20.451)	0.224 (1.866)	50.192** (24.315)	7.351 (15.338)

Table 11.4 Results for the Third Dependent Variable, Fixed and Random Effects Model (continued)

LOGEDU	2.016 (2.288)	1.265 (2.125)	1.937 (2.207)	0.935 (2.157)
LOGINFT	-0.014 (1.349)	0.742 (1.181)	2.008 (1.389)	0.903 (1.323)
Constant		-51.515** (26.513)	-926.483*** (318.492)	-285.271 (193.275)
R Squared	71.93%	18.04%	77.87%	29.79%
Log - Likelihood	-278.451		-263.020	
Likelihood Ratio Test (χ^2)	111.577 (0.00%)		30.861 (0.03%)	
F Test	12.232 (0.00%)		2.947 (0.38%)	
Hausman (9)	29.36 (0.07%)		9.17 (42.18%)	

*significant at 10%, **significant at 5%, ***significant at 1%

Table 11.5 Results for the Fourth Dependent Variable, Fixed and Random Effects Model

Dependent Variable: FDI in the Services Sector

	Model 1 One Way Fixed effects	Model 2 One Way Random effects	Model 3 Two Way Fixed effects	Model 4 Two Way Random effects
LOGGDP	-1.482 (8.109)	-2.229 (7.656)	0.639 (9.177)	0.217 (8.283)
LOGEXP	-2.517 (1.810)	-0.043 (0.458)	-4.766** (2.144)	0.009 (0.468)
LOGUNE	1.012 (1.401)	0.236 (1.065)	1.751 (2.040)	0.158 (1.210)
LOGPEXP	9.701* (5.884)	6.482** (3.359)	4.599 (9.490)	8.443** (3.943)
LOGPINV	-3.613 (2.600)	-3.983* (2.255)	-3.303 (2.782)	-4.039 (2.419)
LOGING	6.140 (4.677)	1.837 (2.382)	0.552 (6.178)	0.850 (2.543)
LOGPOP	-26.322 (32.489)	-1.481 (2.603)	10.967 (41.527)	-3.091 (3.355)
LOGEDU	-2.185 (3.635)	-1.159 (3.264)	-1.795 (3.770)	-1.096 (3.293)
LOGINFT	1.382 (2.143)	1.638 (1.719)	1.485 (2.372)	1.535 (1.860)
Constant		-62.627* (34.168)	-140.215 (543.953)	-51.483 (35.859)
R Squared	62.02%	56.08%	65.38%	55.92%
Log - Likelihood	-338.624		-332.604	
Likelihood Ratio Test (χ^2)	16.979 (15.04%)		12.039 (22.11%)	
F Test	1.256 (25.57%)		1.067 (39.36%)	
Hausman (9)	8.69 (46.62%)		10.01 (34.94%)	

Results

We can see the main results in the following tables, the values in parentheses are the standard deviations, whereas the percentages associated with the hypothesis tests indicate the probability of rejecting the corresponding model. The likelihood ratio and *F* test compares Model 1 with a model without the effects, (a model considering the independent variables), and Model 3 with model 1. The Hausman Test compares the Random effect model with fixed effects, i.e., Model 1 vs. model 2 and Model 3 vs. model 4.

Analysis

Fixed Effects Versus Random Effects (One Way and Two Way)

Four alternative models were estimated for each dependent variable. Model 1 estimates the parameters considering individual effects uncorrelated among each other and captures them as a fixed effect, whereas model 3 takes into account not only the individual effect but also the effect of each period inside the estimation, considering both of them as fixed effects. The comparison between these two models takes into account the values of the log-likelihood, the likelihood ratio and the F test; if the values are close to each other, the model selected is the one that uses less independent variables, due to the size of the sample (130 observations). For the case of the random effects, models 2 and 4 consider that the individual[2] and period effects[3] are correlated and therefore the influence of these effects is random. This approach exploits the serial correlation in the composite error using a GLS framework, which was the estimation used here. The Hausman Test tests the fixed effects estimation versus random effects; in the case of the fixed effects, the null hypothesis (H_0) is that random effects would be consistent and efficient against (H_1) that random effects would be inconsistent, the result of the test is a vector of dimension k (where k is the number of independent variables) which is distributed $\chi^2(k)$. The test compares this value with the critical χ^2 value; when this statistic exceeds the critical value, it reveals that the fixed effects model is better than the random effects, for each case (one-way and two way respectively).

As we can see in the tables 11.2 and 11.3, the values for the Log-likelihood are close in the case of the one-way and two-way models. Further, models 1 and 3 better explain the dependent variables, authorized FDI and realized FDI, than models 2 and 4 (random effects). This suggests that the influence of the regions and the years themselves on FDI

---

[2] For the case of Model 2.

[3] For the case of Model 4.

are uncorrelated and, therefore, can be captured as a fixed effect of the region and the year, although the values of R-squared and log-likelihood are smaller in the case of one-way fixed effects versus two-way. However, we applied the parsimonious principle and chose model 1 for the case of authorized FDI and realized FDI.

Table 11.4 indicates a different situation; in this case, Model 3 is a more powerful one to explain the dependent variable, FDI in the export sector, when it is compared with one-way fixed effects. However, when the comparison is made with the random effects model (model 4), the Hausman value indicates that the latter is a better model. In other words, the influence of the regions and the years is random and cannot be captured as individual effect, hence it is considered in the error term. This result is not completely surprising, since the largest amount of FDI in the export sector is concentrated in a few regions of the country, particularly those regions that have a large amount of natural resources such as mining and forestry. Since the random effects model considers a large number of random draws from the cross-section, the treatment of these effects is as if they were random draws of the population; this is appropriate when there is neglected heterogeneity in the regions concerning this sector, and the heterogeneity of the FDI cannot be captured with fixed coefficients. A similar case happened for the fourth dependent variable, FDI in the services sector; table 11.5 reveals that both one-way and two-way random effects better explain the variable than models 1 and 3, but the R-squared value shows that model 2 is preferred to model 4, and that means that the individual effects are correlated among each other but not the period effects. Further, the effects of the regions are orthogonal with the rest of the explanatory variables, making it necessary to treat them in the error term, which is correlated serially with the "natural" error term. The fact that the services sector is more concentrated in the regions with larger population (about one third of the total population in Chile), supports the idea of random effects, in the sense that the effect of the regions is not fixed for all regions, but rather concentrated in few regions of the population of study. The preferred models for each variable are shown in table 11.6.

Table 11.6 Summary of the Models Chosen for each Dependent Variable

Dependent Variable	Model Chosen	Name of the Model
Authorized FDI	1	One-way Fixed Effects
Realized FDI	1	One-Way Fixed Effects
FDI in the Export Sector	4	Two-Way Random Effects
FDI in the Services Sector	2	One-Way Random Effects

Authorized FDI

From the results shown in table 11.2, we can see that the level of exports, the public expenditure, the average income, the population, the education and the infrastructure are significant variables. This means that the "traditional" variables play a role in the decision of how much foreign investment is permitted in each region, and the fixed effect of each region is also significant although only at a 10% level. The public expenditure, the income and the education have the expected sign, meaning that they are considered as attractive factors of FDI, and the magnitude of these parameters indicates that there is high sensitivity of the authorized FDI to these variables, since the results show directly the elasticities of the dependent variable to the explanatory variables. However, the exports, the population and the infrastructure present an opposite sign than the one expected, and hence, they appear to deflect this kind of FDI. Since this variable is more concerned with decision making rather than actual capital inflow, it is reasonable to think that variables such as population and infrastructure, when they are larger, could be considered as a measure of agglomeration. Chile's small size thus may present a disadvantage. The exports level also shows a negative sign, which is a little surprising, since it was expected that openness or trade would be attractive to FDI. In this case, it seems that as exports increase, authorized FDI would decline, but this also could mean that exports and FDI are correlated with each other rather than with one explaining the other. This variable was not used in lagged form, and thus, there is possibility that the causality of these variables is the other way around, i.e., that the authorized FDI causes the export level to fall.

Realized FDI

When we look at the results for the realized FDI on table 11.3, these differ completely from the previous case, the realized FDI estimation indicates that only the unemployment and the public expenditure are significant variables, with 99% of confidence. Both variables have the sign expected, i.e. the public expenditure shows a positive sign, indicating that it is considered an attractive factor of FDI. Public investment was not significant, although it was thought a better proxy; the unemployment rate shows a negative sign, which indicates that it deflects the actual FDI. The elasticities indicate also a large sensitivity of the dependent variable, especially in the case of the public expenditure. Since it is also a fixed effects model, a closer look at these effects reveals that they are not significantly different from zero, indicating that the differences of the regions themselves do no play a role in the attraction of FDI. An interesting result is that the variables often linked with FDI, such as growth, income and infrastructure, do not play an important role in the attraction of FDI, at least not at the regional level

FDI in the Primary Sector

Looking the results on table 11.4, we can see that the significant variables are the growth of GDP, the exports level, the unemployment rate, the public expenditure and the public investment. The values for the growth of GDP and public expenditure present the expected sign, with a large sensitivity of this kind of FDI to these variables. FDI in the primary sector is characterized mainly by investments in natural resources such as mining and fishing; in some cases, they form a great part of regional GDP. The positive relationship of GDP with FDI indicates that the return on these investments are important for the multinationals and, in the case of public expenditure, this variable acts as a measure of the development efforts in the regions. The level of unemployment has the expected negative sign which it is expected if this variable is considered as an indicator of the quality of the labor force. Every variable that indicates growth and development of the region acts as an attractive factor for investment. An interesting result is the role the level of exports, even though it is significant, it has a negative sign, which means that the elasticity of FDI is negatively related with the level of exports. Again, this could be explained in the sense that since this sector (primary), is mostly export-oriented, the country in general puts greater efforts in promoting exports in sectors. In this case, the level of exports acts as "competition" for the export-oriented FDI maybe because it leads to increase the foreign currency, making the exchange rate unfavorable to the export sector. For the case of public investment, is it reasonable to think that the FDI in the primary sector and this kind of investment might act as substitutes, i.e. the negative correlation between these two variables indicates that if there is public investment in one region then there will be foreign investment in the others, as a way to balance the capital in the regions. However, the causality in each case is not clear, especially for GDP, exports and public investment; these results only indicate that the FDI in the primary sector and the independent variables are correlated in a non-linear relationship.

FDI in the services sector

In the case of the FDI in the services sector, we can see from table 11.5 that the public investment, the public expenditure and the constant are significant, indicating that the proxies used for public incentives are correlated with the dependent variable, but the signs are different. In the case of public expenditure, the sign is positive indicating that the larger the expenditure, the more the FDI will be attracted, with a high level of sensitivity (revealed by the magnitude of the coefficient). For the public investment, the relationship is negative which could be explained in the same sense that these types of investments compete each other. The result of the influence of these variables is interesting, since there might be a positive linear correlation between them, but the fact that they act in opposite ways in this non-linear model indicates that the variables have independent influence on the FDI in the services sector. The constant itself, although significant, shows that if has very little influence, since its magnitude is negative and only significant at 10% level. It is probably also that this FDI had flourished mainly through acquisitions and privatizations, the idea of market-capturing can still be differentiated from pure market-seeking, since the bulk of these investments are in activities related with almost inelastic demand and the attainment of a "secure" market. Market-seeking FDI is the searching for a large size market with downward sloped demand. The mergers and acquisitions took place in sectors such as electricity and water (sanitation is also included in this category) as well as services such telecommunications and finances. Since very few variables explain the dependant variable, it should be considered that the search for more specific determinants, such as costs, and demand-related variables, like consumption and prices, or time-related variables, it could be that the increase of these investments took place in the latter years of the period of analysis. The study of investment in sectors such as water and electricity also need the inclusion of "non-traditional" variables, since, for the specific case of Chile, many of these firms were government-owned, and these investments took place in a specific period of time of Chile, when the government authorized the privatization of such services.

Conclusions

The story of FDI in Chile reveals that direct policies made by Chile in order to attract FDI were slightly different from others applied in countries such as Argentina and Brazil, this difference is visible when comparing the authorized and realized FDI. The traditional variables were significant for the authorized FDI, indicating that the model of FDI that relates comparative advantages for multinationals is put into practice, although in Chile the objective for attracting FDI was not development *per se*, but the control of the debt crisis and inflation and the expansion of the export sector. Hence, part these motives provide the reason why during the early 1990s most of the FDI was concentrated in the mining sector, a sector highly profitable for foreign companies, and also appropriate for expansion of the export sector. However, when considering the realized FDI, the variables were not significant, with exception of two of them, indicating that the regional macroeconomic variables do not play an important role in FDI, but that there are other factors that do not imply the importance of regional location.

The analysis of the determinants at a sector level tends to confirm that even though the usual variables used for explaining FDI might be significant in explaining FDI, the causal relationships could be the other way around and that there is only correlation or even a bi-directional causality. In fact, for the case of the Mining sector, which was the leader in FDI until mid 1990s, some the typical determinants were significant, whereas for the services sector, most of the determinants were shown to be not significant. Hence, as FDI has evolved from the primary to the tertiary sector, the determinants have also evolved, making necessary the search for other factors that could explain the attraction of FDI. Consideration of spatial effects or more specific factors such as trade arrangements, or the inclusion of Chile into to larger trade markets, would need to be tested in future work.

The use of panel data specifications was appropriate and revealed for the main dependent variables (authorized and realized FDI) that the fixed effects specifications were significant. A more extensive analysis of the attraction of FDI in each would require a longer time series to capture some of the effects of infrastructure investment and investments in human capital. The fact that the random effects models were significant for the secondary dependent variables (FDI in the primary and services sector) indicate that there is some kind of concentration of the sector in few regions, i.e. the regions are heterogeneous in terms of FDI in certain sectors such that the fixed effects specification is not able to explain.

For the case of the services sector, we cannot assume that it was market-seeking FDI, since the typical factors considered for this kind of FDI were not significant, hence the suggestion that this type of investment was market-capture FDI. So far, this concept has not been explored extensively, and the results presented here suggest that there are still some factors that need to be considered, from the quality of the data, the specification of the model and the use of other explanatory variables.

References

Agosin, M., Fuentes, J. and Letelier, L. (1994) "Chile: The Origins and Consequences of External Capital." In Jose Antonio Ocampo and Roberto Steiner (eds.) *Foreign Capital in Latin America*. Washington, DC, Inter-American Development Bank.

Armstrong, H. and J. Taylor, (2000) *Regional Economics and Policy*. Third edition, Oxford, Blackwell Publishers.

Asiedu, E. (2002) "On the Determinants of Foreign Direct Investment to Developing Countries: Is Africa Different?" *World Development*, 30, 107-119.

Broadman H. and Sun X, (1997) "Distribution of Foreign Direct Investment in China," *World Economy*, 20, 339-361.

Chen, J-R. (2000) "FDI, International Financial Flows & Geography." In J-Ren Chen (ed.) *Foreign Direct Investment*. New York, St. Martin's Press.

Chen, K., J. Chou, S. Wang and N. Kuo (2000) "Economic Impact of Export processing zones in Taiwan: A CGE analysis." In J-Ren Chen (ed.) *Foreign Direct Investment*. New York, St. Martin's Press.

De Ferranti, D., G. Perry, D. Lederman, and W. Maloney (2002) *From Natural Resources to the Knowledge Economy, Trade and Job Quality*, World Bank Latin American and Caribbean Studies – Viewpoints.

Economic Commission for Latin American And The Caribbean (ECLAC-CEPAL) (2000) *La Inversión Extranjera en América Latina y el Caribe* (Foreign Direct Investment in Latin America and the Caribbean) CEPAL - Unidad de Inversiones y Estrategias Empresariales de la División de Desarrollo Productivo y Empresarial.

Kozlowski P. and J. Weekly (1990) "Explaining Interstate Variations in Foreign Direct Investment in the United States," *Regional Science Perspectives*, 20, 3-25.

Kreinin, M. (1995) "International Mobility of Productive Factors," chapter 9 in *International Economics: a Policy Approach:* Seventh Edition, New York, The Dryden Press.

Lahiri S. and Y. Ono (2003) "Export-Oriented Foreign Direct Investment and Local Content Requirement," *Pacific Economic Review*, 8, 1-14.

O'Huallacháin, B. (1982) *The Relationship Between Foreign Direct Investment and a Regional Industry System: An Analysis of Interregional and Intra-Corporation Linkages of Foreign-Owned Manufacturing Establishments*, unpublished Ph.D. Thesis, University of Illinois at Urbana-Champaign.

Noobakhsh, F., A. Paloni and A. Youseff, (2001) "Human Capital and FDI Inflows to Developing Countries: New Empirical Evidence," *World Development*, 29, 593-1610.

Ruane F. and H. Görg (1996) "Aspect of Foreign Direct Investment in Irish Manufacturing since 1973: Policy and Performance," *Journal of the Statistical and Social Inquiry Society of Ireland*, 27, 37-93.

Scott, P. (1998) "The Location of Early Overseas Multinationals in Britain, 1900-1939: Patterns and Determinants," *Regional Studies*, 32, 489-502.

Smekal C. and R. Sausgruber (2000) "Determinants of Foreign Direct Investment in Europe." In J-Ren Chen (ed.) *Foreign Direct Investment*. New York, St. Martin's Press.

Sun, H. and A. Parikh (2001) "Exports, Inward Foreign Direct Investment (FDI) and Regional Economic Growth in China," *Regional Studies*, 35, 187-196.

Sun, Q., W. Tong and Q. Yu (2002) "Determinants of Foreign Direct Investment Across China," *Journal of International Money and Finance*, 21, 79-113.

Wei, Y., X. Liu, D. Parker and K. Vaidya (1999) "The Regional Distribution of Foreign Direct Investment in China," *Regional Studies*, 33, 857-867.

World Investment Report, (1999) *Foreign Direct Investment and the Challenge of Development,* United Nations.

Zhang, K. (2001) "Does Foreign Direct Investment Promote Economic Growth? Evidence from East Asia and Latin America," *Contemporary Economy Policy*, 19, 175-185.

Index